Christine M. Marwick is former Publications Director for the Center for National Security Studies in Washington, D.C. She is editor of the first six editions, contributing author to subsequent editions of *Litigation Under the Federal Freedom of Information Act and Privacy Act* published by CNSS, and has spoken frequently at conferences and seminars covering FOIA and government information policy. Ms. Marwick is co-author of the book *The Lawless State: The Crimes of the U.S. Intelligence Agencies* (Penguin) and of numerous articles. She was editor of the monthly *First Principles: National Security and Civil Liberties*. Previously, she worked for the *Selective Service Law Reporter*. Ms. Marwick lives in Washington, D.C. with her husband and daughter.

Other Bantam Books in the series
Ask your bookseller for the books you have missed

YOUR RIGHT TO GOVERNMENT INFORMATION

Christine M. Marwick

**General Editor of this series:
Norman Dorsen, President, ACLU**

BANTAM BOOKS
TORONTO · NEW YORK · LONDON · SYDNEY · AUCKLAND

YOUR RIGHT TO GOVERNMENT INFORMATION
*A Bantam Book / published by arrangement with
the American Civil Liberties Union*

Bantam edition / April 1985

ISBN 0-553-24819-7

Published simultaneously in the United States and Canada

*Bantam Books are published by Bantam Books, Inc. Its trademark,
consisting of the words "Bantam Books" and the portrayal of a
rooster, is Registered in U.S. Patent and Trademark Office and in
other countries. Marca Registrada. Bantam Books, Inc., 666 Fifth
Avenue, New York, New York 10103.*

To Richard Talbot Seymour

This legislation springs from one of our most essential principles: a democracy works best when the people have all the information that the security of the Nation permits. No one should be able to pull curtains of secrecy around decisions which can be revealed without injury to the public interest. . . . I signed this measure with a deep sense of pride that the United States is an open society in which the people's right to know is cherished and guarded.

—President Lyndon B. Johnson,
upon signing the
1966 Freedom of Information Act

Acknowledgments

This book would not have been possible without the many people and organizations, including innumerable government employees, whose diligent efforts have helped make freedom of information policy an effective tool for bringing about a government that is responsible to the public. I would particularly like to thank the following people:

Morton H. Halperin, Director of the Center for National Security Studies (CNSS) in Washington, D.C. (which is jointly sponsored by the American Civil Liberties Union Foundation and the Fund for Peace), is responsible for getting the CNSS—and me—into trying to solve the problem of excessive official secrecy. In addition to the center's ongoing work concerning the effect of national security claims on civil liberties, the CNSS has, since 1975, been publishing yearly updates of *Litigation Under the Federal Freedom of Information Act and Privacy Act*, a technical manual for lawyers.

I'm greatly indebted to all the people who have worked with me on past and present editions of this resource. Daniel N. Hoffman's work on CNSS-related studies of national security information policies has been invaluable. I would also like to thank Monica Andres, the CNSS librarian extraordinaire and tracker-down of innumerable bits and pieces of Freedom of Information Act (often abbreviated as FOIA) lore. David Atkins, while a student-intern at the CNSS, worked with me on a concise pamphlet entitled *Using the FOIA: A Step-by-Step Guide*, and much of his work has found its way into this book. Other past CNSS student-interns whose research has directly or indirectly been incorporated in this book are Charles Hatton, Roland Hartley-Urquhart,

Eileen Kennedy, Stacy Sonnett, and Janet Weingarten. Elaine Hulse not only provided excellent typing for the manuscript, but also turned out to be an invaluable editor, with many constructive suggestions on style and form. And most especially, I would like to acknowledge those people who commented with special diligence on the draft of this book: Mort Halperin, David Vladeck, Ann Mari Buitrago (FOIA, Inc.), and, particularly, Harold C. Relyea (the Congressional Research Service and the American University).

I have also had stalwart moral support while writing this book. I want to thank my husband, Richard T. Seymour, whose energy sustained me through the weekends and evenings that the work absorbed, and I would like to thank our friend and neighbor, Richard Breitman, who provided ice cream and sympathy.

Contents

I
Access to Government Records:
The Freedom of Information Act and the
Privacy Act

II
Access to Government Meetings

Appendixes

Preface

This guide sets forth your rights under the present law, and offers suggestions on how they can be protected. It is one of a continuing series of handbooks published in cooperation with the American Civil Liberties Union (ACLU).

Surrounding these publications is the hope that Americans, informed of their rights, will be encouraged to exercise them. Through their exercise, rights are given life. If they are rarely used, they may be forgotten and violations may become routine.

This guide offers no assurances that your rights will be respected. The laws may change and, in some of the subjects covered in these pages, they change quite rapidly. An effort has been made to note those parts of the law where movement is taking place, but it is not always possible to predict accurately when the law *will* change.

Even if the laws remain the same, their interpretations by courts and administrative officials often vary. In a federal system such as ours, there is a built-in problem of state and federal law, not to speak of the confusion between states. In addition, there are wide variations in the ways in which particular courts and administrative officials will interpret the same law at any given moment.

If you encounter what you consider to be a specific abuse of your rights, you should seek legal assistance. There are a number of agencies that may help you, among them, ACLU affiliate offices, but bear in mind that the ACLU is a limited-purpose organization. In many communities, there are federally funded legal service offices that provide assistance to persons who cannot afford the costs of legal representation.

In general, the rights that the ACLU defends are freedom of inquiry and expression; due process of law; equal protection of the laws; and privacy. The authors in this series have discussed other rights (even though they sometimes fall outside the ACLU's usual concern) in order to provide as much guidance as possible.

These books have been planned as guides for the people directly affected; therefore, the question and answer format. (In some areas there are more detailed works available for "experts.") These guides seek to raise the major issues and inform the nonspecialist of the basic law on the subject. The authors of these books are themselves specialists who understand the need for information at "street level."

If you encounter a specific legal problem in an area discussed in one of these handbooks, show the book to your lawyer. Of course, he will not be able to rely exclusively on the handbook to provide you with adequate representation. But if your lawyer hasn't had a great deal of experience in the specific area, the handbook can provide helpful suggestions on how to proceed.

Norman Dorsen, President
American Civil Liberties Union

The principal purpose of this handbook, as well as others in this series, is to inform individuals of their legal rights. The authors from time to time suggest what the law should be, but their personal views are not necessarily those of the ACLU. For the ACLU's position on the issues discussed in this handbook, the reader should write to Librarian, ACLU, 132 W. 43 St., New York, NY 10036.

Introduction

Do I have the right to obtain government information?

Yes. Except for certain categories of information, you have the right of access to any federal government record. In some cases, you even have the right to sit in on certain kinds of official meetings.

This book is a basic do-it-yourself manual for exercising this right to government information. The federal access statutes have been designed so that anyone can use them. You do *not* have to have a lawyer in order to make requests for information.

Sometimes, these statutes operate with the simplicity of a vending machine: you insert your request and out comes the material you wanted. At other times, however, they operate more like a slot machine; you don't always win; that is, you don't always get the information you were seeking. Sometimes, though, the machine is plainly gummed up. Agency personnel may themselves be confused about what they're doing, or the gray area may be subject to different interpretations, or a new administration may introduce tighter policies. That's where this book tries to help. It explains in some detail how these machines work, and how you might be able to tinker with the machine in order to get better results, by simply educating the agency about what your legal rights are.

Which statutes establish a legal right of access to federal government information?

There are four major federal statutes that were set up to provide public access to government information. Their specific provisions are discussed in detail in later chapters.

1. The federal Freedom of Information Act (FOIA) is a general access statute that was first enacted in 1966, in order to allow the public to request access to records that are in the possession of any federal agency. Except for certain categories of information that are specifically protected by exemptions, the agencies are required to release anything that is requested. It's an accepted fact that the FOIA has had a major impact on the flow of information. It is the strongest, most used, most litigated, most effective, and most important of the federal access statutes. As a result, the lion's share of this book is devoted to the FOIA: not only is there more to be said about it, but pound for pound, explanations of the FOIA will carry greater weight in obtaining the release of information. And because of its influence, the FOIA is the subject of more controversy than the other access statutes.

2. The federal Privacy Act (occasionally abbreviated as PA) is intended to protect personal privacy from abuses by the federal government agencies that handle personal information. One means of protection that it sets up consists of granting individuals the right to examine their own personal records. The right of access to these records provided by the Privacy Act, overlaps with the right established by the FOIA, and this book discusses the two of them together. Since the FOIA is a stronger access statute than the Privacy Act, this book gives the former more attention.

3. The federal Government in the Sunshine Act (enacted in 1976) is an "open meetings" law. It establishes a right to attend meetings of the governing boards of some fifty federal agencies. It also establishes the right of access to the records of such meetings. As with the FOIA and the Privacy Act, the Sunshine Act has certain exemptions.

4. The Federal Advisory Committee Act (enacted in 1972) gives the public the right to attend federal advisory committee meetings. The categories of exemptions of the FACA are identical to those of the Sunshine Act, but it is otherwise a weaker open meetings statute.

It is important to realize that these four access statutes are not the only statutory channels provided for establishing a flow of government information.[1] There are innumerable federal statutes that deal in some sense with information policy, and people who want to find out about the workings of government should keep an eye out for these. Some may have a direct effect on the big four—the FOIA, the Privacy Act, the Sunshine Act, and the FACA—since they provide exemptions to each of these. Other statutes will establish that some agency or office has a legal obligation to compile certain kinds of information, such as reports on particular subjects; these statutes may also set up specific procedures by which the material is to be made public. Some statutes, for example, state that reports and records must be published by the government or deposited in the National Archives.[2] In addition to the laws that have access to information as their primary focus, there are many that establish an affirmative right to specific kinds of information.[3] The Ocean Pollution Research and Monitoring Program Act, for example, provides that information on ocean pollution must be disseminated to interested parties.[4] It is important to realize that there are many kinds of federal information that are available just for the asking.

Do I have to know a great deal about how the access statutes work in order to use them?

No. This book does not have to be read cover to cover in order to use these laws. The access statutes often operate in a very streamlined way, and making requests for information can be a very simple and straightforward process.

Under the FOIA and the Privacy Act, there are three phases. (1) You write a letter and wait for a response. (2) If the response isn't satisfactory, you write an appeal letter (which may be simple or complicated, depending on how ambitious you are). (3) If the response to your appeal letter isn't satisfactory, you either forget the matter or look into the possibility of going to court to compel the release of the information. Under the Sunshine and the FACA open meeting statutes, most of your work consists, first, of finding out what meetings are scheduled and are open to the public. Second, if a meeting is closed, you try to persuade the agency or committee to change its mind and open the meetings. Third, if the meeting is still closed, you consider taking the matter to federal court to compel openness.

Since most people are not versed in the ins and outs of bureaucratic procedures, this book sketches out what to do, when to do it, what to expect, and how to guide a request through the various stages of federal paperwork. Only occasionally, particularly in dealing with the kinds of information the access statutes exempt, does the book get into some of the technicalities of legal cases.

What is the historical background of the federal access statutes?

While the process of exercising your right to government information may sometimes seem cumbersome, it is useful to remember that not long ago the public had virtually no right to such information.[5] To a certain extent, any discussion of public access statutes is a discussion of reforms: reforms worked out in the past and, hopefully, reforms will make things proceed more smoothly and rationally in the future.

While the Bill of Rights set up certain protections for debate (freedom of speech is, after all, a form of information policy), it was silent on the matter of freedom of information. Certainly the American government had controversies over secrecy from the very beginning.[6] But the nature of government has changed greatly since then. At one time, for instance, there was no Justice Department, but only an attorney general, and in such a situation the paper flow was very different from what it is with a bureaucracy staffed by thousands. The institutions of government changed dramatically over the years, in both size and impact, but there was for a long time no reciprocal shift in the public's ability to find out what the government was doing. Individuals were increasingly accountable to the government, but the government was not increasingly accountable to individuals. The public had to settle for what it found out through official releases, through unofficial leaks, through congressional investigations, and, sometimes, through the evidence extracted when the government was a party to a court action or administrative adjudication.

It was haphazard access at best. Yet much information was of acute importance, whether to a public interested in finding out what the policies on some issue might actually be, or to an individual anxious to see what his own personal files contained. Often, an agency's rules, regulations, and prior decisions were kept secret—adding up, in effect, to the concept of "secret law," which members of the public might inadvertently run afoul of.

In the 1950s, the problem of citizen access to information

had reached such proportions that the term *freedom of information* was increasingly heard, and lively and lengthy congressional inquiries into the problem began.[7] At that time, disclosure law (then contained in Section 3 of the Administrative Procedure Act,[8] was extremely vague and allowed the agencies to adopt stringent—and, in effect, arbitrary—standards for release. Only if the relevant official decided that release would "benefit" the public, or be "compatible with the welfare of society," and if the material was not deemed "confidential for good cause found," would release be considered. The requester had to be, in the eyes of the official, "properly and directly concerned," but even a desire to see one's own personal records did not necessarily constitute such a concern. In practice, officials too often felt that responding to information requests was inconvenient to the agency, and therefore not compatible with the welfare of society.[9]

The congressional inquiries had no difficulty in concluding that the balance of power that controlled the flow of information was unfair, unjust, and counterproductive. But the FOIA took shape only slowly, and all the while the agencies argued that an open records statute would threaten effective government. It was not until 1966, that the Freedom of Information Act, the first of the four main federal access statutes, was enacted. The adverse result that the bureaucrats had predicted, never materialized. Lacking time limits under which the agencies had to respond to a request, or ways to recoup lawyers' fees in a court battle, or keeping search and copying fees in proportion to the size of the request, or other provisions that would provide real teeth for a public trying to use the act, the FOIA was instead riddled with loopholes that left much of its implementation up to the goodwill of the agencies. And that goodwill too often lacking, the original FOIA produced relatively little material.

Yet the concept of access to government information was an idea that was catching on. When the Federal Advisory Committee set out to correct some of the problems that had developed in the administration and use of executive branch advisory committees, one of the solutions incorporated was the right to attend the meetings of such committees, together with the right to obtain committee records under the provisions of the FOIA.

It was Vietnam, the Pentagon Papers, and Watergate that educated the public and Congress about many of the threats that excessive secrecy—and the concomitant lack of official accountability—posed to the well-being of the government itself. And the need for an access statute with real teeth had been underscored by the considerable creativity that many agencies had exercised in devising loopholes in order to evade the intent of Congress in the 1966 act. In 1974, the FOIA was given a major overhaul. Loopholes were plugged, and the ability of citizens to enforce their FOIA rights themselves was upgraded substantially. President Ford used his veto power against the amendments, asserting that placing time limits upon agency responses was "unworkable" and that increasing the power of the courts to review national security claims was "unconstitutional." Congress disagreed, and liberals and conservatives voted together to override the veto.

The momentum behind the 1974 amendments carried forward into other new legislative activity. The Privacy Act was passed shortly after the FOIA amendments in 1974, and the Government in the Sunshine Act (along with another improvement in the FOIA and amendments for the FACA) was enacted in 1976.

None of this should be made to seem too comfortably settled, however. While many agencies have accepted the idea of open government as embodied in the access statutes, other agencies continue to lobby for loopholes to get special exemptions.

The political swing that took place in the 1980 national election, with the installation of the Reagan administration and the change of climate in Congress, brought with it a variety of legislative proposals which, if enacted, would cut back in a few places on the public's right to government information.[9] There is a real paradox here, since a general distrust of "big" government was one of the issues that generated the results of the election, yet these access rights have provided a concrete way in which "big" government can be kept in line.

As of this writing, it is too early to tell just how far the pendulum will swing on the question of rights to government information. One of the things that makes the situation difficult to predict is that those agencies that have been lobbying hardest for access cutbacks have not, to date, been able to show that their work has actually been hurt by the access statutes.[10] This lack of proof has not, however, prevented alarming claims from being made.

So far, the most far-reaching changes would involve (1) an extension of the time limits that have to elapse before you can go to court; (2) some changes in the fees that agencies could charge; and (3) making broader exemptions for some intelligence and law enforcement records.[11] Other proposals include limiting some of the agencies' power to release certain kinds of business records. Another factor that makes the future of access laws difficult to predict is that it is not necessary to amend the four primary access statutes themselves in order to limit access to specific kinds of information. Agencies can sometimes get what might be called backdoor amendments to the acts—other statutes may be enacted that allow them to withhold information that would otherwise be available under the federal access statutes.[12]

As this book explains different aspects of the access statutes, it will try to point out a few of the changes that are under discussion. But please bear in mind that it is very easy for an administration to ask for a change in an existing law, and a far harder matter to actually get what it wants. The principle of freedom of information has many protectors. The possible changes that are mentioned here are just that—only possible changes. It is far from certain that they will ever be enacted. They are mentioned so that, if the law in fact does change, and if some of these changes affect you, you will have some idea of where you stand.

Has the implementation of the FOIA changed over the years?

Yes. With the exception of some backsliding with the Reagan administration, the federal bureaucracy seems to be gradually getting used to the fact that the FOIA means what it says. The government itself has made increasing efforts to explain the acts to its employees, and at the same time, the routine handling of government paperwork has had to become more rational. Government filing systems have had to be refined so that FOIA requests could be more easily handled, and at the same time they have become better suited to meeting the agencies' other needs as well.

While there is still a great deal of agency resistance to the access statutes, there has also been increasing compliance.[13] As the public continues to make use of these statutes, this process of educating federal employees to be more responsive to the public will continue.[14]

All these developments are, however, very much a matter of administrative policy and political climate. The attitude in the White House can have great influence on whether the agencies will take an open or a closed posture. And the attitude in Congress will determine whether Capitol Hill will make the effort to push an administration to be more open, or whether an administration will push Capitol Hill to allow its operations to be more closed.

Should I feel hesitant about using the laws that give me the right to government information?

There is no reason why you should be shy about exercising these rights, any more than there is a reason to be shy about exercising rights like voting.

As a member of the public, you should feel free to throw yourself headlong into the whole process. The chances of getting at least some useful information are very good although you will probably encounter some frustration along the line. Perhaps the best way to approach the process of using the access laws is to look at it as an education in how government agencies operate. In a very real sense, these access statutes will introduce you to a corner in the world of government regulations, procedures, filing systems, and thinking. Deciphering the inner workings of some agency can be a challenge, and it is public spirited for you to do so. When agencies are open to the public, they are also responsive to the public. Sometimes (with a little luck), members of the public end up being able to participate unofficially in the process of government by being watchdogs looking for such problems as inefficiency, mistakes, prejudices, and abuses.

As part of this process, you should not be shy about contacting your representatives in Congress for help and letting them know about problems in how an agency is implementing the access laws. This is one way of emphasizing to Capitol Hill that the access statutes are worth the resources that they take to administer, and that, as a service to their constituents, these laws should be safeguarded and strengthened.

What is the best approach for gaining access to government information?

Every request for access to information is different, but it is useful to keep in mind a few rules of thumb and general caveats. These appear here and there throughout this book, but it is useful to summarize them at the outset so that you can be aware of them.

1. There are relatively simple procedures for calling this right to information into play, but you should be prepared to find that things often work out differently in practice than they do in theory.

2. Not all agencies or officials are alike. Some are resolutely open and cooperative, while some are extremely creative at finding ways to avoid releasing information.

3. Do not be afraid to question the agencies and their officials. Sometimes they don't know what they are doing; sometimes they will play on your presumed ignorance in order to avoid producing information; and sometimes they can be very skillful at finding loopholes and gray areas in your right of access. This book tries to give you the means to argue about whether some piece of information is actually in one of the gray areas.

4. The current situation is subject to change on short notice. Agencies regularly revise their regulations and make personnel changes. Administrations change, and with them the attitude toward openness will change as well. The courts have an enormous number of access cases pending before them, and decisions are always coming down and shifting the shades of gray around. Congress enacts new laws or changes old ones, and the agencies are almost always asking Congress for changes and for special exceptions for their particular files.

5. The access statutes give the public the right to sue in court if an agency seems to be withholding information improperly. If you can muster the resources to go to court and have a fair case, you shouldn't be shy about challenging agency decisions. The access statutes were designed to be enforced by the same people who use them—the requesters.

6. The access statutes provide an enforceable legal right, but if you can gain access to material through some informal channel that you happen upon, there's no reason not to use that channel. It never hurts to get on the phone and talk with somebody in an agency (particularly its public relations office); some agencies have a policy of being very cooperative.

If an agency says that certain information or documents are exempt from disclosure, shouldn't I take their word for it?

No, but many people feel intimidated because the statements that the agencies make sound authoritative. Agencies will not suggest that something withheld may actually be in a legally uncertain gray area. You should remember that the law says that it is the courts—and not the agencies—which are supposed to make the final decision about what falls under a particular exemption. And the government officials who make decisions about withholding records are, in the last analysis, just normal, average people. They make mistakes in interpreting what the law allows them to withhold—and when the matter goes to court, the government loses about half the time. In some agencies, the people processing requests have never been properly trained and do not understand what the access statutes require.[15] Sometimes, they have no idea what the agency's own regulations for handling information actually are. (Some classifiers in the Department of Defense, for example, thought that the term *administrative convenience* was reason enough for not complying with the classification standards and procedures laid out in the executive order on classification of national security information.[16])

Will I be able to get useful information?

Yes. Sometimes material is released without any deletions. But even if the material is full of deletions and withholdings, you can frequently get clues to other supplemental documents, reports, and records, which you can then track down. And even partial documentation is better than no documentation at all.

The press, for example, was at first rather skeptical about the FOIA. They generally assumed that it would produce little that their own, informal sources could not get for them. But, by now, press use of the information statutes has become routine. It turns out that simply having a document that has already been released provides a good starting point for asking the informal sources for comment and clarification.

How accurate will the information that I receive be?

All that you can assume is that the documents that you get are, in fact, copies (minus possible deletions, which are supposed to be indicated) of the records that the agencies have.[17]

The material contained in these records may or may not be reliable, however. Agency information may be mistaken, distorted, or inaccurate. Officials make honest errors, or leave records which will make them look good and others look bad. Government records, in short, are produced by fallible human beings. And, certainly, the fact that something may be contained in a document that was formerly "top secret," or in records that the agency fought to withhold, does not mean that the material is necessarily true, or even very interesting.

Are agencies ever misleading regarding my legal rights to information?

Yes, and therefore you should not blindly accept what officials processing your requests say. Many requesters have been told things that were absolutely incorrect or, at best, misleading.

Take the example of one requester who stated, after some two months of correspondence failed to produce any of the material he had requested, that he intended to exercise his right to appeal the denial of his request. The agency wrote back, "A requester has the right to appeal the denial of specific documents. Since no documents have been denied to you at this point, there is no 'right of appeal of any adverse determination' in this case." This response, quiet simply, was wrong. While it is true that in this particular case no "adverse determination" had been made, it is also true that the FOIA sets up other grounds for appeal. The 1974 amendments to the FOIA give you the right not only to appeal actual denials, but also to appeal (and, indeed, to sue) if the time limits set out in the statute are not met. (See chapter 5.) In this case, the agency's response implies that the *only* basis for writing an appeal letter is an actual "adverse determination"—a letter from the agency denying the requester the material asked for.

In such a situation, you, the sophisticated requester, simply write an appeal letter anyhow, and cites the section of the statute that establishes the right to appeal violations of the FOIA's time limits. It is likely that the person at the agency who wrote the misleading letter did not actually understand, or was familiar with, the law on FOIA appeals, and this, then, is a situation in which it is your job to educate agency personnel.

How consistent is the government's implementation of the access statutes?

Not consistent at all; there is great variation from official to official, from agency to agency, and from situation to situation regarding how much material and what kind of material is released.

One official processing a particular FOIA request might find the subject matter embarrassing and look for a possible basis for withholding the material; another official might find that the same material supported goals that he approved of, and would readily release the material. Some officials seem to have a better attitude toward openness than others. And some agencies have adopted policies designed to facilitate openness (training employees about legal requirements, liberal regulations, frequent fee waivers, and so on), while others have designed their procedures so that release is harder to come by (having appeals processed by the same person who initially denied release, for example). Some agencies have adopted very informal access policies—at the former Department of Health, Education, and Welfare (HEW), for example, FOIA requests could even be made orally, something that even the statute doesn't require.[18] (The HEW has since been split into two agencies: the Department of Health and Human Services (HHS) and the Department of Education.) Some agencies regularly process requests within the statutory time limits, while others delay responding for months or even years.

In one of the happy surprises that shows what a good attitude can accomplish, the Department of Defense has what is probably the best FOIA/PA record in the federal government. It has accomplished this in spite of the disadvantages of being a huge agency, having to deal with a great deal of classified national security information, and having more than 60,000 FOIA/PA requests every year. About 80 percent of the requests it receives are granted in full within 10 days; by contrast, the CIA, a smaller agency receiving far fewer requests, has a 2- to 3-year backlog for processing. The Department of Defense, as might be expected, has rarely been troubled with FOIA lawsuits.[19]

Do I have to understand legal citations in order to use the access statutes?

No. You don't have to master legal citations in order to use the federal access statutes effectively, but neither should you be intimidated by them. Agencies will sometimes toss such numbers at the public; the public can just as easily learn to play the game, so you will sometimes find technical-looking citations in this book. Sometimes these are in the text itself, but usually they are found in the footnotes. If you use them in your correspondence with an agency, remember to copy them *exactly*. They all look alike until you realize that the most insignificant punctuation can make for large differences in meaning.

Take the citation for the Freedom of Information Act as an example. It is usually written as "5 U.S.C. Section 552." (If the word *section* is abbreviated, the citation is shortened to "5 U.S.C. Sec. 552" or "5 U.S.C. §552.") This cite means that the text of the FOIA can be found at Section 552 in Title 5 of the United States Code. The U.S. Code is the compilation of all the federal statutes. It's divided into *many* volumes and is found in law libraries. Title 5 of the Code groups together the laws that control how the government is supposed to be administered.

There are subsections and subsubsections and so on within each section of the Code, and this is where things are most likely to be confusing until you get used to it; for instance, 5 U.S.C. Section 552(b)—note the parentheses around the small *b*—refers to the subsection of the FOIA that states the kind of information the agencies can withhold (these are called the exemptions). But 5 U.S.C. § 552b—note that the small *h* is not enclosed by parentheses—is the citation for the federal Government in the Sunshine Act. (There are other variations as well—too many to go into here.) In a lot of ways, this system is much like the methods used to cite book, chapter, and verse in the Bible.

There are other legal citations that appear in the footnotes of this book. If you want to look up this material, the librarian at a law library would be able to help you. This reference material is cited for your convenience, but, again, you can ordinarily use the acts effectively without delving into these matters.

In addition, you should be aware that if the FOIA, or any other statute, is later amended, the various provisions within it may be rearranged and renumbered.

What other sources of information might provide access to

the same kind of information that I might seek under the access statutes?

There are innumerable useful sources of government information that have nothing to do with the access statutes. It can be very handy to make use of these: they may be less time-consuming and cheaper; they may also provide more of the facts that you want. At the very least, checking some of these alternative sources will often give you the background that you might need in order to write more precise requests for information under the access statutes. And if you cannot dislodge what you want through the formal request process, these other sources may be your last recourse.

First, there are the obvious sources such as libraries, the National Archives, the Government Printing Office (GPO), and the uncounted thousands of official reports and statements handed out by the various agencies to the general public. (Most agencies have a Public Affairs Office to help you.) In addition, somewhere on Capitol Hill there are members of Congress who sit on a congressional committee that is responsible for overseeing the same kind of agency activity that you want to get information about. The committees and subcommittees necessarily limit themselves to questions that have relatively important policy implications, but they have the advantage of being able to subpoena information that might be exempt under the access statutes. The offices of individual senators and representatives do not have subpoena power, but they do a lively business of trying to help constituents. You should feel free to contact this useful resource.[20] Also on Capitol Hill are the House and Senate Document rooms (which have copies of bills and reports that might not be available from the various committees), and from the General Accounting Office (GAO), which issues reports.

Nor should you be shy about using the telephone to call federal offices and simply ask what you want to know. It is true that it can sometimes be very difficult to find the right person in the right office, but once you do, the people that you reach are often very helpful. In other words, this book, by its nature, tends to focus on the adversarial side of the process of getting information out of the government, but what you want to know is often there for the asking. Depending on what you want, you could try to get it the easy way first.

One former FOIA official in the Department of Justice has suggested a number of other unofficial avenues for getting information. As you might infer, these suggestions typically work best in areas where you have a business interest in the material; such interests often develop specialized networks of knowledgeable contacts. At the very least, these suggest how creative people can be about finding out what they want to know.

1. Try to attend conferences and seminars in the subject area of your interest; you are likely to meet agency personnel there.

2. Try to consult former agency personnel and others who might know something about the subject area.

3. Try to find out if someone has sued the government in a non-FOIA lawsuit and obtained evidence on the subject; see if you can work out a cooperative agreement.

4. Issue a public statement about agency activities that may bring out the information that you want when the agency decides to explain or rebut.[21]

NOTES

1. Perhaps the most useful bibliography of materials on the broad range of federal government information is Harold C. Relyea and Elaine R. Tomchik, *Managing Official Information—Accountability and Protection in the Federal Government: A Selected Bibliography* (Report No. 80–183 COV) (Washington, D.C.: Congressional Research Service, Oct. 15, 1980).

2. The material available through the GPO is diverse, extensive, often extremely interesting, and very accessible to the public. For information on ordering, write to the Superintendent of Documents, U.S. Government Printing Office, Washington, DC 20402

Another government office set up to sell the government documents to the public is the National Technical Information Service, 5285 Port Royal Rd., Springfield, VA. 22161. It sells reports from government-sponsored research.

The National Archives is located at 8th and Pennsylvania Ave. N.W., Washington, DC 20408 and publishes material explaining how to make use of its resources.

There are also a number of privately published books that offer considerable information on finding an enormous range of data in federal agencies (and from other sources as well). Harry J. Murphy,

Office of Security, CIA, *Where's What: Sources of Information for Federal Investigators* (New York: Quadrangle, n.d.) (declassified, Aug. 1975); Congressional Quarterly's *Washington Information Directory* (Washington, D.C.: Congressional Quarterly, updated yearly).

3. In fact, there are so many statutes that control some aspect of the public's right to information that no one has successfully compiled a list of all of them. To get an idea of the diversity, see U.S. Congress, Committee on House Administration, *Information Policy: Public Laws from the 95th Congress*, 96th Cong., 1st sess., Jan. 31, 1979, p. v. This compilation of legislation containing access provisions, both major and incidental, is apparently the first time that such a review has been undertaken. It is limited, however, to only those statutes enacted in 1977 and 1978.

4. *Id.* at 6.

5. There is a loosely defined common law right to "public records," which applies to the legislative, judicial, and executive branches of government. This means that while it is not possible to get documents under the FOIA from Congress and from the courts, in some circuits there is nonetheless a very limited common law right that is sometimes enforceable. The key issue is whether a given document is in fact a "public record." You are on far more tenuous ground when asserting a right to such materials when the government contests it. *Schwartz* v. *Dept. of Justice*, 435 F. Supp. 1203 (1977); *U.S.* v. *Mitchell*, 179 U.S. App. D.C. 293, 551 F.2d 1252, 1257 (1976); *Courier-Journal & Louisville Times Co.* v. *Curtis*, 335 S.W.2d 934, 936 (Ky. 1959), *cert. denied*, 364 U.S. 910 (1960); 66 AM JUR. 2d *Records and Recording Laws*, §15 (1973). For the historical background of the FOIA, with comparison to other countries, *see* Harold C. Relyea, "Freedom of Information Policy Developments in the U.S.," *Transnational Data Report*, vol. V., no. 2 (1982).

6. Daniel N. Hoffman, *Governmental Secrecy and the Founding Fathers* (Westport, Conn: Greenwood Press, 1981).

7. A book generally credited with having first focused public attention on the problem of access to government information is Harold L. Cross, *The People's Right to Know: Legal Access to Public Records and Proceedings* (New York: Columbia U.P., 1953). It deals with federal, state, and local information policies in both the administrative and judicial processes of government, but not with the issue of national security information.

8. 5 U.S.C. §1002.

9. *See, e.g.*, Relyea, "Freedom of Information in the 1980s: Policy Changes on the Horizon," *First Principles*, Feb. 1981, pp. 5–7 (*First Principles* is available from the Center for National Security Studies, 122 Maryland Ave., N.E., Washington, DC 20002); Relyea, "Freedom of Information Act Faces Uncertain Future," *Legal Times of Washington*, Aug. 3, 1981, p. 30; Rep. Glenn English, "Cut Access to Government Data?" *U.S. News and World Report*, Jan. 18, 1982, reprinted, *First Principles*, Mar. 1982, p. 16; Floyd Abrams, "The

Public Value of Information Is Merely 'Trivial': So Says the Reagan Administration," *First Principles*, May/June 1983, p. 5, (adapted from Apr. 21, 1983 testimony before joint hearings, U.S., Congress, House, Judiciary Subcommittee on Civil and Constitutional Rights and the Post Office and Civil Service Subcommittee on Civil Service).

10. *See, e.g.*, Christine M. Marwick, "Freeing the CIA from Freedom of Information: Why?" *First Principles*, Jan./Feb. 1980, pp. 1 ff.; Center for National Security Studies Report No. 106, "The CIA and the Freedom of Information Act"; Athan G. Theoharis, "The Freedom of Information Act and the Intelligence Agencies," *Government Publications Review*, Vol. 9 (1982): 37–44; Mark H. Lynch, "The FOIA and the CIA," *First Principles*, Sept./Oct. 1983, pp. 1–4.

11. *See, e.g.*, §774 and § 1324, 98th Cong., 1st sess. (1983).

12. Three such backdoor amendments enacted at the close of the 96th Congress are the Federal Trade Commission Improvement Act of 1980 (P.L. 96–252), the Shippers' Export Declarations Law (P.L. 96–275), and the Nuclear Regulatory Commission Appropriations Authorization Act (P.L. 96–295). *See FOIA Update*, vol. II, no. 2 (Winter 1981): 2. *FOIA Update* is published by the Office of Information Law and Policy, U.S. Department of Justice, Washington, D.C. 20530

13. Comptroller General of the United States, *Timeliness and Completeness of FBI Reponses to Requests under Freedom of Information and Privacy Acts Have Improved* (GAO Report GGD–78–51) (Washington, D.C.: General Accounting Office, Apr. 10, 1978), p. 51.

14. *See generally Comptroller General of the United States, id., An Informed Public Assures that Federal Agencies Will Better Comply with Freedom of Information/Privacy Laws,* (GAO Report LCD–80–8) (Washington, D.C.: General Accounting Office, Oct. 24, 1979).

15. Comptroller General of the United States, *Government Field Offices Should Better Implement the Freedom of Information Act,* (GAO Report LCD–78–120) (Washington, D.C.: General Accounting Office, July 25, 1978).

16. Comptroller General of the United States, *Continuing Problems in DOD's Classification of National Security Information,* (GAO Report LCD–80–16) (Washington, D.C.: General Accounting Office, Oct. 26, 1979).

17. As of this writing there is one exception to this. The Consumer Product Safety Commission (CPSC) is supposed to verify complaint records before these are released. Legislation is pending which would, if enacted, change this. *See, e.g.*, U.S. Congress, House, *Report 98–114 on H.R. 2668*, 98th Cong., 1st sess., 1983.

18. Comptroller General, *Government Field Offices, supra,* note 16, at 24.

19. *Department of Defense Annual Report on the FOIA,* available from The Director, FOI and Security Review, OASD (Public Affairs), The Pentagon, Washington, DC 20301.

20. Sen. William Cohen and Kenneth Lasson, *Getting the Most Out of Washington: Using Congress to Move the Federal Bureaucracy* (New York: Facts on File, 1982). *See supra* note 2.

21. Robert L. Saloschin, "Sailing Against the Wind: How to Encourage Agencies to Grant Your FOIA Request," 1 *Government Disclosure Service* (Prentice-Hall) para. 7017, p. 7060.

I

Access to Government Records: The Freedom of Information Act and the Privacy Act

I

The General Provisions of
the Freedom of Information Act and
the Privacy Act

**Which statute should I use to request government records—
the Freedom of Information Act or the Privacy Act?**

It depends on what kind of information is in the records
and who you are.

The federal Freedom of Information Act (FOIA)[1] is a broader
access statute than the Privacy Act, and therefore can be used
in all situations. The FOIA gives any member of the public
the right of access to *all* records in the custody of the federal
executive branch *unless* those records are covered by one of
the exemptions specified in the act. You do not have to have
any reason or personal interest in making the request, and,
under present law, can be a foreigner.[1a]

The federal Privacy Act[1b] provides access only to *personal*
records in the custody of the federal executive branch or in
the custody of a contractor who handles systems of records
covered by the Privacy Act for a federal agency. Under the
Privacy Act, there is a much *broader* range of exemptions
that an agency can rely upon to withhold information. In
order to make a Privacy Act request, you must be either the
subject of the records or the subject's legal guardian. In
addition, you must be either a U.S. citizen or a permanent
resident alien.[2]

If this seems confusing to you, you are not alone. There has
been a good deal of debate about the "interface" between the
FOIA and the Privacy Act, which do not mesh as easily as
they might have. At one point, some commentators were
arguing that the Privacy Act restricted access rights that had
been strengthened by the FOIA amendments, passed only a few

3

months earlier.[3] However, the Privacy Act states that information that is available under the FOIA cannot be withheld under the Privacy Act,[4] and that information that is available to an individual under the Privacy Act, cannot be withheld under FOIA exemptions.[5] In other words, releasing personal files to the subject of those files is not a violation of privacy under the FOIA exemptions that protect personal privacy. Therefore, both the Privacy Act and the FOIA give individuals access to their personal files, and personal privacy is protected by the FOIA exemptions for privacy, which are discussed later.

In most ways, the FOIA offers greater access to personal files as well as general records—its exemptions are narrower. The Privacy Act, for example, entirely exempts the personal files held by the CIA and the FBI; but under the FOIA, no agencies are entirely exempt. By the same token, the Privacy Act permits an agency to withhold "any information compiled in reasonable anticipation of a civil action or proceeding."[6] An agency could withhold personal records under the Privacy Act if, for example, it were considering initiating a lawsuit against the subject; the same records might, however, be available under the FOIA, unless the agency could apply one of the narrower FOIA exemptions.

The Privacy Act's procedures for making access requests are also weaker then those of the FOIA. The Privacy Act does not put limits on the time the agency has in which to respond to a request for information; nor does the Privacy Act require agencies to set up a procedure for handling appeals for records that have at first been denied. Under the FOIA you need only to "reasonably describe" what is wanted; under the Privacy Act, you are supposed to specify the record system to be checked.

After some dispute between the Justice Department and the congressional overseers of the FOIA and the Privacy Act, the Justice Department adopted a policy whereby agencies should process requests for information under whichever of the two statutes would give you greater access.[7]

So the best rule of thumb for deciding under which law to request information is this: if the request is for any kind of government records that do not personally deal with you, make your request under the FOIA; if the request is for personal records relating to you, cite both laws so that you can get the greatest disclosure. This book will discuss the two records acts together, for they are often implemented together. Indeed, most government offices that handle requests for records are called FOIA/PA offices. If this text refers to the FOIA/PA you will know that it is referring to some meshed aspect of the federal records statutes that applies to both acts. If the text refers to just the "FOIA," you'll know that the particular point under discussion refers to rights available under only the Freedom of Information Act. If the text refers to the "Privacy Act" or "PA," you will know that the particular point deals only with the Privacy Act.

How does the Privacy Act protect privacy?

In addition to its access provisions, the Privacy Act has a number of other provisions, not shared by the FOIA, of which you should be aware:

1. It places limits on how personal records can be used.
2. It allows you to have records amended (either corrected or expunged) if they are not "accurate, relevant, timely or complete."[8]
3. It provides that if you are adversely affected by a government record that is not "accurate, relevant, timely or complete," you may sue in federal court for an amendment of the records and/or an award of at least $1,000 in damages.[9]
4. It protects First Amendment rights (freedom of speech and religion) by prohibiting any agency, including law enforcement and intelligence agencies, from maintaining records on how people exercise these rights, *unless*
   (1) the agencies are authorized to do so by another statute;
   (2) the subject of the records has granted permission; or
   (3) the First Amendment information is actually pertinent to an authorized law enforcement activity.[10]

These provisions are not elaborated upon in this book, which limits itself to the art of gaining access to government records. An Avon/ACLU publication, *Your Right to Privacy*, by Trudy Hayden and Jack Novik, covers the full scope of Privacy Act issues.[11]

Is information that is exempt from disclosure under the Privacy Act (and/or the FOIA) also exempt from the other protections of the Privacy Act?

No. The fact that records may be exempt from mandatory disclosure does not relieve the agencies of the other provisions of the Privacy Act. First Amendment data, for example, is protected, and personal information in government files must be accurate, timely, and relevant to a legitimate government purpose.

The effect of the access exemptions may mean that you might not be able to obtain access, under the FOIA and the Privacy Act to your files in order to check them for accuracy, timeliness, and relevance, but if you do obtain access through other sources (through some other kind of civil suit, for example), you still have the right to sue for correction, expungement, and damages under the Privacy Act.

Can the FOIA/PA be used to obtain information that was compiled to determine whether I will be hired as a federal employee, accepted into the military service, promoted, qualified to obtain a federal contract, or given a security clearance for handling classified information?

Yes, the Privacy Act gives access to information relating to the subject's "suitability, eligibility, or qualifications" for such federal benefits or privileges. However, the Privacy Act provides an exception for withholding information that would reveal the identity of a confidential source.[12]

Such material also overlaps somewhat with one of the exemptions of the FOIA, if they reveal an official's advice or opinion in regard to making decisions about federal employees or applicants. [This exemption, governing certain kinds of information found in internal government memoranda, is codified at 5 U.S.C. §552(b)(5), and referred to as the (b)(5) exemption. [see chapter 4.] Likewise, the (b)(6) exemption could also be used to protect the official's privacy.

Information used to determine military promotions can also be obtained under the Privacy Act unless that information would reveal a confidential source.[13]

What agencies are covered by the FOIA/PA?

The FOIA/PA share a broad definition of what agencies are covered. In addition to the offices ordinarily thought of as agencies, these include many other organizations within the executive branch of government.

Congress helped clarify the status of many ambiguous entities by stating, in the legislative history, that they were to be covered. The Executive Office of the President is considered an agency for the purpose of the FOIA and the Privacy Act, and includes the Office of Management and Budget (OMB), the National Security Council (NSC), the Federal Property Council (FPC), and similar offices. Government corporations are also covered by the FOIA/PA. Examples include the St. Lawrence Seaway Development Corporation, the Federal Crop Insurance Corporation, the Tennessee Valley Authority (TVA), and the Inter-American Foundation. Government-controlled corporations are likewise considered agencies under the FOIA/PA. Examples include the National Railroad Passenger Corporation (Amtrak) and the Postal Service.[14]

The status of many government-related entities is less clear since Congress made no specific mention of them. Two general criteria have been important to the courts in determining whether an entity is an agency under the FOIA/PA. Agencies have the legal authority to make decisions and are not relatively independent of the federal government.

Therefore, if an entity does not make decisions—if it merely functions as a consultant—it is not an agency under the FOIA/PA.[15]

Other agencies are too autonomous relative to the federal government to be agencies, even though they make decisions, use federal funds or have some direct organizational connection to the government. Thus, the American Red Cross, in spite of the fact that it operates under a congressional charter and that its board of governors is appointed by the President, is not considered an agency because it is not run under federal control or with federal appropriations.[16] Likewise, the Trust Territory of the Pacific Islands, in spite of the fact that it is supervised by the Department of the Interior, has been held not to be an agency because it performs purely local government functions for non-U.S. citizens.[17] Corporations that receive federal funds but are neither chartered nor controlled by the federal government, such as the Corporation for Public Broadcasting (CPA), are excluded from FOIA/PA coverage in order to help protect its independence under the First Amendment (freedom of the press). By contrast, an organization such as the Federal Home Loan Mortgage Corporation (FHLMC), which is a "government-controlled corporation," and doesn't involve First Amendment values, is considered an agency.[18]

Are the records of the President and his staff available under the FOIA/PA?

The records of the President and of "the President's immediate personal staff or units in the Executive Office whose sole function is to advise and assist the President," are exempt under the FOIA/PA.[19]

However, in 1978, Congress passed an act governing presidential records. These new provisions separate the records of the President and the Vice President into two categories—personal records and presidential records.

Under the Presidential Records Act of 1978, the official records of the President and Vice President after January 20, 1981, will be subject to FOIA review by the archivist of the United States.[20] If the President has not designated them as "restricted," the records can be reviewed after five years; otherwise, they become subject to review after twelve years. In addition, the Presidential Records Act specifies that Exemption 5 of the FOIA will not apply to presidential records. In other words, while the advice and discussion that leads up to decisions and policies in all other agencies is *not* available under the FOIA because of Exemption 5 (see the discussion in chapter 4), similar advice leading to the decisions and policies of the President and Vice President *will* be available under the Presidential Records Act.

Are Congress or the federal courts covered by the FOIA/PA?

No. Congress chose to exempt both itself and the courts when it enacted the FOIA and the Privacy Act.[21]

When Congress was considering the creation of the FOIA, it was focusing upon information access problems involving the executive branch agencies and the public, as well as the broad authority that the Administrative Procedure Act had permitted regarding the withholding of records. A direct application of the FOIA/PA to Congress would be complicated by the "speech and debate" clause of the Constitution, which gives members of Congress and their staffs considerable immunity from questions pertaining to their legislative activities. Congress is, however, continuing to review its status.[22] A law authorizing broader access to court records would, of course, present problems with the separation of powers doctrine.

Both Congress and the courts, of course, produce a vast

amount of material that is available for the asking. Huge quantities of their proceedings are available in libraries. And both courtrooms and congressional proceedings are almost always open to the public on a space available basis.

Is material at the Library of Congress available under the FOIA?

The Library of Congress is part of the legislative branch rather than the executive branch of the federal government and, therefore, is not generally covered by the requirements of the FOIA.[23] However, the Copyright Act of 1976, provides that the Copyright Office (which is an integral unit within the Library of Congress) shall be subject to the provisions of the FOIA to the extent specified in Copyright Office regulations.[24]

In addition, the Library of Congress has adopted a policy that closely follows that of the FOIA. Its general regulations provide access to "evidence of the organization, functions, policies, decisions, procedures, operations, or other activities," rather than to provide access to the library's collections themselves, which are available through the regular library services. Library information regulations exempt the records developed by the Congressional Research Service and by the Congressional Law Library.

A request for material should be addressed to the Chief, Central Services Division, Library of Congress, Washington, DC 20540.

Are materials available from the General Accounting Office (GAO) under the Freedom of Information Act?

As a support arm of Congress, the General Accounting Office (GAO) maintains that it is not required to comply with the FOIA. It has, however, adopted regulations that parallel the FOIA, although these permit broader exemptions than those of the FOIA; for example, all investigatory records compiled for law enforcement are exempt.

The GAO maintains a public reading room at 441 G Street, N.W., Washington, DC 20548. If the material sought is not available in the reading room or as a GAO publication,[25] a written request for access may be made. The GAO requires that you use GAO Form 339, Request for Access to Official Record, which is to be sent to the Records Management & Services Officer, Office of Administrative Services, General Accounting Office, Washington, DC 20548.

Appeals are to be addressed to the Comptroller General of the U.S., 441 G St., N.W., Washington, DC 20548.[26]

Do the FOIA/PA cover the governments of the District of Columbia or the U.S. territories?

No. However, the District of Columbia has a similar FOIA.[27]

Are government contractors or grant recipients covered by the FOIA/PA?

Generally, no. But personal records in the possession of government contractors are covered by the provisions of the Privacy Act if the contract with the agency involves the operation of a "system of records to accomplish an agency function."[28] In other words, the contractor must actually be managing some system of agency records that contains personal data covered by the Privacy Act. In this limited situation, such records would be available under the Privacy Act, but not under the FOIA.

Otherwise, neither contractors nor the recipients of federal grants are considered "agencies" covered by the access statutes. Even when an agency has the authority to obtain records from a grantee upon request, it is not required to do so. The fact that the records may be the subject of an important public debate does not alter this.[29]

Of course, any records the agency actually has in its possession concerning its contractors or grantees are subject to review and release under the access statutes.

What governmental bodies are not covered by the FOIA/PA?

The federal Freedom of Information Act and the federal Privacy Act apply only to the executive branch of the federal government, so they cannot be used to acquire information from the files of state and local governments. (However, most states and many municipalities have privacy and open records statutes of their own, which you can check in law compendiums.[30] These may be quite different from the federal statutes. For additional information on these state statutes and local ordinances, check with your state attorney general or secretary of state, or your city's corporation counsel.)

Many records dealing with state and local governments are in the files of federal agencies, which are available under the federal FOIA/PA. In addition, school records are often available by making requests under the Buckley Amendment; the latter is a federal statute.[31]

In addition, the Privacy Act gives certain agencies blanket exemptions to the access provisions. (This will be discussed later.)

Does the Privacy Act permit access to the files of the Secret Service?

No. The Privacy Act exempts records relating to the protection of the President and other selected officials.[32] Secret Service records are, however, subject to review under the FOIA.

And can the Privacy Act be used to get personal data from the CIA?

No. The Privacy Act exempts the CIA entirely.[33] Such records are, however, subject to review under the FOIA, and the CIA has chosen to exercise its discretion and to process Privacy Act requests. As of this writing, the CIA has been lobbying to exempt all but personal records from the provisions of the FOIA.

And can the Privacy Act be used to get personal data from law enforcement agencies?

No. Each agency whose principle function is the enforcement of criminal laws has a broad exemption under the Privacy Act.[34]

For law enforcement agencies that do not have enforcement of criminal laws as their principle function (the Securities and Exchange Commission, for example), records can be obtained under the Privacy Act only (1) if the records in question have been used to deny a person "any right, privilege, or benefit that he would otherwise be entitled to by Federal law"; and (2) if the release would not disclose a confidential source.[35] Records concerning employment or a federal grant are examples of the kinds of benefits that require review under the Privacy Act, even if held by a law enforcement agency.

However, the FOIA's (b)(7) exemption for certain law enforcement records is narrow enough that it does in fact provide a good deal of access to such material. (See chapter 4.)

Does the FOIA require agencies to publish the materials that I might want?

Yes, some kinds of information must be published. Although the focus of this book is to explain how to obtain government information by writing requests to agencies for specific documents, federal access laws have publication requirements that have been very important. Much information about agency regulations, operations, programs, and policies is published in the *Federal Register (Fed. Reg.)* and the *Code of Federal Regulations (CFR)*. Still more is readily available in the public "reading rooms" that most agencies now maintain.

The *Federal Register* can be a useful resource since it contains material on agency operations, including a regularly updated index to each agency's FOIA policies and related materials. As discussed later, it contains notices about Sunshine meetings. The *Federal Register* is available in most major libraries and all law libraries.

The *Code of Federal Regulations* is a compilation of all agency regulations, including, of course, those dealing with the FOIA, the Privacy Act, the Sunshine Act, and the Federal Advisory Committee Act, and is available in law libraries.[36] A particularly useful reference tool in the *CFR* is the "Finding Aids" volume. Ask your librarian to acquaint you with the *CFR* and the updating material in its supplements and in the *Federal Register*.

Does the Privacy Act require that agencies publish information about their records systems?

Yes. The Privacy Act requires that each agency publish in the *Federal Register* a descriptive list of the record systems from which information about individuals may be retrieved by the use of a personal identifier.[37] (A personal identifier may be, for example, a name, a government employee number, a Social Security number, or even a fingerprint.) This list, which must be updated every year,[38] permits you to check over the systems and to specify which ones you think will contain personal data.[39]

In practice, there are two problems with the way this works out. First, the *Federal Register* descriptions are sketchy at best; some authorities have described then as a "virtually indecipherable mass."[40] (Even so, they may give you enough of a hunch to make an educated guess or two.) Second, agencies can maintain systems that are full of personal data out exempted from publication—if they limit their indexing system to nonpersonal identification. The system of records on Project X, for example, may contain a detailed description of John Jones's role in the project, but if the file system index relates only to the subject matter of the project, and does not include cross-references with personal identifiers to the people involved, then the system would not have to be listed in the *Federal Register*. (Such personal records, however, might be easily retrieved by someone who learned from Jones's personnel file that he had been involved in the project.)

Is there an advantage to going to the *Federal Register* to find out what record systems each agency has?

Yes. This allows you to determine what record systems you should specifically request—it allows you to plan your request strategy. The FBI, for example, has a central record system and a separate system for recording its electronic surveillances. However, unless you specify that you want a check of the electronic surveillance index (the ELSUR Index), the FBI does not routinely check it. So while it is not necessary to do any research in the *Federal Register*, it can help you write a more comprehensive request.[41] It is the position of the General Accounting Office (GAO) that agencies *ought* to inform you that not all records systems have been searched when the agency receives a general request for all records about you. But the GAO maintains that agencies do not have a legal *obligation* to do so.[42]

In the alternative, as discussed in chapter 2, you can try calling or writing to an agency's FOIA/PA Office or Public Information Office for copies of, or citations to, this information. Many agencies will routinely hand out this information.

What kinds of information does the FOIA require agencies to publish?

Basically, the FOIA requires agencies to publish data about their organization, operations, and policies that will have an effect on the public. The purpose is to put an end to the concept of "secret law," which was a problem before the FOIA reforms. Under the old information section of the Administrative Procedure Act, an agency could make a decision or embark on a program, and the members of the public who were affected could get no solid explanation of what precisely the rules of the game were. Unless the particular agency chose to enlighten it, the public was left to guess blindly whether it was going to run afoul of the unstated agency regulations.[43] Since the FOIA, the courts have held that "secret law is an abomination," and ruled that any precedents, policies, or interpretations that the agencies use in making decisions *must* be available to the public.[44]

As a matter of practice, agencies have often argued that some particular item does not actually fit the publication requirements because it does not actually apply to the public. However, if the agency cites some unpublished regulation, form, policy, or what have you, in its dealings with a member of the public, it has defeated its own argument. With a very few exceptions, you have a right to see whatever authority they are citing or relying on.[45]

The FOIA specifically lists the following kinds of information that the agencies must publish in the *Federal Register:*

1. how the agency is organized
2. how the public can get information from the agency
3. descriptions of agency functions
4. formal and informal procedures that determine agency functions
5. rules of agency procedures
6. descriptions of agency forms, and where to get the forms
7. agency instructions concerning the scope and contents of its papers, reports, or examinations
8. agency rules for implementing federal laws
9. general agency policies that affect the public

Is there any information concerning agency policies, functions, procedures, and so on that is not published in the *Federal Register,* but which is available elsewhere?

Yes. The full range of materials that is covered by the FOIA publication requirements include all final opinions in cases that affect agency actions, any and all policy statements and interpretations, and any and all staff manuals (except for certain manuals dealing with law enforcement), and instructions that will affect members of the public. (See chapter 4.) As a practical matter, this body of information is too voluminous for all of it to be published in the *Federal Register*. As a result, the FOIA requires that any such material that is not published in the *Register* must nevertheless be made available to the public for inspection and copying. Most agencies have handled this by setting up reading rooms where the complete collection of this material can be found. Reading rooms sometimes have unusual schedules for when they are open to the public; it is therefore best to check ahead. The FOIA also permits agencies to make such material available by selling printed copies.

In addition, the FOIA requires that all information that is covered by its publication requirements must be adequately indexed (at least four times a year); the index must also be published or otherwise made available to the public.[47]

What happens if an agency does not publish or make available the information just discussed?

If an agency does not publish material or make it otherwise available, the government cannot use that material, policy, or rule, or whatever, to the detriment of a person who would be "adversely affected" by the failure to make it public. If the IRS, for example, did not publish a description of some income tax form, you could not be penalized for not having known about it. In addition, the FOIA requires "timely notice" of such rules, regulations, forms, policies, and so on, in order to be valid, such materials must be published *before* they go into effect.

If the agency fails to meet these requirements, then any person who would be adversely affected may go to court to stop the particular agency action or policy.[48]

Are the agencies required to disclose information about how they implement the FOIA?

Yes, the FOIA itself requires that each federal agency submit to Congress a report every year detailing how the agency has handled its obligations under the FOIA.[49] These reports are available from the Public Affairs Office of each agency and must include—

1. the number of FOIA requests the agency turned down and the reasons for these determinations;
2. the number of administrative appeals that you made, and the agency's reasons why it denied the appeals;
3. the names, titles, and positions of the officials responsible for the denial of records under the FOIA;
4. the record of FOIA cases in which agency officials

were cited by a court as possibly having withheld information "arbitrarily or capriciously," together with a record of the disciplinary action taken as a result of the court's finding;[49a]

5. copies of all agency rules that implement the FOIA;

6. copies of each agency's fee schedule and account of the fees collected;

7. other data describing the agency's efforts to implement the FOIA.

The Congressional Research Service of the Library of Congress has been producing an overview of each year's reports. These can be very useful if you are curious about the track record of a particular agency or agencies. Ask your senator or representative for a copy of the latest version of this study.

In addition, each year the Attorney General is required to submit to Congress a report that lists (1) the FOIA cases; (2) the exemptions involved in each lawsuit; (3) the end result of each case; and (4) the costs, fees, and penalties to the agency in each. The Attorney General's report is also supposed to describe the Justice Department's efforts to encourage the agencies to comply with the FOIA.[50]

Are federal prisoners considered members of the public and thereby affected by the publication requirements?

Since prisoners have fewer civil rights than the rest of the public, federal agencies have avoided publishing information that affects only prisoners. However, in spite of this resistance, the courts have so far held that prisoners are members of the public under the publication requirements of the FOIA. Legislation has been proposed that may, however, cut back on the access rights of convicted felons.[51]

Can documents released under the FOIA be read at the agency, without having to go through the entire request procedure and pay for the copies of the materials?

In some cases, yes. You can find out whether an agency has a public reading room by either asking the FOIA/PA office or by checking the agency's regulations in the *CFR*. The following agencies with the Justice Department have public reading rooms: the Justice Department, the U.S. Attorneys and U.S. Marshals, the Bureau of Prisons, the U.S. Board of Parole, the Community Relations Service, the Law Enforcement Assistance Administration (LEAA), and the FBI.[52] Some agencies keep on hand in their reading rooms material that has previously been released under the FOIA in response to requests and that are of particular interest to the public. The FBI's reading room in Washington includes over seventy "preprocessed" FOIA materials, including files on the surveillance of the American Civil Liberties Union (ACLU), the Kennedy assassination, Malcom X, the Rosenbergs, and the Women's Liberation Movement.[53]

What is the definition of an *agency record* that falls under the provisions of the FOIA?

The language of the statute provides no definition of just what an agency record is, and the situation is more complex than one might think at first.

As already explained, not every government-related entity is an agency covered by the FOIA, and obviously records held by nonagencies are not accessible. But what is the status of documents that are connected somehow to both an agency and a nonagency? The courts have fashioned a working definition of agency records that turns on whether something has been created by, obtained by, and/or under the control of, a federal agency. These criteria are best explained by way of examples.

If an agency has never obtained the raw data behind a study that it funded but that was conducted by a nonagency (for instance, an outside contractor), then the agency is not required to obtain that raw data when it is requested under the FOIA.[54] Even though they were, for a time, housed at the State Department, the notes of Henry Kissinger's telephone conversations while he was National Security Advisor, are Department of State records because they had not been generated by, used by, or under the control of, the agency.[55] A transcript of a secret congressional hearing (that is, a congressionally generated document) is not an agency record although the CIA has a copy in its possession, since it was shown that Congress had intended to maintain control over the document.[56] However, the mere fact that an agency creates a document for a congressional inquiry is not sufficient to establish congressional control,[57] nor is a letter that is written after congressional documents are transferred to the CIA.[58] Similarly, questionnaires filled out by senators for the use of the Attorney General are agency documents because, among other things, the senators had never indicated a desire to retain control.[59] Presentence reports, which are generated by the sentencing court (like Congress, the courts are not agencies within the meaning of the FOIA/PA) for use by the Parole Commission, are considered agency records because the commission exercised control over them.[60]

The handwritten notes that agency employees write during the course of their work have a rather ambiguous status, even though they are generated by agency employees on agency time and are found within the physical confines of an agency office. Because handwritten notes that no one ever bothers to transcribe are perhaps uniquely suited to being categorized as the kind of predecisional material protected by the FOIA's Exemption 5 (see chapter 4), such notes can often be withheld even if they are considered agency records. However, there is no blanket exemption for handwritten notes. (If there were, it is probably fair to say that the work load of government typists would fall off dramatically.) What determines whether or not notes are agency records are such things as their "personal nature," the degree to which the notes are (or are intended to be) circulated within the agency, and whether the notes were meant to be temporary or permanent records.[61]

What kinds of items are considered agency records available under the FOIA?

Initially, the 1966 FOIA only gave access to government "files." With the 1974 amendments to the FOIA, this was changed to apply to *records*—a much broader term. By doing this, Congress set out to make it harder for agencies to withhold entire files.[62] But government records are more than simply files full of paper. The FOIA also gives access to records such as film, X-ray film, and computer tapes. Physical objects, such as the rifle used to kill President Kennedy, are not considered records,[63] largely because they are not reproducible.

A word of warning about computer tapes and printouts is in order, however. Since computer time is very expensive, fees for computerized data can be quite high (be sure to check out the fees in advance). In addition, the tapes and printouts may not necessarily contain the data that you want in the form you need. Unfortunately, it seems that you cannot compel an agency to write a new program in order to retrieve precisely the information that is being requested.[64]

Does the FOIA require that an agency compile a record if none has existed before the request?

It depends on whether the records that are requested already exist in some form. An agency, for example, will have to copy a requested report, but it will not be required to write one that does not already exist. In one case, a court compelled an agency to compile a list, because the requester could in fact have gotten the material by asking for all the files.[65] However, you should expect both that agencies will strenuously resist putting together such compilations, and that search fees will be costly.

In response to a request for personal files under the Privacy Act, what kinds of records must an agency search?

The Privacy Act concerns records that deal with personal information. This includes, but is not limited to, data such as "education, financial transactions, medical history, and criminal or employment history." The records must include an individual's "name, or the identifying number, symbol, or other identifying particular assigned to the individual, such as a finger or voice print or a photograph."[66] And, for data to be covered by the Privacy Act, it must be contained in a "system of records" from which it can be retrieved by such personal identifiers.[67]

Taken together, this means that there may well be records concerning an individual that would not be checked in a request under the Privacy Act. A system of records is covered only if it is indexed in some way that would permit an official to use a personal identifier to retrieve information about an individual. Some files may be set up differently. They might be organized according to, say, technical specifications, even though those files might contain personal data on individuals who are, in fact, identified by name. If the system is not cross-referenced or indexed according to people involved, the record system would not be covered by the Privacy Act. However, the Privacy Act would still require that the information be accurate, timely, and relevant.

When you are making a request for your personal files, it is useful to consider what kinds of records, in addition to the data banks of personal records, might contain personal information. If you were or are a government employee, for example, are there any project records that might contain information on you that you would want to look at? These project records could then be specifically identified for a search made under the FOIA.

If some part of the material that I want is, in fact, properly exempt, can the agency withhold everything else that I have requested?

No. The 1974 amendments to the FOIA have made it clear that agencies *must* release "segregable portions" that remain after the material that is exempt from release has been deleted.[68]

According to a Justice Department memorandum, an agency must release any remaining material that "is at all intelligible" after the deletions have been made. And if there are any "doubts about the intelligibility or responsiveness of remaining nonexempt material," those doubts "should be resolved in favor of release."[69] Agencies regularly forget about this, however, and both your initial request for material and your appeal letters should remind them that you expect this provision to be adhered to. (See chapter 4).

NOTES

1. 5 U.S.C. §552.
1a. *See generally* Morton H. Halperin, ed., *The 1984 Edition of Litigation under the Federal Freedom of Information and Privacy Acts* (Washington, D.C.: Center for National Security Studies, 1983); U.S., Congress, House, Committee on Government Operations, Subcommittee on Government Information and Individual Rights, and U.S., Congress, Senate, Committee on the Judiciary, Subcommittee on Administrative Practice and Procedure (Joint Committee Print), *Freedom of Information Act and Amendments of 1974 (P.L. 93–502): Sourcebook: Legislative History, Texts, and Other Documents,* 94th Cong., 1st sess., 1975 (hereafter cited as *1974 FOIA Sourcebook).* As of this writing, there are a number of legislative proposals which, if enacted, would limit the use of the FOIA to United States persons and permanent resident aliens. *See e.g.,* §774, 98th Cong., 1st sess. 1983.
1b. 5 U.S.C. Section 552a.
2. For background on the Privacy Act, see Charles C. Marson, "The Privacy Act," in *1984 Litigation,* Halperin, ed., *supra* note 1; Office of Management and Budget, *Privacy Act Implementation: Guidelines and Responsibilities,* 40 Fed. Reg. 28,948 (July 9, 1975); U.S. Congress, House, Committee on Government Operations, Subcommittee on Government Information and Individual Rights, and U.S., Congress,

Senate, Committee on Government Operations (Joint Committee Print), *Legislative History of the Privacy Act of 1974, S. 3418 (Public Law 93–579): Sourcebook on Privacy*, 94th Cong., 2d sess., 1976 (for sale by the Superintendent of Documents, U.S. Government Printing Office, Washington, DC 20402, for $12.45). The Privacy Act also set up a two-year commission to study privacy problems; its results are published in U.S. Privacy Protection Study Commission (Linowes Commission), *Personal Privacy in an Information Society* (Washington, D.C.: Government Printing Office, 1977).

3. *See* U.S., Congress, *Congressional Record*, Oct. 9, 1975, pp. S. 18144–51, which reprints the correspondence of Sen. Edward Kennedy concerning alleged conflicts between the two acts. At one point the Justice Department contended that the Privacy Act, even though it was passed only a few weeks after the FOIA, had the effect of repealing your access to your own files under the FOIA. The Justice Department backed down on this. *See also* Note to "The Freedom of Information Act's Privacy Exemption and the Privacy Act of 1974," 11 *Harv. Civ. Rts./Civ. Libs. L. Rev.* 596 (1976).

4. 5 U.S.C. Section 552a(b)(2).

5. 5 U.S.C. Section 552a(q).

6. 5 U.S.C. Section 552a(d)(5). As of this writing, there is proposed legislation that would, if enacted, place similar restrictions on FOIA use. *See e.g.*, U.S., Congress, Senate, Committee on the Judiciary, *Freedom of Information Reform Act: S. 774*, 98th Cong., 1st sess., 1983, S. Rept. 98–221, p. 29.

7. U.S., Congress, Senate, *Congressional Record*, Oct. 9, 1975, p. S. 18, 151.

8. 5 U.S.C. Section 552a(d)(2).

9. 5 U.S.C. Section 552a(g)(1)(C)and(D).

10. 5 U.S.C. Section 552a(e)(7) reads that agencies maintaining records covered by the Privacy Act shall "maintain no record describing how any individual exercises rights guaranteed by the First Amendment unless expressly authorized by statute or by the individual about whom the record is maintained or unless pertinent to and within the scope of an authorized law enforcement activity."

11. *See also* Marson, *supra*, note 2.

12. 5 U.S.C. Section 552a(k)(5).

13. 5 U.S.C. Section 552a(k)(7).

14. *See* 5 U.S.C. Section 552(e); U.S., Congress, House, *Amending Section 552 of Title 5, United States Code, known as the Freedom of Information Act*, 93d Cong., 2d sess., 1974, H. Rept. 93–876, p. 8, reprinted in *1974 FOIA Sourcebook, supra* note 1, at 128.

15. *Washington Research Project v. Dept of HEW*, 504 F.2d 238, 248 (D.C. Cir. 1974), *cert. denied*, 421 U.S. 963 (1975).

16. *Irwin Memorial v. American National Red Cross*, 640 F.2d 1051 (9th Cir. 1981).

17. *Gale v. Andrus*, 643 F.2d 826 (D.C. Cir. 1980).

18. *Rocap v. Indiek*, 539 F.2d 174 (D.C. Cir. 1976).

19. U.S., Congress, Senate, *FOIA Amendments, Conference Report,* 93d Cong., 2d sess., 1974, S. Rept. 93–1200, p. 15. The conference approved the result reached in *Soucie* v. *David,* 448 F.2d 1067 (D.C. Cir. 1971). *See also* 5 U.S.C. Section 552(e).

20. Public Law 95–591; 92 STAT. 2523; 44 U.S.C. Sections 2201–2207.

21. Harold C. Relyea, "Access to Congressional Records," Freedom of Information Center Report No. 428, School of Journalism, University of Missouri of Columbia, Oct. 1980; *Paisley v. CIA,* 712 F.2d 686 (D.C. Cir. 1983).

22. U.S., Congress, Senate, Committee on Governmental Affairs, Subcommittee on Oversight and Government Management, *To Eliminate Congressional and Federal Double Standards: Hearing on S. 1112,* (1979).

23. *Kissinger* v. *Reporters Committee for Freedom of the Press,* 445 U.S. 136 (1980).

24. Public Law 94–553; 90 STAT. 2541; 17 U.S.C. 101 et seq.

25. A list of GAO publications is available from the Publications Section, General Accounting Office, Washington, DC 20548.

26. *See* 4 *CFR* Part 81.

27. U.S., Congress, Senate, Committee on the Judiciary, Subcommittee on Administrative Practice and Procedure, *Freedom of Information: A Compilation of State Laws,* 95th Cong., 2d. sess., 1978, has a detailed treatment of the District of Columbia FOIA. It is available from the U.S. Government Printing Office for $5 (stock no. 052–070–04741–1). *See also* James T. O'Reilly, *Federal Information Disclosure* (Colorado Springs: Shepards, McGraw-Hill, 1977) chap. 5, p. 4.

28. 5 U.S.C. Section 552a(m).

29. *Forsham v. Harris,* 445 U.S. 169 (1980).

30. For a brief summary of state freedom of information and privacy laws, *see* Wallis E. McClain, ed., *Summary of Freedom of Information and Privacy Laws of the Fifty States* (Washington, D.C.: Plus Publications, 1978). The texts of the state information laws are reprinted in *Freedom of Information, supra* note 27.

31. The Family Educational and Privacy Rights Act (Buckley Amendment), 20 U.S.C. §1232g. Simply put, the Buckley Amendment gives students and their parents a right of access to school records if the school has received any federal funds (which most schools have). *See* Alan H. Levine and Eve Cary: *The Rights of Students* (New York: Avon, 1977), pp. 108–114.

32. 5 U.S.C. §552a(k)(3); *see* 18 U.S.C. §3056.

33. 5 U.S.C. Section 552a(j)(1).

34. 5 U.S.C. Section 552a(j)(2).

35. 5 U.S.C. Section 552a(k)(2).

36. To use the *CFR* first find out which volume contains the regulations of the agency that you are interested in. Each volume has a list of the titles; check them for the subject area that you are inquiring about. If you don't find what you want, check the monthly *Federal Register*

(Fed. Reg.) Subject Index, or use the table of changes in the *CFR* sections to find the changes that have been published in the *Federal Register*. The librarian should be able to help.

37. 5 U.S.C. Section 552a(e)(4).

38. 5 U.S.C. Section 552a(f).

39. The Office of the Federal Register publishes a compilation entitled *Protecting Your Right to Privacy*.

40. *See* O'Reilly, *supra* note 27, Chap. 5, p. 4.

41. U.S., Congress, House, Committee on Government Operations, Subcommittee on Government Information and Individual Rights, *FBI Compliance with the Freedom of Information Act: Hearing*, 95th Cong., 2d sess., 1978, pp. 23, 26, 27.

42. *Id.* at 69.

43. The term *secret law* was coined during the congressional hearings that led up to the enactment of the 1966 FOIA. *See* Kenneth Culp Davis, *Administrative Law of the Seventies* (Rochester, N.Y.: Lawyer's Co-operative Publishing Co., 1976), §3A. 6–4, p. 71.

44. *NLRB* v. *Sears, Roebuck & Co.*, 421 U.S. 132, 153 (1975).

45. *See* the discussion in chap. 4 for an explanation of the FOIA's (b)(2) exemption as applied to investigative manuals for more details.

46. 5 U.S.C. Section 552(a)(1).

47. 5 U.S.C. Section 552(a)(2).

48. *See* U.S., Congress, Senate, *Amending the Freedom of Information Act*, 93d Cong., 2d sess., 1974, S. Rept. 93–584, p. 9. *See also* Davis, *supra* note 43, at 72–75; *Morton v. Ruiz*, 415 U.S. 199 (1974).

49. 5 U.S.C. Section 552(d).

49a. 5 U.S.C. Section 552(a)(4)(F).

50. 5 U.S.C. Section 552(d). The Office of Information Law and Policy, U.S. Department of Justice, Washington, DC 20530, publishes a list of all FOI cases, which is of course more comprehensive than the report for any one year. *The Administration of the Freedom of Information Act: A Brief Overview of Executive Branch Annual Reports for 1978* (Washington, D.C.: Congressional Research Service, Library of Congress, 1978) (as of this writing, reports are also available for 1975, 1976, and 1977).

As of this writing, there is proposed legislation which, if enacted, would shift the yearly due date of these yearly reports from March 1 to December 1 of each year, and require that the reports cover the fiscal year rather than the calendar year. These changes would not alter the substance of the reporting requirement. *See, e.g.*, U.S., Congress, Senate, *Freedom of Information Reform Act*, supra note 6.

51. *See National Prison Project of the ACLU Foundation, Inc.*, v. *Sigler*, 390 F. Supp. 780, 701 (D.D.C. 1975) (Department of Justice hearings may become precedents and are therefore covered); *Ramer* v. *Saxbe*, 522 F.2d 695, 698–700 (D.C. Cir. 1975) (Bureau of Prisons policies must be published because of the impact on prisoners); *Pickus* v. *U.S. Board of Parole*, 507 F.2d 1107 (D.C. Cir. 1974) (guidelines affecting prisons are not merely internal management

policies). The National Prison Project of the ACLU Foundation, 1346 Connecticut Ave. N.W., Washington, DC 20036, has available, up-to-date information on FOIA laws concerning prisoners. *See also* O'Reilly, *supra* note 27, at chap. 6, pp. 29–30.

52. 28 C.F.R. §16.2.
53. "FOIPA Preprocessed List," available from FOI/Privacy Branch, FBI, Washington, DC 20535.
54. *Forsham v. Harris,* 445 U.S. 169 (1980).
55. *Kissinger v. Reporters' Committee for Freedom of the Press,* 445 U.S. 136 (1980).
56. *Goland v. CIA,* 607 F.2d 339 (D.C. Cir. 1978), *cert. denied,* 445 U.S. 927 (1980).
57. *Paisley, supra* note 21.
58. *Holy Spirit Assn. v. CIA,* 636 F.2d 838 (D.C. Cir. 1980).
59. *Ryan v. Dept. of Justice,* 617 F.2d 781 (D.C. Cir. 1980).
60. *Carson v. Dept. of Justice,* 631 F.2d 1008 (D.C. Cir. 1980).
61. *Porter County Chapter of the Izaak Walton League, Inc. v. Atomic Energy Commission,* 380 F. Supp. 630 (N.D. Ind. 1974); *British Airports Authority v. Civil Aeronautics Board,* 531 F. Supp. 408 (D.D.C. 1982); *Conoco Inc. v. Dept. of Justice,* 521 F. Supp. 1301 (D. Del. 1981), *aff'd,* 687 F.2d 724 (3d Cir. 1982).
62. *1974 FOIA Sourcebook, supra* note 1, at 451.
63. *"Attorney General's Memorandum on the Public Information Section of the Administrative Procedure Act"* (1967), p. 23.
64. *Prescott v. U.S.,* No. 75-1137 (9th Cir. 1976). *See* O'Reilly, *supra* note 27 at chap. 9, p. 9.
65. *Disabled Officers* v. *Rumsfeld,* 428 F. Supp. 454, 456–57 (D.D.C. 1977).
66. 5 U.S.C. Section 552a(a)(4).
67. 5 U.S.C. Section 552a(a)(5).
68. 5 U.S.C. Section 552(b).
69. *"Attorney General's Memorandum on the 1974 Amendments to the Freedom of Information Act"* (1975), pp. 14–15.

II

Writing an FOIA/PA Request

Who is entitled to records under the access provisions of the FOIA?

The FOIA states that "any person" can request records under the provisions of the act.[1] This means that under current law the act can be used by individuals, foreigners, corporations, and associations, provided that they follow the procedures for making requests and pay the fees (unless granted a fee waiver) for searching and copying records. These requirements will be discussed in more detail later in this chapter. And, of course, you are not entitled to information in categories that are exempt from mandatory disclosure.

Thus far, the courts have carved out only one category of persons who do not have enforceable rights under the FOIA—fugitives from justice. Agencies are not required to process the FOIA requests of a felon who fled after conviction.[2]

What all this means is that you do not have to explain to anybody either why you want a particular piece of information, or why you are important enough to bother with: the fact that you have written an FOIA request is enough by itself to get you in the door. In fact, it is sometimes best that you not tell an agency who you are or what your interest is. Agency professionals, for example, are seldom delighted about taking time away from their work load to hunt for something for a student term paper. And although student status is supposed to have no effect on access rights, as a practical matter of psychological strategy, if you say something that exasperates the searcher, he might just decide not to carry the hunt to every last available file cabinet. There are only two situations

25

in which who you are makes an important difference in your favor: when you request personal files, and when you want to ask for a fee waiver. These situations are discussed later.

As mentioned earlier, there have been proposals in Congress that would, if enacted, limit who can use the FOIA. One proposal, for example, includes prohibiting FOIA requests by foreign nationals, allowing the Attorney General to place limits on FOIA use by incarcerated felons, and delaying the processing of requests from persons who are engaged in an ongoing civil or criminal judicial proceeding or an administrative adjudication.[3]

And under the Privacy Act?

As explained in chapter 1, access under the Privacy Act is narrower than under the FOIA. The Privacy Act applies to systems of records concerning individuals; it defines an *individual* as a "citizen of the United States or an alien lawfully admitted for permanent residence."[4] This means that illegal immigrants, or people with student, tourist, or other temporary visas, are not protected by the Privacy Act and do not have access to their personal records under its provisions. (However, under current law such people could still get access to their personal records under the FOIA, and private information about them would still be protected by the privacy exemptions of the FOIA, which are discussed later.) This definition of an *individual* also means that organizations, such as corporations, are not covered by the Privacy Act, although personal data about the individuals within any organization would have the full privacy protections of the FOIA and the Privacy Act. But here again, there is a qualification: when an individual mentioned in the agency files has been acting in an "entrepreneurial capacity," he may not be able to use the Privacy Act to gain access to such records.[5] This same category of entrepreneurial records would of course be available under an FOIA request. Although corporations have no safeguards under the personal privacy protections of the federal access statutes, their confidential business information is nevertheless protected. (See chapter 4.)

And who is entitled to get personal records under the access provisions of the FOIA and the Privacy Act?

To be entitled to receive agency records that contain intimate personal data, you must be the subject of the records, or the legal guardian or parent of the subject of the records,[6] or be authorized by the subject of the records to receive the records. Authorizations (also known as privacy waivers) to receive another individual's records cannot be coerced or inferred or obtained without an explanation to the individual of his or her privacy rights.[7] This means that organizations such as corporations and labor unions are not entitled to access to the agency records about their employees or members unless the subjects of the records have explicitly authorized such access. The privacy protections do have certain exceptions, however. (See chapter 4.)

And who is entitled to records concerning a person who is dead?

For most purposes, under the Privacy Act, a deceased person is probably not an "individual."[8] (See also chapter 4.)

Can a legal minor or a person who is legally incompetent use the Privacy Act?

There is no reason why a minor or anyone else cannot request access to his or her own records. However, if the request has to be taken to court, the legal guardian must decide to file the suit.

What fees can an agency charge for an FOIA request?

The 1974 amendments to the FOIA permit agencies to charge only for the direct costs of searching for, and copying, requested records.[9] All agencies are required to publish a "fee schedule" showing their charges for copying and for searches (including computer searches) by their professional and clerical staff. Bear in mind that fees can be quite costly, especially with large requests. Under current law, agencies are not permitted to charge for the time spent reviewing the records to determine if any material is properly exempt from mandatory disclosure. (See chapter 5.) There are, however, legislative proposals which, if enacted, would allow the agencies to charge for the time that is spent reviewing the records—unless the request is made for noncommercial research purposes, by the news media, or by a nonprofit group that intends to make the information public.[10]

And what fees can be charged for a request processed under the Privacy Act?

The Privacy Act permits agencies to charge fees only for the "actual costs" of copying records.[11] This means that agencies cannot charge for the time that is spent on searching for, or reviewing, the documents, but only for the cost of copying them. Therefore, with many agencies, costs for requests for personal files can be greatly reduced by asking for them under the Privacy Act rather than under the FOIA. (Unfortunately, the Privacy Act exemptions are broader and you may not get as much information.)

What are the fees for a request made under the FOIA/PA?
Most agencies (but not all) have adopted a policy of charging search fees if a request is made under both the FOIA and the Privacy Act. Copying fees can be charged under both acts.

How much are the fees for an FOIA search likely to be?
There is no easy way to answer this. Much depends on how easily the information is located, which in turn depends on how efficient that particular part of an agency's filing system is. In addition, fee policies vary greatly from one agency to the next. To find out how a particular agency's fees break down, you should ask its FOIA/PA office for a copy of its "fee schedule." As of this writing, searches by clerical staff range from about $3.00 to $7.00 per hour, and those by professional staff range from about $6.00 to $15.00 per hour. (Clerical staff typically handle routine requests for files that are in the main filing system of the agency. Professionals, however, will handle requests that require some knowledge of the subject matter of the request in order to identify and/or locate the documents.) Costs for computer searches may involve items for various aspects of the search. One agency, for example, charges $8.75 per hour for FOIA-related keypunching, $14.00 per hour for programming, and $65.00 per hour for computer time. (Depending on an agency's policies, you may not be able to get a special computer program written to retrieve your data, regardless of your willingness to pay for it.) Duplication fees also vary, but they typically run between $.05 and $.10 per page.

Search fees also vary depending on whether the contents of an entire file clearly respond to your request, or whether a file or files would have to be searched in order to determine whether they had some documents covered by your request.

If the fees seem high talking with the agency employees who are handling your FOIA request can sometimes be useful in order to learn how the files are arranged; you may then be able to rewrite your request so that the search is simpler for them and cheaper for you. Ask that you be notified of the fees in advance before asking the agency to go through with processing the request.

Can I be charged search fees if an agency finds little or no material that I have asked for, or if all the material is exempt?

Yes, if it is an FOIA request, agencies can charge for all search costs. However, the Justice Department has recommended that search fees be waived if the unsuccessful search was conducted at a minimal cost to the agency. The Department of Justice has also recommended that fees be charged for unsuccessful searches only if you were given fair notice that this might happen.[12]

Bear in mind that if an agency finds any material at all, no matter how inconsequential, it will be considered a successful search. The fact that none of the material is very interesting or useful does not make a search unsuccessful. You have no guarantee of quality or quantity in exchange for the fees you pay. The National Technical Information Service (NTIS) of the Department of Commerce, for example, has a set fee of $125 per computer tape; the amount of information is immaterial.

What do I do if I expect that I will only want a few documents out of the many that an agency may have on some topic?

You have three options.

First, you can specify what you don't want as well as what you do want. If you are not interested in seeing what newspaper clippings a particular agency, such as the FBI, may have on you, for instance, then you should say so. (One controversial figure ended up paying the FBI $600 for copies of what turned out to be 6,000 newsclips on him.) Unfortunately, there is no way to request that the agency send only the "interesting" documents, and a great many in any given category may be nothing but the fruits of bureaucratic paper-shufflings.

The second option is to ask to inspect the material that is

found in response to your request so that you may select the material you want copied. Some agencies will allow this as a matter of routine; others, however, will deny it as a matter of routine. You should ask for this option only if you are willing and able to travel to the place where the records are kept. (You would still pay search fees, but could limit copying fees this way.)

A third option, as mentioned earlier, is to find out if the material has already, been requested and released and if it is now available in a reading room. (See chapter 1.) If so, you can make arrangements to review it and select what you want. (You would not have to pay search fees, and could limit copying fees as well.)

If I want to inspect the documents rather than pay for copies, or if I want to inspect the documents before deciding whether to buy copies, can I get the agency to ship them to a government office in the city where I live?

No. However, you should find out whether the agency has a local office that would have copies of the documents.

How do I decide where to address an FOIA/PA request?

The easiest place to start is with your telephone directory. Most agencies have field offices or regional offices in most major U.S. cities. A quick phone call should produce the address and phone number of the agency's Public Affairs or Freedom of Information Office (bear in mind that the precise titles of these offices vary a fair amount from one agency to the next).

It might be more complicated to find out which agency handles the kind of information you want. For instance, it may not be obvious whether some economic information is covered by the Treasury Department or by the Office of Management and Budget (OMB). Once again, the Public Affairs or Freedom of Information Office should be helpful, although they do sometimes make mistakes.

To help track down a likely agency or agencies, you might consult *The United States Government Organization Manual*, which describes the function of each agency and its bureaus. [13] There are also private publications that provide instructions on obtaining information from the government. [14] The staffs of your congressional representatives might also be able to suggest which agency covers what you are interested in. A list of agency addresses is printed in the Appendix. However, it is not exhaustive, and, furthermore, addresses change frequently.

If you guess wrong and address your FOIA/PA request to an agency that does not actually have the records you want, most agencies will forward the request to the proper agency. This will cause a delay, but will not invalidate your request. However, it is possible that an agency may not be able to determine what agency might have material that you want. Often, a number of agencies will each have their own records on some subjects—for example, the CIA, the State Department, the Department of Defense, the National Security Council (NSC), and the National Security Agency (NSA) may all be interested in a given foreign event. If you anticipate that more than one agency will have records that you want, there is no reason why you cannot write to each. Bear in mind, though, that search and copying fees will mount because they will be charged by each agency.

When should I send a request to agency headquarters, and when to the field offices?

When in doubt, it is usually safe to address requests to headquarters, but generally field or regional offices have a great deal of interesting information. Headquarters receives information according to institutional and bureaucratic needs; field offices collect information that they work with on a daily basis. Therefore, if you are interested in the operations of the agency in a given locality, you should forward your requests to field offices as well as to headquarters. In the case of the IRS for example, virtually all records relating to any given taxpayer would be found at the local office where that person's tax returns are sent. Headquarters records consist primarily of administrative and policy materials.

In the case of the FBI, you must write to the field offices, and not to the headquarters in Washington, D.C. Even when you ask the bureau headquarters to check specific field office records, the FBI will not do so.

You should be aware of the fact that field offices are often unfamiliar with FOIA/PA laws and prone to making mistakes in their interpretations of what is or is not available.[15]

How long may the agencies take to respond to an FOIA request?

The 1974 amendments to the FOIA provide that an agency

must determine whether to comply with an FOIA request within 10 working days of receiving the initial request letter. The agency response must notify you of the determination, the reasons for the determination, and your right to write an administrative appeal letter if any material is withheld.[16] An agency can take an additional 10 working days in "unusual circumstances."

As of this writing, there are proposals in Congress which, if enacted, would extend the time limits somewhat, allowing an additional 30 days in unusual circumstances.[17]

And how about a Privacy Act request?

The Privacy Act, unlike the FOIA, does not provide explicit time limits for the agencies' responses to Privacy Act requests. As a result, the FOIA is clearly the stronger law when it comes to enforceable time limits—this is one reason why it is generally wise to make requests for personal records under *both* the FOIA and the Privacy Act, so that the FOIA time limits come into effect.

However, most agencies have issued regulations that require that Privacy Act requests be acknowledged within ten working days, and that the records themselves must be made available within thirty working days.[18]

If you make a request under the Privacy Act alone (in order to save on search fees, for example) but there are excessive delays in responding to a request, it is always possible to write the agency another letter and inform them that you wish your letter to be treated as a FOIA/PA request, rather than exclusively as a Privacy Act request; this would bring the more stringent FOIA time limits into effect. This will not ordinarily speed up the time that the agency takes, but it will clarify your standing to sue for enforcement of the FOIA time limits, if that is your intention.

If the agency turns down my original request and I appeal, how long can it take to respond to the administrative appeal letter?

An agency must respond to an FOIA administrative appeal letter within 20 working days. The agency's response must inform you that you can seek judicial review (that is, file a lawsuit) if all or some of the records are still withheld.[19] Again, an agency can take 10 additional working days in "unusual circumstances." The Privacy Act does not set up procedures for administrative appeals, but many agencies have established them when they issued their Privacy Act regulations. You can call the agency's FOIA/PA Office for an explanation of their regulations, or you can check them in the *Federal Register (Fed. Reg.)* or the *Code of Federal Regulations (CFR)*. In the alternative, you can simply adopt the FOIA procedures.

As mentioned earlier, there are legislative proposals before Congress which, if enacted, would allow an agency to take up to an additional 30 days in unusual circumstances.[20]

What are the "unusual circumstances" that allow an agency to take longer to respond?

The FOIA specifies that an agency can legitimately take an additional ten working days to respond to either an initial request or an appeal letter in one of three situations:

1. the documents are not located in the office where the request was sent and must be obtained from another office;[21]
2. the request is for a voluminous amount of material;[22]
3. the agency must consult with another agency, or with two or more of its own components, before it can determine whether the material can be released.[23]

Various legislative proposals have suggested also adding several additional reasons that would qualify as unusual circumstances. These include situations (1) where the agency head states in writing that the deadlines cannot be met for a particular request without significantly disrupting the performance of a statutory agency function; (2) where submitters of information must be notified that their information has been requested (see chapter 4); and (3) where a large number of requests has created a substantial backlog of unprocessed requests.[24]

What can I do if the agency does not respond within the time limits?

The FOIA gives you the right to take the agency to court for violating the time limits of the statute.[25] The federal court may then order the agency to process the request within a specific time frame. However, since the judicial process is expensive and time-consuming (at the very best, it will take several months; often, it takes one to three years), it is usually better to be patient, unless you have an urgent need for the material.

If you need to press the time limits, there are four slightly different situations in which you may file an FOIA lawsuit in order to speed up the processing of your request.

1. For an initial request: the agency misses the ten-working-day deadline and does not claim additional time for "unusual circumstances." (Instead of filing suit, it is almost always better to write an administrative appeal letter.)

2. For an initial request: the agency claims the additional time allowable in unusual circumstances, but misses this extended deadline. (Again, it is almost always better to write an administrative appeal letter.)

3. For an administrative appeal: the agency misses the twenty-working-day deadline and has already used up, in processing the initial request, the extra time allowed in unusual circumstances.

4. For an administrative appeal: the agency misses the twenty-working-day deadline and fails to notify you that it will be taking the additional time permitted in unusual circumstances.

(For information on agency delays, see chapter 3; for writing administrative appeals, see chapter 5; and if you are considering filing a suit, see chapter 6.)

When should I make an FOIA/PA request?

Ideally, you should make a request for information as soon as you realize that you are interested in the particular material. Delay may allow material to be destroyed, forgotten, lost, or misappropriated.

Federal statutes permit the destruction of records except for those that document the "essential transactions of an agency" or have important historical, legal, administrative, or research value. Sometimes, views on what should be preserved differ considerably, and it is possible to go to court to challenge a systematic destruction program, as has been successfully done in regard to FBI files.[26]

But even if the files are not in danger of being destroyed, common sense dictates making requests while the topic is still fresh in the memories of the employees who dealt with it.

In addition, if a federal employee improperly removes government documents from an agency before you file your FOIA request, you cannot sue under the FOIA in order to obtain access, at least if there is no evidence that the transfer was done in order to avoid an FOIA request. This situation occurred when a former secretary of state gave his telephone records, subject to special access restrictions, to the Library of Congress, which is not subject to the FOIA. The Supreme Court held that even where such a transfer of agency records might be improper, the agency (in this case the Department of State) could not be sued under the FOIA for withholding material that is no longer in its possession.[27]

Should I hire a lawyer to write an FOIA/PA request letter for me?

No. In most cases there is no need to. Letters requesting FOIA/PA access are very easy. Since a lawyer would probably charge about a hundred dollars to write a request letter, and since a nonlawyer can write a perfectly good request letter simply by following the forms, there is no need to hire a lawyer.

What form should an FOIA/PA request letter take?

Some agencies will provide a standardized "demand" form for you to fill out, but it is very easy to write a request letter of your own. There are sample form letters in Appendix A, which you can copy or adapt to your own request. Also, some organizations have produced their own fill-in-the-blank form letters, which their members have successfully used to request material under the FOIA or the Privacy Act.

A few general points should be kept in mind:

1. An FOIA/PA letter doesn't have to be erudite (even fill-in-the-blank form letters are fine), but it does have to be legible. It should be typed, or at least printed *very* clearly.

2. Be sure to date your request. Time limits can be important, and some agencies file their requests by date. You will also want to refer to the date of your letter in your future correspondence with the agency.

3. Be sure to keep a copy of all your correspondence

with the agency. This will be very helpful in writing administrative appeals and going to court.

4. If your request is for files where there may be some privacy interests that the government should protect, you will want to have your signature notarized and include any identification that the agency requires. You may want to attach to your initial request letter a privacy waiver from other persons, or you may want to wait until the agency actually denies records by citing privacy exemptions.

Does a request for information have to be made in writing?

A few agencies have voluntarily adopted informal, oral procedures for making FOIA requests, but other than that, all FOIA requests must be made in writing. Under the Privacy Act, requests may be made orally. In either case, written requests are better because it is easier to enforce your rights when you have documentation of your efforts.

Of course, as described in the Introduction, you might be able to use other, less formal avenues for getting the same kind of information. Some officials, if they know that the material would be available under the FOIA anyway, will just send it to you so that they don't have to bother with handling a formal FOIA request.

How precisely must an FOIA request describe the records wanted?

The answer is that an agency must search for records if the FOIA request "reasonably describes" the material sought.[28] The legislative history of the 1974 amendments states that a "reasonable description" is one that "would be sufficient if it enables a professional employee of the agency who was familiar with the subject area of the request to locate the record with a reasonable amount of effort."[29] This means that an agency cannot refuse to process FOIA requests simply because you do not know the particular file number, precise title of a report, or exact date of some agency decision.

On the other hand, common sense dictates that you should give the agency as detailed and precise a description as possible of the material you want. Vague descriptions only make it easy for the agency to say that a record does not exist. Nor should an agency have to engage unnecessarily in guessing games as to which particular set of documents you actually want. And finally, the vaguer the description, the longer the search will take and the higher the search fees will be.

If there are published accounts citing the material that you want—newspaper clippings, articles, congressional reports, books, memoirs, or agency reports—provide these specific references. If possible, attach to your request a copy of the newsclipping or page where the material you are requesting is described.

If you know that the records (or portions of them) have already been released, be sure to say so—this should reduce or even eliminate the search fees. If possible, give data to identify the release: the name of the original requester, the date of release, and the release number (if any).

Give any specific identifying information that you might have: the subject, date, and title of the record; who wrote it and to whom it was addressed; and the office where it originated.

In planning a request strategy; it is a good idea to think concretely about the "search logic" that an agency employee might follow in fielding a request. For example, if you are listing a series of topics on which you want material, determine the real scope of what you want. If you are interested in records on, say, "mail opening and surveillance," an agency might respond by sending only those records that deal with *both* mail opening and surveillance, but nothing that would deal with just one or the other. It can be useful to use the "and/or" phrasing to describe the material that you want, if you really want an inclusive search.

Obviously, what is a "reasonable description" to one person may be quite unreasonable to another, particularly to the person whose job is to search the files. The General Accounting Office (GAO), as of April 1978, felt, for example, that "where a requester asks the FBI if it has 'any file on me,' " a search of only the Bureau's Central Records System would be an adequate response, even though many files are not indexed in that system. In other words, unless there were an intent to conceal the existence of some records, an agency could limit its search to the most likely file system.[30] In order to get around this problem, you should be as specific as possible in your description, and it may help to do a little research. (The discussion in chapter 4 compares the file systems of the FBI and the CIA. This gives just two examples of how differently agencies can organize their records.)

Besides providing a reasonable description of what I am requesting, what other points should my letter include?

The sample request letter in Appendix A contains a number of points that will show that you are sophisticated about the legal provisions of the FOIA/PA. Sometimes, an agency will take such letters more seriously in order to save paperwork itself later on.

If you have omitted these points from FOIA or Privacy Act requests, the omission does not invalidate the request, but these details save time by clearing up matters at the outset.

1. A request letter should state which statute you are making a request under. As you know by now, FOIA is 5 U.S.C. Section 552, and the Privacy Act is 5 U.S.C. Section 552a. (See the beginning of chapter 1 if you missed that explanation.) If you are requesting personal files under both acts, cite them both.

2. Remind the agency that if some portion of the material is exempt, the acts require them to release "segregable portions"—that is, everything that is left after the exempt material is deleted.

3. You are entitled to know the grounds (that is, the exemptions) on which the request is being denied or material is being deleted. State that you want a detailed justification of the withholdings.

4. State that if the agency's response is not satisfactory, you will write an administrative appeal (see chapter 5). Ask for the name of the official to whom such appeals should be sent. (Agencies are required to give you this information even if you forget to ask for it.)

5. Straighten out the costs in advance. You should either make it clear that you are prepared to pay all reasonable search and copying fees, or you should state that if the fees are over some amount that you specify, that you want to be notified before the request is processed. (The agency will probably notify you of the costs beforehand anyhow.)

6. If you want to avoid some of the copying costs (but not, of course, the search costs, if it is an FOIA request), your letter should include a request to see the documents rather than having copies made. If you think that you will want to select some documents for copying, you should say so. (Do not ask to inspect the documents first

if you are not prepared to go to the place where they are located.)

7. If you think that you may qualify for a fee waiver, you should request one in your initial request letter. (See the discussion on fee waivers later in this chapter.)

8. State that you would like the agency to contact you if they need to clarify some aspect of your request. Make sure they have your address and daytime phone number. (If you move while your request is being processed or is waiting in line at an agency that has a lengthy backlog, make sure that you notify the agency of your new address and daytime phone. Enclose a copy of your initial request letter to make sure they know who you are.)

After I have sent a written request under the FOIA or Privacy Act, can I follow up by telephoning the agency?

Yes. In fact, this is often a good idea—it can be useful to establish a "contact" in the office handling the FOIA/PA requests. There are some useful procedures to keep in mind when following through via the telephone.

1. Be cordial. The human touch often works better than the legal argument. In spite of publicity to the contrary, bureaucrats can be very nice people.

2. Be sure to take notes on what was said, the date(s) on your phone conversation(s), and, most important, the name of the person you spoke to.

3. Follow up each conversation by sending a letter to the official you spoke to. This letter should say that you are writing to confirm your conversation on that date. It should carefully restate any agreements, definitions, time schedules, fees, and so on that might have been agreed upon. A follow-up letter will do three things: (1) it will remind the official what was agreed upon; (2) it will provide a written record when your request file is passed on to other personnel; and (3) if there has been a misunderstanding in the phone conversation, the letter will alert both you and the agency in time to set things straight.

4. If the agency does not follow through with what had been agreed to, you will be able to bring up this failure in the future. It will also help show a court that you made every effort to work out reasonable arrangements

for processing your request, but that the agency refused to follow through on its promises.

Are there special problems involved in making a request for voluminous materials?

Yes. A request for a huge amount of material involving thousands of documents is far more complex than a simple request for, say, a specific report or file. And if a request is "overbroad," it can be denied.[31] Even if you could afford to pay for such a mass of material, you cannot ask for all the records of a given agency, or even within a particular filing system or computer memory bank. This does not mean, however, that you *cannot* make a request for a huge number of documents—the FOIA release of documents in the Rosenberg espionage case numbered over a hundred thousand items. What it does mean is that you must think about strategy questions when formulating a large request.

Ordinarily it is better planning to write a series of separate requests for smaller sets of records than to write one request for "everything relating to" a given subject; you can then cite specific records that are referred to in the earlier batches of material that you get.

Sometimes it saves time to write smaller requests. In many agencies, huge requests will be processed separately from more modest requests. The FBI, for example, considers anything over fifteen volumes of information (two hundred pages per volume) as a "project" case. Typically, the FBI will negotiate in order to narrow the scope of the request.[32]

Not only does this help keep search and copying fees manageable, but narrow requests generally get better cooperation from agency officials. Remember, FOIA requests are fielded by human beings on the other end, and officials can get overwhelmed and confused, just like anyone else. If your request is broad, it is a good idea to be willing to discuss the scope of your request with the agency; this should be included in your request letter.

In the interests of keeping your requests narrow, it is sometimes a good idea to describe not only what you want, but also what you are *not* requesting. (Often people do not realize how much material they are asking for.) If you're researching problems with nuclear reactors, for example, could you limit the request to one or a few named plants rather than to all the plants nationwide? You can always request more material later on. Or, if you want records on housing problems of, say, the elderly, can you break the request down into geographic regions, or economic factors? (Sometimes it will be a good idea to discuss such factors with someone at an agency to determine how categories are broken down so that a request can be written to reflect the filing system and make the search far easier.)

There is an exception, however, to the general rule that a series of small requests is better than one large one. At agencies such as the FBI and the CIA there are large backlogs, tolerated by the courts, and your requests may wait in line for two or three years before they are processed. In such a situation, planning a series of follow-up requests might add decades to your wait. Therefore, at a backlogged agency, you would be better off starting with broad requests. If time is important to you, a call to the agency's FOIA/PA office should provide you with an estimate of how long processing takes, and you can plan the scope of your requests accordingly.

Can I make an FOIA request that would require an agency to mail automatically, as they become available, any new material that fit a particular description?

No. The FOIA does not require agencies to establish mailing lists to keep you informed of new developments. If you want new material, you must write a new request.[33]

What kind of information should I include in a request for my personal files?

First, the request has to give the agency enough identifying information so that there is no confusion about whether they are sending John Jones's records to the correct John Jones. And second, the request should give the agency clues as to where to look.

Requests should include such facts as your birth date, place of birth, nationality, and Social Security number. Other facts might sometimes be relevant: previous names, nicknames, previous addresses, and (if you're writing to an agency that would be likely to have an interest in such facts, such as the CIA or the State Department) dates and places of travel abroad.

If your name is relatively common, include enough information to distinguish you from other people with the same or a similar name.

If your name is frequently misspelled, you might ask the agency to check under various possible misspellings.

In some agencies, such as the FBI, the political surveillance files of women may be filed under their husbands' names. (Sometimes the FBI has mistaken roommates and lovers for spouses and filed accordingly. Therefore, if the FBI claims it has no files on a particular woman, she may want to request a check under the name of Mrs. John Jones.)

If you had a particular relationship with an agency—if you were an employee or participated in some program or worked on a contract—you will want to mention that fact and, if possible, give an employee identification number.

You may also want to state what cities and states you have lived in and on what dates. Often files are available only at the regional or field offices and not at the agency headquarters; in that case, it is often a good idea to write to the relevant offices around the country, as well as to headquarters.

If I believe that an agency may have earlier violated my privacy (by conducting a political surveillance of me, for example), how much identification of my activities should I give?

This is a difficult situation. For the vast majority of people who have been politically active, there is no file, as such, under their names. These people will probably be mentioned in the files relating to the organizations they belonged to and the activities they took part in. The FBI's "See Reference" index might very well contain cross-references so that these organizational files could be checked. However, the usefulness of this index is obviously limited, because Bureau informers listed participants of many activities only by nicknames, or by misspelled names, and they certainly did not have access to reliable identifiers, such as Social Security numbers.

If you think that the FBI (or any other agency) may not have a file or an index under your name, you may have to give it additional information about your activities. You might want to tell it, for example, what organizations you belonged to and when, or what activities or demonstrations you participated in. You would then get the records from those files.

This obviously makes many people extremely uneasy, given the record of improper and illegal actions that some agencies took against people who were exercising their First-Amendment rights.[34] One solution is to offer more information only after finding out whether the agency does have records retrievable under your name. (If the FBI has a file on you in particular, it will ordinarily contain everything of interest to you, and there will be no practical need to check other files.) This tactic will require additional time, of course.

If you do decide to volunteer additional information about your activities, you should take care to respect the privacy of the individuals that you knew—don't provide additional personal information about them without their consent.

If I write a request for my files to an investigative agency, will that agency start a file on me?

In order to process an FOIA/PA request, a government agency must begin an *administrative* file to contain papers relating to your request. This is a typical, routine office procedure; it is not an *investigation* of you as an individual. So far, there have been no allegations that these FOIA/PA files for requests have been turned into a "watchlist" or blacklist for harassment by the agencies.

If I think that I may have been the subject of specific intelligence programs by an intelligence agency, should I mention this?

Yes. This is particularly helpful at the CIA, which (unlike the FBI) does not have a centralized filing system.

When should an agency be asked to waive or reduce fees?

The FOIA permits agencies to waive or to reduce fees when "furnishing the information can be considered primarily benefiting the general public."[35] It is up to the discretion of the agency to decide whether to waive or reduce fees, but the agency decision can be reviewed by the courts.

Not surprisingly, agencies and requesters regularly disagree on whether a particular release would be of primary benefit to the public, or to the private interests of the requesters themselves. It is useful to look at the history of the fee waiver question in order to explain how to approach asking for a waiver.

This provision is one of the 1974 amendments to the FOIA. Before that, the Justice Department had recommended using the search and copying fees to "discourage frivolous requests."[36] Agencies had a habit of deciding that far too many requests were "frivolous," and the 1974 amendments set out to correct this situation. The legislative history of the 1974 amendments states that "fees should not be used for the purpose of discouraging requests for information or as obstacles to disclosure of requested information."[37] Congress added the fee waiver provisions because it did not want fees to be an obstacle that would prevent all but wealthy corporations from using the act. As a result, if you are indigent, you can sometimes obtain fee waivers because, lacking money for fees, you would otherwise be unable to use the act.[38]

In spite of this, agencies have not necessarily been very generous in granting fee waivers and reductions, even where both the information and the requester have fit the criteria for granting waivers. Looking at how the fee waiver provisions have been implemented since 1974, congressional inquiries have concluded that, "most agencies have been too restrictive with regard to granting fee waivers for the indigent, news media, scholars, and nonprofit public interest groups."[39] Indeed, during the Reagan administration, guidelines were issued that in effect urged agencies to move toward adopting a more restrictive policy toward waivers. The guidelines have been faulted on Capitol Hill for not mentioning the principle of liberal construction and for instead emphasizing the agency's view of the public's need for the requested information; the agency should not, as the guidelines advise, be in the business of trying to decide whether there is genuine public interest, or whether the requested records would in fact be a valuable contribution to that interest.[40] As of this writing, there is proposed legislation which, if enacted, would counter the guidelines and clarify congressional intention.[41]

How do I write a request for a waiver or for a reduction of fees?

The first thing is to decide whether the release of the material that you are requesting would benefit the general public. If you believe that it would, then your job is to explain that in your initial request letter. Keep in mind that if the material is being requested for commercial purposes—if it would be of financial benefit to you—then it will not qualify as being of benefit to the general public (except perhaps in very extraordinary circumstances where the information reveals, say, fraud or impropriety). This question of financial benefit does not apply to the press; even though one purpose behind writing a book or article is to make money, publication is considered something that will benefit the public. (Unfortunately, many agencies do not routinely consider writing a book or an article as something that is automatically of benefit to the public.)

Since agencies must publish in the *Code of Federal Regulations* (*CFR*) their criteria for granting fee waivers or reductions, you may want to check the regulations so that your request can reflect their particular formula. The FOIA/PA Office of some agencies will send you a copy of these regulations if you ask. Generally speaking, there are a variety of criteria that ordinarily appear in the regulations.

You must be able to explain that there is genuine public interest in the subject that the documents cover. You would want to cite ways in which related aspects of the subject have received public attention in the past—other books, articles, official investigations, scholarly inquiries, and so on. With some agencies, you may have some difficulty in explaining how a general public interest in, say, political surveillance by intelligence agencies, translates into specific public interest in the political intelligence records compiled on you personally.

Another argument that might demonstrate public interest is whether other people are likely to be requesting the same information; if so, it would be unfair for the first requester to pay the entire search fee. In such a situation you might want to focus on asking for a fee reduction rather than a complete fee waiver.

If you know of others who have received the same documents and gotten a waiver or reduction of fees, say so and be specific.

Explain precisely how the public is interested in the material and how you intend to make the records public. Will you, for instance, be publishing articles or books about their contents? Are you a journalist, historian, or other kind of researcher? Will you make the records available to the public by giving them to a library? (If so, try to include a letter from a librarian stating their interest in adding the documents to their collection.)

If you are writing on behalf of a nonprofit, tax-exempt organization, say so. It is sometimes useful to include the organization's tax-exemption number.

If you are prepared to save copying costs by going to the location of the documents and reading them without copying, try to make arrangements to do so. Be sure to find out during what hours of the week you would be able to review them; some agencies have unusual time restrictions and you will want to know all of this in advance.

State that since these documents are of interest to the public, others will undoubtedly be requesting them, and that it is unfair to have the first requester pay the full burden of the search costs.

These points are incorporated into the sample fee waiver letter in Appendix A. They apply equally to an initial request for a fee waiver and to an administrative appeal of an initial denial of a fee waiver. (See also chapter 5.)

How much do fee waiver policies vary from agency to agency?

How successful these arguments in favor of a fee waiver will be varies greatly from one agency to another. At some agencies—such as the FBI—it seems that, at least to date, there are virtually no arguments (short of the intense and continuing public attention focused on a topic such as the Rosenberg and Hiss cases) which are deemed to be of benefit to the public. The FBI's policy is that they will consider waiving fees for personal files only in "very exceptional and well known cases."[42] The CIA, on the other hand, has adopted a policy of routinely waiving fees chargeable for similar personal files. However, the CIA has been extremely reluctant to grant fee waivers for FOIA requests for subject matter files. By contrast, other agencies, such as the HEW under the Carter administration, found enough public benefit in almost all requests that fee waivers were granted as a matter of routine.[43]

Many agencies routinely waive fees for small requests (generally under twenty-five dollars), on the theory that the bookkeeping that would be necessary to collect the fees would cost the agency more than the fees that they would collect. Some agencies, however, have been extremely stubborn about granting fee waivers, even when it ended up costing them more money to collect than to waive. This policy, however, has been changing. You should keep your representatives in Congress informed when agency policies on fee waivers are running counter to the intent of Congress.

If an agency does not waive or reduce fees for a request that is in the public interest, what recourse do I have?

You should write an appeal letter (see chapter 5); the official who handles the appeal may be swayed by additional policy arguments and waive the fee. If this fails, you can file suit and the courts can review a refusal to waive or reduce fees as an abuse of agency discretion.[44]

Can an agency refuse to waive fees because they say that little will ultimately be released?

No. The courts have held that the release of even one sentence could be of great importance to the public and would justify a fee waiver. Recent congressional attention to this issue has supported the position that agencies may not refuse to waive fees simply because they claim that there would ultimately be many deletions.[45]

NOTES

1. 5 U.S.C. Section 552(a)(3).
2. *Doyle v. Dept. of Justice*, 494 F. Supp. 842 (D.D.C. 1980), *aff'd*, 668 F.2d 1365 (D.C. Cir. 1981), *cert. denied*, 455 U.S. 1002 (1982).
3. *See, e.g.*, U.S., Congress, Senate, *S. Rept. 98–221 on S. 774*, 98th Cong., 1st sess., 1983.
4. 5 U.S.C. Section 552(a)(2).
5. *Shermco Industries* v. *Sec'y of the Air Force*, 452 F. Supp. 306, 314–315 (N.D. Tex. 1978) *rev'd on other grounds*, 613 F.2d 1314 (5th Cir. 1980) ("the rights of proprietorships, businesses and corporations are not intended to be covered by this Act"). Other courts have rejected this view. *See, e.g., Zeller* v. *U.S.*, 467 F. Supp. 487 (E.D.N.Y. 1979) ("Congress's express findings and statement of purposes simply do not support the entrepreneurial exclusion from the Privacy Act that is embodied in the OMB Guidelines.")
6. 5 U.S.C. Section 552a(h).
7. U.S., Office of Management and Budget, *Guidelines for Implementing Section 552a of Title 5*, 1975, p. 20.
8. *Id.* at 10.
9. 5 U.S.C. Section 552(a)(4)(A).
10. *See* S. Rept. 98–221, *supra* note 3, at 7.
11. 5 U.S.C. Section 552a(f)(5).
12. "Attorney General's Preliminary Guidance Concerning the 1974 Freedom of Information Act Amendments" (Doc. 11, 1074), p. 11.
13. The U.S. Government Organization Manual is available from the Superintendent of Documents, Government Printing Office, Washington, DC 20402. It is also available in most libraries.
14. Harry J. Murphy, Office of Security, CIA, *Where's What: Sources of Information for Federal Investigators* (New York: Quadrangle, n.d.)

(declassified, Aug. 1975); U.S., Congress, Senate, *Congressional Quarterly's Washington Information Directory* (updated yearly).

15. *See generally* Comptroller General of the United States, *Government Field Offices Should Better Implement the Freedom of Information Act,* GAO Report LCD–78–120 (Washington, D.C.: General Accounting Office, July 25, 1978).

16. 5 U.S.C. Section 552(a)(6)(A)(i).

17. S. Rept. 98–221, *supra* note 3, at 12.

18. *See, e.g.,* 40 *Fed. Reg.* 28957–58 (July 9, 1975).

19. 5 U.S.C. Section 552(a)(6)(A)(ii).

20. S. Rept. 98–221, *supra* note 3.

21. 5 U.S.C. Section 552(a)(6)(B)(i).

22. 5 U.S.C. Section 552(a)(6)(B)(ii).

23. 5 U.S.C. Section 552(a)(6)(B)(iii).

24. S. Rept. 98–221, *supra* note 3.

25. 5 U.S.C. Section 552(a)(6)(C).

26. Jonathan Kwitney, "Hot Issue: FBI Agents Rap Policy of Burning Files, Link It To Public Access Acts," *Wall Street Journal,* Sept. 27, 1978, pp. 1, 21. In *American Friends Service Committee* v. *Webster,* 485 F. Supp. 222 (D.D.C. 1980), *aff'd* 720 F.2d 29 (D.C. Cir. 1983), the court ordered preservation of FBI records in accordance with the federal statutes controlling the disposal of records: the Archival Administration Act (44 U.S.C. Section 2101 *et seq.*); the Records Management by Federal Agencies Act (44 U.S.C. Section 3101 *et seq.*); the Disposal of Records Act (44 U.S.C. Section 3301 *et seq.*).

27. *Kissinger v. Reporters Committee for Freedom of the Press,* 445 U.S. 136 (1980).

28. 5 U.S.C. Section 552(a)(3).

29. U.S., Congress, House, H. Rept. 93–876, 1974, p. 6.

30. U.S., Congress, House, Committee on Government Operations, Subcommittee on Government Information and Individual Rights, *FBI Compliance with the Freedom of Information Act,* 95th Cong., 2d sess., 1978, p. 39.

31. Id. at Senate, Committee on the Judiciary and Committee on Government Operations, *Privacy: Hearings,* 93d Cong., 2d sess., 1974, vol. I, p. 1150.

32. Comptroller General, *Timeliness and Completeness of FBI Responses to Requests Under Freedom of Information and Privacy Acts Have Improved,* (GAO Report GGD–78–51) (Washington, D.C.: General Accounting Office, Apr. 10, 1978), pp. 35–36.

33. *Nolen v. Rumsfeld,* 535 F.2d 890 (5th Cir. 1976), *cert. denied,* 429 U.S. 1104 (1977); *Lybarger v. Cardwell,* 577 F.2d 764 (1st Cir. 1978); *Herrick v. U.S. Customs Service,* 709 F.2d 41 (11th Cir. 1983).

34. For a summary of improper intelligence operations, *see* Morton H. Halperin et al., *The Lawless State: The Crimes of the U.S. Intelligence Agencies* (New York: Penguin, 1976). The Center for National

Security Studies, 122 Maryland Ave., N.E., Washington, DC 20002, has additional publications on this subject.

35. 5 U.S.C. Section 552(a)(4)(A).

36. "Attorney General's Memorandum on the Public Information Section of the Administrative Procedure Act" (1967).

37. U.S., Congress, Senate, *Conference Report*, S. Rept. 93–1220, p. 8; reprinted in U.S., Congress, House, Committee on Government Operations, Subcommittee on Government Information and Individual Rights, and U.S., Congress, Senate, Committee on the Judiciary, Subcommittee on Administrative Practice and Procedure (Joint Committee Print), *Freedom of Information Act and Amendments of 1974 (P.L. 93–502): Sourcebook: Legislative History, Texts, and Other Documents*, 94th Cong., 1st sess., 1975.

38. *Blue v. Bureau of Prisons*, C75–2092A (N.D. Ga., Order of Aug. 10, 1976), *rev'd on other grounds*, 572 F.2d 529 (5th Cir. 1978). *But see Rizzo v. Tyler*, 438 F. Supp. 895 (S.D.N.Y. 1977).

39. U.S., Congress, Senate, Senate Committee on the Judiciary, Subcommittee on Administrative Practice and Procedure, *Agency Implementation of the 1974 Amendments to the Freedom of Information Act*, 95th Cong., 2d sess., Mar. 1980, p. 90 (Committee Print), cited with approval in S. Rept. 98-221, note 3 above, p. 9.

40. S. Rept. 98–221, *supra* note 3, at 10–11. *See also* Letter from Representative Glenn English concerning the Department of Justice Fee Waiver Guidelines of Jan. 7, 1983, printed in *First Principles*, Mar./Apr. 1983, pp. 4–5. *First Principles* is available from the Center for National Security Studies, 122 Maryland Ave., N.E., Washington, DC 20002.

41. *See e.g.*, S. Rept. 98-221, *supra* note 3.

42. Comptroller General, *supra* note 32, at 33. For the time being, the FBI has adopted policies that virtually eliminate the granting of fee waivers. *See e.g.*, Letter from Quinlan Shea, Director of the Office of Privacy and Information Appeals, to Monica Andres, Center for National Security Studies, Washington, D.C., Aug. 22, 1979.

43. Comptroller General, *supra* note 15 at 34.

44. For an example of FOIA fee waivers, the policies of selected agencies, and congressional oversight of the question, *see* U.S., Congress, Senate, Committee on the Judiciary, Subcommittee on Administrative Practice and Procedure, *Freedom of Information Act: Hearings on Oversight of the Freedom of Information Act*, 95th Cong., 1st sess., Sept. 15, 16, Oct. 6, Nov. 10, 1977, pp. 785–822. *See also Eudey v. CIA*, 478 F. Supp. 1175 (D.D.C. 1979).

   For a comprehensive discussion of problems with FOIA fee waivers and possible ways of improving the situation, *see* John E. Bonine, *Public Interest Fee Waivers Under the Freedom of Information Act: A Report to the Administrative Conference of the United States* (Washington, D.C., Administrative Conferences of the U.S., Nov. 7, 1980).

45. S. Rept. 98–221, *supra* note 3, at 9–10, citing *Eudey, supra* note 44; *Rizzo, supra* note 38.

III

Agency Responses: General

What are the responses that an agency is likely to give to an FOIA/PA request?

It is possible, of course, that you may, within the statutory time limits, get the information that you want from the agency, and either be charged a manageable fee or be granted a fee waiver. Some agencies, such as the Department of Defense, have had excellent records of handling FOIA/PA requests, which shows that even a huge agency with a heavy request load can meet both the spirit and the letter of the information laws. But in many agencies, requests run afoul of bureaucratic reactions. You should be prepared to expect a number of alternative responses to crop up and you should not get discouraged on the first round. It is often possible to dislodge the information you want if you are persistent.

In this chapter and the next, we deal with the problems that are likely to come up when using the FOIA/PA. (Exemption claims are treated in chapter 4.) These two chapters should be read with an eye for possible arguments that might later become the basis of your administrative appeal letter(s) or lawsuit. (It is always useful to be thinking two or three steps ahead.) Another thing to keep in mind is that you should feel free to make follow-through contacts with the agencies: often, you will be able to negotiate with, explain to, and otherwise educate the officials with whom you are dealing. Too often, these officials have not been given adequate guidance by their agencies about what the federal access statutes require of them.[1]

Time Limits

How long can I expect the agencies to take in answering my FOIA request?

There is no set answer to this. The length of time for a response varies from agency to agency, from administration to administration, and from time to time.

As mentioned earlier, the law says that the initial response to an FOIA question must be made within 10 working days, except in special situations. (Of course, you must also take into consideration extra days in the mail, and some agencies have notoriously inferior internal delivery systems.) Many agencies consistently take longer than this, and some offices within an agency take longer than others. Across the government as a whole, figures on the FOIA time limits are good: one study indicated that some 86 percent of FOIA requests received a response within ten days.[2] As mentioned in earlier chapters, as of this writing there are various legislative proposals that, if enacted, would give agencies more time in which to respond.

What should I do if the agency tells me to wait?

The first letter you will receive from an agency may simply acknowledge that the request has been received and is being processed. It may announce that your request has been assigned a "wait number," and it may also give you an estimate as to when the material you are after will be processed—that is, searched for, and, if located, reviewed for release.

Although the FOIA gives you the right to sue in federal court to force the agency to comply with the time limits, it is ordinarily best to be patient and to try to deal with the bureaucratic process. Unless you have an urgent need for the records,[3] judges typically are more helpful if you can show that you made every reasonable attempt to get the agencies to comply *before* taking the matter to the courts.

There are, however, a number of steps that you can and should take. It is a good idea to write or call the FOIA/PA Office and try to get a date by which they promise to have your request processed. (It is at this time that you start establishing your "contact" at that office with the official who has primary responsibility for fielding your request.) This may also be the best time to begin asking questions about the agency's filing system and search procedures. Inform the agency that if your request is not processed by the promised date, you will view the delay as a denial of the records and will write an appeal letter. (See chapter 5.)

Be sure you maintain records of your correspondence and conversations with the agency about delays. These records will be needed in writing an appeal letter or going to court.

Searches for Requested Materials

What should I do if the agency tells me that my description of the material that I want was not specific enough?

If an agency informs you that your description of what you want is not specific enough, give it the benefit of the doubt and rewrite the request. You might want to write or call the official processing your request to find out what kind of details the agency would need to track down the material.

If the request is for personal files, this usually means that you haven't given enough information for the agency to be able to distinguish one person from another in their files. (See chapter 2.)

What do I do if an agency writes back and tells me that it has no records?

So far, it seems that the agencies are being fairly straightforward and are not intentionally denying that they have files when in fact they do. But there is always a possibility of human error or of halfhearted searches. Your first response, of course, is to provide more information concerning the topic under request so that the agency staff has a better idea about what it is looking for and where to look. (Again, you might try to discuss this problem with an official at the agency to determine how the records, if they exist, might be filed.) Consider doing some more research. For instance, do congressional hearings, news reports, court records, articles, or scholarly accounts give a clearer description of the material you want?

You should, however, be alert to terminology that implies that the records don't exist, when the actual situation is somewhat different. If an agency response is at all ambiguous, it should be pursued; you have a right to ask for clarity.

An agency, for example, might simply say that they do not have the files or that the files are "unavailable," and hope that you will leave the matter there. This sort of response should be pursued. If that agency does not have the records, find out who does. Have they been transferred to the Federal Records Center where obsolete files are stored? If so, the records should be retrievable. If the records have been transferred to another federal agency, find that out; you can send off an FOIA/PA letter to that agency. Are the records at a field office of the agency? If so, ask that your request be sent there, or write the field office directly. If the records have been transferred to a private contractor, you should find out the date of that transfer. If it was done after your FOIA request was made, then there is a reasonable presumption that the transfer was made in order to avoid responding to your request, and this would be grounds for suit. [4]

And finally, if your effort to clarify these points does not produce satisfactory results at the initial request level, you should repeat them in an administrative appeal letter.

This ongoing correspondence may be rather exasperating and rather frustrating, but it can turn out to be worthwhile. One organization, for example, ended up getting an additional 9,800 documents from the FBI after they had originally been told that everything on the organization had been released. [5] You should also bear in mind that very often the filing systems are simply dreadful. (It is sometimes said that one unanticipated benefit of the FOIA has been that agencies now have to improve their filing systems so that they are workable.)

If they cannot find records, some agencies fail to inform requesters of appeal rights because they do not consider a "no records" response to be a denial. [6] You should write an appeal letter anyhow.

If the agency persists in claiming that the requested material doesn't exist, and if you think that you can convince a court that it *has* to exist (or else that the agency simply hasn't been doing its job), then you should not let the agency put you off easily.

What do I do if the agency says that they have no personal records on me?

This happens with surprising frequency. The first thing to do is to write back and give more information to identify yourself. The second thing to do is to ask what filing systems they have checked and whether the agency files include a cross-referencing index.

The FBI's cross-reference index, for example, produces something called See References. As of this writing, the FBI has a policy that if the index shows See References that might refer to you, it will send a letter that includes the following paragraph:

> If you believe your name may have been recorded by the FBI incident to the investigation of other persons or some organization, please advise of the details describing the specific incident or occurrence and time frame. Thereafter, further effort will be made to locate, retrieve, and process any such records.[7]

Obviously, this is a very open-ended request for additional information, and in case you want to check up on improper political surveillance, it seems to be seeking much the same information that the discredited surveillance programs had been compiling.

You have several options. You can request that the FBI check out all additional See References that *might* refer to you. (This might, however, run up several hundred dollars of search fees; you should either state your willingness to pay such fees up to some figure, or request an estimate of what the search fees would be.) Or, you can write back and give the FBI some specific information about your activities, in order to narrow the number of See References it would have to check. If you decide to ask for a general check of all likely See References, this eliminates part of the problem of divulging specific information about yourself to an agency that has misused such data in the past. Even so, you must provide enough identifying information to the FBI so it can determine whether you are, in fact, *the* John Jones who did attend a particular meeting rather than another person with the same or a similar name.

It is also possible that an agency may have records concerning your activities, but that they are not referenced, however vaguely, under your name. If you worked on a government contract, for instance, you may be mentioned throughout the files on that contract, but the index may not be designed to take account of that fact. Such records would not be available under the Privacy Act (since your name would not be retrievable by an individual identifier), but you could ask for an FOIA review of such contract records. To make sure that references to you were not deleted on privacy grounds, you would want to establish that you were in fact the John Jones mentioned in the records.

Some agencies have not been informing people making FOIA requests for their personal files that requesters have a right to write an administrative appeal letter when their request is denied in full or in part. These agencies will typically announce that an FOIA request is being processed under the Privacy Act, but do not then inform you that appeals procedures remain available under the FOIA.[8] (The Privacy Act does not provide specific appeal rights.) You should feel free to write an FOIA appeal whether or not you are informed of that right.

Can I sue in court if I do not believe that the agency really does not have the records that I want?

Yes, although this is obviously more difficult than a lawsuit where the agency admits to having the documents, but refuses to turn them over. But there are several procedures that can be used to confirm the nonexistence of records, and sometimes, under pressure of a lawsuit, officials do manage to find material that had been unavailable before.

Your lawyer can "take discovery" (usually sworn written statements or oral testimony made under oath) to find out whether a credible effort had been made to search for the records.[9] You can also use the discovery process to find out whether there are other records, perhaps not fitting the precise description given in the request letter, but that would in fact provide some or all of the information that is wanted.[10]

And, of course, informal avenues can be explored. Do you or your lawyer personally know any present or former agency employees who might be able to shed some light on the question of whether the documents exist, and if so, where they might be? (See the Introduction for suggestions on unofficial access, and chapter 6 for a discussion of FOIA lawsuits.)

Destruction of Material

What happens if an agency tells me they have destroyed the files that I am requesting?

The government does have a policy of routinely destroying old files that are no longer in use. But some files have been destroyed mainly because the data they contain will prove embarrassing to the agency. The greater bulk of J. Edgar Hoover's "personal" files, for example, were destroyed, as were the CIA drug-testing files, and the files from the National Security Agency (NSA) on domestic targets. Unfortunately, once the files are destroyed, the government cannot be ordered to reconstruct them,[11] although one court did in fact order the files to be reconstructed in a case where the destruction took place after the suit was filed.[12] Sometimes, of course, reconstruction might be impossible.

If the files have been destroyed, ask for the date of the destruction, and under what regulations the destruction was carried out. When government material is destroyed, that fact is supposed to be duly documented; you can ask for the specific records authorizing the destruction. And since material that is of historical interest is supposed to be preserved, if your request includes such material you should ask for an explanation of its loss. Sometimes, when an agency looks around for its internal documentation, it will discover that the material still exists.

If there is evidence of improper destruction, you might be able to gain some leverage with the agency, although ordinarily once material is gone, it is gone forever. But at the very least, if there is a problem of improper destruction of government records, the National Archives and the congressional oversight committees should be informed of the situation.

What do I do if I am afraid that the agency might destroy the files?

Simple: just make an FOIA request for the records you want. Although there have been some slipups on this point, once an FOIA request has been made, the records are supposed to be immediately pulled off the roster of records slated for destruction. This power to stop destruction of documents is one of the extra advantages of the FOIA/PA.[13] If you think the records you are requesting might be destroyed, you should ask in writing for a specific assurance that, pending the resolution of your FOIA/PA claim, they not be.

Fees

How do the agencies handle the charging of search and copying fees?

Your initial request letter should ordinarily state that you are willing to pay fees up to a certain dollar figure, and that if the fees are above that you should be contacted.

Many agencies will write off small fees (usually those less than twenty-five dollars), because it would cost more in administrative time to collect fees than to waive them. If the fees are not waived, most agencies will contact you regardless of what you state in your initial request letter. They will want either a commitment that you will pay the search fee they estimate, or a deposit of approximately half the estimated cost of the search.

Do agencies ever charge excessively high fees?

Yes. Although Congress specified in passing the 1974 amendments, high fees were not to be used as a deterrent to FOIA requests, there are indications that it still happens.[14] Sometimes, within a single agency there are no uniform criteria for charging fees; the fees for two different requests for the same material may vary by as much as several thousand dollars.

Sometimes, of course, high search fees are legitimate, but it is also true that there is no quality control on the search procedures used.

To be certain that the fees you are being charged are in line with the established policies of a particular agency, you should check the agency fee schedule. (See chapter 2).

Can I negotiate about a fee that seems excessively high?

Yes. Begin by negotiating with the official who is handling your initial request. Try to determine what the search procedures will be, and whether there is any way you can redefine or narrow your request so as to substantially reduce the fees. If your original request asked for everything on, say, Angola, you might decide to limit it to a particular year or city or set public figures. You might limit your request to reports, summaries, or analyses that might have been prepared on Angola for, say, the secretary of state or the White House or Congress. Sometimes you will discover that, without realizing it, you have asked for more material than you could possibly read, much less pay for.

Sometimes, agencies will embark on search procedures that are unnecessarily complicated. The FBI, for example, has asked individual requesters seeking their personal files if they were willing to pay as much as several hundred dollars for a search of *all* cross-references to their names. If the subject has a file under his name, this is ordinarily unnecessary, since most things of interest will be in that file.

What arguments should I make when negotiating a waiver or reduction of fees because release would benefit the public?

Chapter 2 explains the criteria for obtaining a fee waiver. These should be included, at least briefly, in your initial request letter and can be elaborated upon in your later negotiations and appeals. If you failed to ask for a fee waiver in your initial request letter, you can bring it up later by writing a separate letter later on.

While your initial request letter may have treated the request for a fee waiver quite briefly, as negotiations proceed you may want to explain in as much detail as possible why release would benefit the public. Also, you should state that if the fee waiver or reduction is denied, you will appeal that denial.

Can an agency deny a request for a waiver of search fees because it believes that few or no documents will, after being located and reviewed for exempt material, be released?

No. If the information meets the criteria for being of benefit to the public, the agency is supposed to waive the search fees even if little or nothing is likely to be released. In some instances, even one document out of a great many pages may have very significant interest to the public.[15]

Can I write an administrative appeal letter if the agency does not grant a waiver or reduction of fees?

Yes.[16] Your appeal letter should include all the arguments you initially made, plus any additional elaborations you might care to make. In addition, you might want to ask for an itemization of the fees, since agencies do occasionally make mistakes. Sometimes they have ended up charging not only for the search and copying, but also for the review of the documents, which is, under current law, a violation of the FOIA.

If the fees are sufficiently exorbitant to make filing a lawsuit worthwhile, and if you believe that you have the legal resources to go to court, you may want to say so in your appeal letter. The agency's refusal to waive fees can be reviewed by the courts as an abuse of discretion.[17]

If I simply cannot afford the search and copying fees (even where those fees might be reasonable) can I get the fees waived or reduced?

Since the FOIA holds that disclosure is in the public interest, and since the legislative history states that costs are not supposed to be a deterrent to disclosure, it is sometimes possible for an indigent (such as a prisoner or, presumably, a welfare recipient) to get the fees reduced or waived, even where no clear benefit to the general public is likely to follow release.[18] Therefore, an indigent should add a paragraph to requests and appeals, explaining why he qualifies for a fee waiver or reduction.

If I am making my FOIA request for commercial purposes, what recourse do I have if I am charged excessive fees?

While commercial requests are not considered as being of benefit to the public and, therefore, cannot qualify for a fee waiver, commercial requesters are nevertheless protected from exorbitant fees. The same options for keeping fees in line are available to commercial requesters as to others.

First, you can cut or eliminate copying costs if you can review the documents before selecting a few for copying.

Second, you can request an itemization of the fees that are being charged. As just mentioned, agencies have occasionally made mistakes, either typographical errors in the bills or in charging for the review of documents (in addition to the search and copying fees), which they are not permitted to do. Nor are agencies permitted to charge more than "the direct costs" of search and duplication.[19] If the costs are inflated, the agency is violating the law.

And as with all other ways that an agency might violate the letter or the intent of the law, you can and should let congressional oversight committees know about the problems.

NOTES

1. Comptroller General of the United States, *An Informed Public Assures that Federal Agencies Will Better Comply with Freedom of Information/Privacy Laws*, GAO Report LCD 80–8 (Washington, D.C.: General Accounting Office, Oct. 24, 1979), p. 2.

2. ———*Government Field Offices Should Better Implement the Freedom of Information Act*, GAO Report LCD 78–120 (Washington, D.C.: General Accounting Office, July 25, 1978), p. ii.

3. *Cleaver* v. *Kelley*, 427 F. Supp. 80 (D.D.C. 1976) (expedited the processing of a FOIA request for the FBI files of a former Black Panther facing criminal charges); *Liew* v. *CIA*, Civ. No. C–78–2546 SAW (N.D. Cal., order of Feb. 21, 1979) (expedited the processing of material possibly relevant for civil trial); *Exner* v. *FBI*, 542 F.2d 1121 (9th Cir. 1976).

4. James T. O'Reilly, *Federal Information Disclosure* (Colorado Springs: McGraw-Hill, Shepards, 1977), section 7.08, Chap. 7, p. 24.

5. Interview, May 1978, with Margaret Van Houton, Staffer, American Friends Service Committee, Program on Government Surveillance and Citizens Rights, 1501 Cherry St., Philadelphia, PA. 19102.

6. Comptroller General, *Government Field Offices, supra* note 2, at 25–26.

7. U.S., Congress, House, Committee on Government Operations, *FBI Compliance with the Freedom of Information Act;* Subcommittee on Government Information and Individual Rights, 95th Cong., 2d sess., 1978, p. 70.

8. *See* Comptroller General, *supra* note 6.

9. *Weisberg* v. *Dept. of Justice*, 543 F.2d 308 (D.C. Cir. 1976).

10. *National Cable Television Assn.* v. *FCC*, 479 F.2d 183 (D.C. Cir. 1973).

11. *Nolen* v. *Rumsfeld*, 535 F.2d 890 (5th Cir. 1976).

12. *Levine* v. *U.S.*, No. 73–1215–Civ–CA (S.D. Fla., Order of Mar. 22, 1974) (*slip op.* at 10–14).

13. *American Friends Service Committee* v. *Webster*, 485 F. Supp. 222 (D.D.C. 1980).

14. U.S., Congress, Senate, Committee on the Judiciary, Subcommittee on Administrative Practice and Procedure, *Freedom of Information Act: Hearings on Oversight of the Freedom of Information Act*, 95th Cong., 1st sess, 1977, pp. 785–822. [hereafter cited as *Oversight Hearings*].

15. *Eudey* v. *CIA*, 478 F. Supp. 1175 (D.D.C. 1979).

16. This right to appeal fees is not explicit in the language of the FOIA, but it has been inferred from the legislative history and is established as a matter of practice.

17. *See Fitzgibbon* v. *CIA*, Civ. No. 76–700 (D.D.C., Jan. 10, 1977), reprinted in *Oversight Hearings, supra* note 14, at 785–822 generally, for examples of arguments and correspondence dealing with refusals to waive or reduce fees; *Allen v. FBI*, 551 F. Supp. 694 (D.D.C. 1982).

18. *Blue* v. *Bureau of Prisons*, C75–2092A (N.D. Ga., Order of Aug. 10, 1976), rev'd on other grounds, 570 F.2d 529 (5th Cir. 1978). Other decisions, however, have not been found in favor of indigents. *See Rizzo* v. *Tyler*, 438 F. Supp. 895, 900 (S.D.N.Y. 1977); *Jester* v. *Dept. of Justice*, Civ. No. 79–1347 (D.D.C. Aug. 24, 1979); *Mills* v. *McCreight*, Civ. No. 78–2168 (D.D.C. Sept. 27, 1979) (1 *Govt. Disclosure Serv.* [P-H] Para. 79,151).

19. 5 U.S.C. Section 552(a)(4).

IV

Agency Responses: Exemption Claims

What should I do if the agency claims that some or all of the information I have requested is exempt from mandatory disclosure?

Both the FOIA and the Privacy Act permit the agencies to withhold certain categories of information if that information falls under certain specific exemptions. Agencies frequently make mistakes, however, and will withhold material that is not properly exempt. Sometimes, and with some agencies, sweeping claims seem to be made because the officials do not believe that you will pursue the matter.

This chapter will try to explain the ins and outs of proper and improper exemption claims; it will keep one eye on the appeals process, because any time you think that the agency has overstepped its authority and withheld something improperly, you should write an administrative appeal letter. And if the agency still does not release the information that you want, you should consider whether you have grounds for a lawsuit to compel the agency to release the records.

In many cases, the discussion is far more detailed than will be necessary to persuade an agency to release the material. In other instances, even though your legal arguments may be solid, an agency may stubbornly persist in withholding material. However, this detailed discussion also tries to help you decide whether it is worth your while to consult an attorney and go to court.

Finally, bear in mind that these things change. The parameters of an exemption are controlled by court decisions, and new ones are always coming down. In addition, the definition of the exemptions can be changed by legislative amendment.

Does an agency letter that denies some or all of the information that I have requested have to inform me of my rights?

Yes. A letter from the agency that denies you any of the information that you have requested must tell you the following things: (1) the specific exemption of the FOIA or Privacy Act that permits withholding; (2) the name and title of the responsible official(s); and (3) the official to whom such denials can be appealed.[1]

How reliable are claims that some material is properly exempt under the FOIA/PA?

There is no real answer to this question. Attitudes toward disclosing information vary from agency to agency, and from official to official. There are many instances where the same file has been obtained under the FOIA by two separate requesters and yet the two releases had very different deletions.

It sometimes becomes clear that officials with FOIA authority may have only foggy notions of the standards for withholding information. For instance, when one State Department official was questioned during the course of an FOIA lawsuit, he inadvertently revealed that he did not know the operative definition of "Confidential" information.[2]

If you think agency explanations of a withholding do not make much sense you should trust your instincts and do not be shy about writing appeal letters to agencies. Too often the officials themselves do not know the details of the FOIA/PA requirements. They regularly forget that under the FOIA they must release any "segregable portions" and that the act explicitly states that when an exemption claim is contested in court, the government must meet a heavier burden of proof that the exemption is correctly invoked. If the agency fails to establish that the claim is correct, then the material must be released.

What should I do if the agency informs me that it is withholding *all* of the material that I requested?

If the agency is withholding literally *all* of the material that you have requested, it is likely that it is not implementing the "segregable portions" provision of the FOIA. Any portion of the material that is not *specifically* exempted must be separated from the material that can be deleted, and these separable portions must be released to you.[3]

If this happens, you should write an appeal letter to remind them of this provision. In your appeal letter, you may want to include some argument drawn from the discussion of the exemptions that follows. For example, if the agency denies an entire report by citing the (b)(5) exemption for advice, you should write an appeal reminding the agency that all the *facts* contained in the report are not protected by (b)(5).

In your appeal, you should remind agency officials that the government's policy on releasing material after exempt portions are deleted is that "remaining material . . . must be released if it is at all intelligible," and that any doubts "should be resolved in favor of release."[4]

What should I do if the agency releases some, but not all, of the material I requested?

Partial releases should be carefully scrutinized for any signs of improper withholding—that is, deletions that seem too encompassing or that do not seem to actually fit under one of the exemptions discussed in this chapter. Remember that each individual deletion is a partial denial, and each can be appealed and can be grounds for a suit.

Can an agency withhold information that has already been made public?

Ordinarily, no. Release of the information to one person requires release of that information to everyone. Prior release of information is a waiver of the exempt status of the material.[5] But there is some gray area here. Much depends on how the information was made public, to whom it was given, and in what circumstances it was released.

If the release was strictly informal—through "leaks" and without official approval—the material can still be withheld by the agency under the relevant exemptions.

If the information has already been made public officially in some form (such as being put into evidence in a lawsuit or discussed in an official report), then it is ordinarily considered to have been released. But in some cases, the fact that people outside the agency have seen the material in some limited context (for instance, where professional courtesy has been extended to a lawyer who has been permitted to examine confidential business material) may not be considered a prior release per se.[6]

And, of course, the fact that personal files have been released to the subject of those files does not constitute a release to the public.

If the material has been given to a congressional committee, does this mean that the material cannot be properly exempt under the FOIA/PA because it has already been made public?

No. If the agency gave the documents to a congressional committee because of an official request, this does not constitute a release.[7] The congressional committee may, of course, choose to make the data public in some form, but neither the committee nor the agency can be *compelled* to release such data under the FOIA/PA.

What are the FOIA exemptions?

Briefly, the FOIA exemptions fall in nine categories, some of which overlap.

Since agencies use the legal citations to these exemptions when they withhold information, you will have to be able to figure out the citations as well. As explained in the Introduction, the citations to the various parts of the statute are not difficult once you become familiar with them. The exemptions are listed in subsection (b) of Section 552 of Volume 5 of the U.S. Code—our familiar 5 U.S.C. Section 552. Subsection (b) is in turn broken down into nine categories of information that an agency is permitted to withhold.

The (b)(1) exemption for *national security* [5 U.S.C. Section 552(b)(1)]

The (b)(2) exemption for *internal* agency *rules* [5 U.S.C. Section 552(b)(2)]

The (b)(3) exemption for material exempted by other *statutes* [5 U.S.C. Section 552 (b)(3)]

The (b)(4) exemption for confidential *business* information [5 U.S.C. Section 552(b)(4)]

The (b)(5) exemption for certain *internal* government *memoranda* [5 U.S.C. Section 552(b)(5)]

The (b)(6) exemption for protecting *personal privacy* [5 U.S.C. Section 552(b)(6)]

The (b)(7) exemption for certain records of *law enforcement investigations* [5 U.S.C. Section 552(b)(7)]

The (b)(8) exemption for regulation of *financial institutions* [5 U.S.C. Section 552(b)(8)]

The (b)(9) exemption for *oil wells* [5 U.S.C. Section 552(b)(9)]

If you receive a letter from the agency denying your entire request, the explanation will typically consist of little more than a recitation of these numbers (for example, "This material is exempt for disclosure under exemptions (b)(1), (b)(3), and (b)(6)").

If you receive a partial release consisting of documents with gaps in the text where deletions have been made, the gaps should have notations showing which exemption(s) have been claimed for each segment that has been removed. These notations are ordinarily rather cryptic and may very well not follow the standard form for citations to the statute. For instance, instead of writing in a gap the full, formal citation of, say, "5 U.S.C. Section 552(b)(1)," the note may read "(b)(1)" or "b1" or "X1" (X being an unofficial but much used abbreviation for "exemption").

How about the Privacy Act? What kinds of material does it exempt from mandatory disclosure?

Like the FOIA, the Privacy Act exempts certain categories of information from its disclosure provisions.[8] And as with the FOIA, the release of information is still discretionary. Even though an agency might have legal grounds for withholding material, it can still choose to release information about an individual to that person. Unlike the FOIA, the Privacy Act does provide criminal penalties if the agency improperly releases personal information to other parties;[9] therefore, officials are very cautious about making discretionary releases of personal information.

Because of the overlap between the FOIA and the Privacy Act, and because material that can be withheld under the Privacy Act exemptions is nevertheless often available under the FOIA, the Privacy Act exemptions are not of great importance. As a result, the Privacy Act exemptions do not need to be discussed separately, and the relatively detailed explanations of the FOIA exemptions will refer briefly to the comparable Privacy Act provisions.

The (b)(1) Exemption for National Security

Are national security secrets available under either the FOIA or the Privacy Act?

No. If information on national defense and foreign policy (usually called national security information) is *properly* classified, the agencies may withhold it under the FOIA's (b)(1) exemption, which holds that the act does not apply to matters that are "(A) specifically authorized under criteria established by an Executive order to be kept secret in the interest of national defense or foreign policy and (B) are in fact properly classified pursuant to such executive order."[9a]

The Privacy Act also exempts systems of records that are "subject to the provisions" of the FOIA's national security exemption.[10] This means that while personal records can be requested under the Privacy Act, access to such material is controlled by FOIA law if there is any question of national security being affected.

What is the history of the FOIA's (b)(1) exemption?

The 1966 version of the FOIA, as interpreted by the Supreme Court, did not require that information be *properly* classified—any information that was stamped "Confidential," "Secret," or "Top Secret," following the procedures laid out in the executive order on security classification, was exempt from FOIA release, no matter how "cynical, myopic, or even corrupt that decision [to classify the material] might have been."[11] After the many controversies involving overclassification (including the Pentagon Papers and Watergate), Congress overrode a presidential veto in 1974, to amend the (b)(1) exemption. The law now requires that national security information be *properly* classified before the agencies are entitled to withhold it by claiming it is a national security secret protected by the exemption.

Do the agencies still overclassify information?

Yes, which is one reason why you should feel free to argue about whether material is properly classified.

A succession of official inquiries have found that overclassification has been, and remains, a serious problem. Recent General Accounting Office (GAO) investigations found that the mechanisms for overseeing the classification system continue to be inadequate. The GAO found, for example, that while the Nixon executive order to reform security classification (E.O. 11652) required that agencies report the number of classification actions taken, these reports were woefully inadequate. The Interagency Classification Review Committee set up to oversee the Nixon reforms lacked independence, authority, and staff. For instance, the Committee's 1977 annual report listed some 4.5 million classification actions; but the GAO's review concluded that the true number of classification actions came to at least 70 million, and possibly over 100 million.

In 1978, President Jimmy Carter issued an executive order on classification to correct overclassification problems exposed by Watergate and by the intelligence scandals. His directive (E.O. 12065) contained some improvements over the Nixon order. Even so, the GAO concluded that this order did not solve the problem of overclassification either, and a subsequent GAO report found an overclassification error rate of 24 percent in a sample of Defense Department documents.[12]

In 1982, Ronald Reagan revoked the Carter executive order and issued E.O. 12356.[13] This new order has generated considerable controversy because it made no effort to address the acknowledged problem of overclassification, and, at the same time, permitted the classification of more material than ever.[14] As of this writing, the Reagan executive order is the basis for classification reviews under the FOIA. Since three of the last four Presidents have revised the classification system, President Reagan's successors in office may well decide to do likewise. Therefore, the (b)(1) exemption is the most easily altered, for, as presently written, it can be changed without new legislation.

Is any national security information actually being declassified and released in response to FOIA requests?

Yes. While it is true that the agencies continue to overclassify, it is also true that the FOIA amendments have produced useful, interesting, and relevant information. Agencies may not be declassifying everything that they should, but they are definitely declassifying material, and it is worth writing FOIA requests for documents even though there is a possibility that some or all of them might be properly classified.[15] Therefore, you should not be shy about requesting material that might relate to national security. In a sense, all they are doing is asking for a "declassification review," which is a very routine procedure.

What is the legal basis for the security classification system?

As mentioned, information is properly classified if it meets the criteria set out in the most recent executive order on classification. As of this writing classification standards are contained in President Reagan's E.O. 12356.

Since many people are not familiar with "executive orders," a word of explanation about them is in order here. Executive orders are issued by the President; they generally deal with some aspect of government that the federal laws do not address. Unlike statutes, which can be changed only through the complex process of passing new laws, a sitting President can change past executive orders or add new ones at any time.

While the FOIA states that the criteria for classifying national security secrets will be established by the President and set out in an executive order, there is no reason why Congress could not decide to enact a classification system of its own, or to set forth specific standards in the FOIA. If Congress were to choose to do so, the new legislation would then supersede whatever executive order may have been in effect at the time.[16]

The espionage laws, first enacted in 1911 and revised several times since, also provide protection for national security information. But it is worth noting that the espionage laws say nothing about "classified" information, and the courts have held that the simple fact that a given document has been stamped "Classified" does not determine whether it is protected by the espionage laws. The prosecution must prove that the material itself is actually the kind of privileged national security information meant to be covered by the espionage laws.[17]

What are the different levels of national security classifications?

Like earlier orders, E. O. 12356 sets out a three-tiered classification system—"Confidential," "Secret," and "Top Secret" —based on the degree of damage that agency officials believe would ensue if the information were released. The order states that " 'Confidential' shall be applied to information, the unauthorized disclosure of which reasonably could be expected to cause damage to the national security."[17a] The next higher tier of classification is "Secret"; this stamp is supposed to be used only if such damage to the national security could be "serious." The highest tier, "Top Secret," is supposed to be reserved for material where the damage to national security would be "exceptionally grave."

Since the FOIA and the Privacy Act permit agencies to withhold any material that is properly classified "Confidential" or above, Confidential is the only classification standard that counts when someone is requesting material. Under this standard, material can be classified and withheld even if the possible damage would be extremely slight.[18]

Ultimately, then, classification boils down to hunches and differences of opinion. You should not feel awed by the mystique of the classification stamp; you should feel free to argue with agencies in your appeal letters and in your lawsuits that an agency's opinion may, in fact, be wrong, overblown, or not reasonable. If an agency denies information under a national security claim that doesn't seem to make sense, you should, in the administrative appeal letter, try to get the agency to explain why it is *reasonable* to expect that release would cause damage.

What categories of information can be classified?

Section 1.3(a) of the Reagan executive order lists nine specific categories of classifiable information, plus a tenth catchall category. These are

(1) military plans, weapons, or operations;

(2) the vulnerabilities or capabilities of systems, installations, projects, or plans relating to the national security;

(3) foreign government information;

(4) intelligence activities (including special activities), or intelligence sources or methods;

(5) foreign relations or foreign activities of the United States;

(6) scientific, technological, or economic matters relating to the national security;

(7) United States Government programs for safeguarding nuclear materials or facilities;

(8) cryptology;

(9) a confidential source;

(10) other categories of information that are related to

the national security and that require protection against unauthorized disclosure as determined by the President or by agency heads or other officials who have been delegated original classification authority by the President.

What kinds of information may *not* be classified?

Section 1.6(a) of E.O. 12356 provides that documents may not be "classified in order to conceal violations of law, inefficiency, or administrative error; to prevent embarrassment to a person, organization, or agency; to restrain competition; or to prevent or delay the release of information that does not require protection. . . ." This does not mean, however, that agencies *have to* release information that involves illegalities, inefficiency, error, or embarrassment. If an agency can find some other basis for classifying such information, the material can still be withheld; for instance, an agency could argue that embarrassing information could short-circuit diplomatic negotiations.

E.O. 12356, Section 1.6(b), provides that "basic scientific research information not clearly related to the national security" may not be classified.[19]

Can information be reclassified even though it has already been declassified and disclosed?

Yes. Under Section 1.6(c) information that has already been declassified and disclosed may be reclassified if the information still requires protection, and if "the information may reasonably be recovered."[20]

What agencies are permitted to classify information "Confidential"?

Section 1.2 of E.O. 12356 provides that the President may give classification authority to any officials of his choice by publishing notice in the *Federal Register*. Past practice has established classification authority for at least the following agencies:

Agency for International Development (AID)
Arms Control and Disarmament Agency
Central Intelligence Agency (CIA)
Department of
    the Air Force
    the Army

Commerce
Defense
Energy
Justice
the Navy
State
Transportation
the Treasury
Export-Import Bank of the United States
General Services Administration (GSA)
International Communications Agency (ICA)
National Aeronautics and Space Administration (NASA)
Nuclear Regulatory Commission (NRC)
Overseas Private Investment Corporation

Is information ever too old to be properly classified?

Technically, no. Section 1.4(a) of E.O. 12356 provides that "information shall be classified as long as required by national security considerations." This provision allowing material to be classified indefinitely replaces provisions in Carter's E.O. 12065 that established certain time frames for automatic declassification review.[21]

As a practical matter, however, the older the material is, the better your chance for getting it released. If applicable, appeal letters should stress the age of the documents.

Are agencies permitted to use the security exemption to refuse to confirm or deny whether some material exists?

Yes. Section 3.4(f)(1) of E.O. 12356 permits agencies to do this when they decide that "the fact of its [the document in question] existence or non-existence is itself classifiable under this Order." The CIA in particular makes use of this option, and also has a (b)(3) statute (discussed later) which reinforces this prerogative.

Does the classification system take into consideration situations where it might be more important that the public know about something than that the agency keep it secret?

No. The Reagan order eliminated one of the reforms in the preceding Carter order, which had set up an explicit "balancing test" for situations where release might involve some damage to the national security, but where it is more important that the public know what is going on. (For example, one can imagine a situation in which it might be more important that the public know that a particular nuclear reactor was seriously flawed than to conceal the technical basis for the defect.) Eliminating the balancing test from the order also removes the consideration of the public's interest in the material as a basis for an FOIA lawsuit.[22]

However, agencies should be reminded that the FOIA exemptions are discretionary, even in the national security arena. The classification standard applies only to harm from "*unauthorized* disclosures." An FOIA release would be an authorized disclosure if the appropriate agency official chose to release the material. Indeed, every administration has regularly released information that could technically have been classified; administrations ordinarily do this when they can use the information to build support for its policies.

Can agencies classify information after it has been requested under the FOIA?

Yes. Section 1.6(d) of E.O. 12356 permits agencies to classify documents when they are being reviewed for release under an FOIA request.

If this is done, it is supposed to be "accomplished personally and on a document-by-document basis" by upper echelon officials.

Are there any special provisions that control access to national security information originating in the White House?

No. The Carter executive order on classification had set up a special review system for classified information originating with the President or with people acting on his behalf (such as the White House staff), but the Reagan executive order revoked this. It specifically exempts such material from the Mandatory Review procedures. As discussed in chapter 1, the presidential offices are exempt from the FOIA, except as provided in the Presidential Records Act of 1978.

Does the executive order on security classification provide any avenues outside the FOIA for appealing decisions to withhold information under the (b)(1) exemption?

No. Section 5.2(b)(6) of E.O. 12356 gives the director of the Information Security Oversight Office the authority to "consider and take action on complaints and suggestions from persons within or outside the Government with respect to

the administration of the information security program."
However, under the Reagan order, the Director no longer
has the authority to order that improperly classified information be declassified.

After an administrative appeal under the FOIA is turned
down, you can choose to write a complaint or suggestion
under this section. However, since the Director lacks the
power to order declassification, your complaint or suggestion
is unlikely to accomplish more than letting the office know
that you are unconvinced by agency (b)(1) claims.

**Do the procedures outlined in the executive order (such as
the limits upon who has authority to classify documents)
have to be followed in order for documents to be properly
classified under the FOIA's (b)(1) exemption?**
Yes, and you should make certain that agencies have followed
the proper procedures. The legislative history of the 1974
amendments shows,[23] and court decisions have in some instances held, that unless the various procedural requirements
of an executive order on classification have been met, the
material is not properly classified and must be released.[24]

**What recourse do I have if an agency refuses to declassify
material that does not seem properly classified or that is
vital to public debate?**
You can sue in federal court, asking the judge to exercise
the power of *de novo* review of whether the material is
properly classified.[25] (See chapter 6, "Going to Court.") In a
de novo review, the judge has the power to order the release
of improperly classified material.

It was because of this point that President Ford vetoed the
1974 amendments to the FOIA. Congress passed the FOIA
amendments over the veto, but this fact has not prevented a
succession of government lawyers from claiming that the
FOIA does not give judges the power to overrule the classification decisions of executive branch officials as to whether
material is properly classified. The influential District of Columbia Circuit Court of Appeals, which handles the bulk of
FOIA cases involving (b)(1), has issued a decision reaffirming
that the FOIA's legislative history means what it says it
means—namely that judges have the same authority with
(b)(1) claims that they do with other areas of FOIA litigation.[26]

You should be warned, however, that the courts have so far

been unwilling to exercise this authority. Instead, they have placed greater emphasis on the statement in the legislative history of (b)(1) that the courts should "accord substantial weight to an agency's affidavit concerning the details of the classified status of the disputed records."[27]

Even so, it should be emphasized that going to court in (b)(1) cases has produced much useful information. Even though there have been few instances in which courts have ordered information released over the (b)(1) claims of the agencies, a good deal of useful information ends up being released voluntarily by the government, in order to simplify the litigation. In addition, the discovery process (which will be discussed later) also generally produces interesting information.

Some types of information that might be covered by the (b)(1) exemption, might also be covered by the (b)(3) exemption for material protected by various other statutes. This will be discussed later.

The (b)(2) Exemption for Internal Agency Rules

Are documents showing internal agency rules and practices available under the FOIA?

Ordinarily, yes, but there are some limitations on access. Under (b)(2), the FOIA does not apply to matters that are "related solely to the internal personnel rules and practices of an agency."[27a]

Obviously, the crux of the matter is whether something is "solely" of interest to the agency. In this the courts have been sympathetic to requesters—which stands to reason, since requesters are not likely to bother with a request and lawsuit for something that is of no interest to them. In practice, this means that only "minor and trivial matters" can be withheld,[28] and that this exemption cannot apply to matters that are of "genuine and significant public interest."[29] Some examples of information that the courts have held *cannot* be withheld include summaries of the Air Force Academy's handling of honor code violations,[30] agency Evaluations of Personnel Management,[31] training manuals for Occupational, Safety, and Health Administration (OSHA) compliance officers,[32] and property appraisal and disposal records.[33]

Can law enforcement manuals be withheld under (b)(2)?

As of this writing, law enforcement manuals are a category of material that has been subject to conflicting decisions by different circuit courts. On the one hand, the release of such manuals might help someone circumvent the law; on the other hand, if they are not released such manuals might establish "secret law," and the public does have an interest in knowing how law enforcement is implemented. There is speculation that this question will either go before the Supreme Court or produce a legislative change in the FOIA in order to resolve the conflict.

In the influential D.C. Circuit, the leading case now holds that (b)(2) applies if release "significantly risks circumvention of agency regulations or statutes." However, at the same time, the (b)(2) exemption cannot be used to withhold material that would amount to secret law.[34] Thus, there appears to be a balancing test to govern the competing interests. Some examples of manuals that courts have held *can* be withheld under the (b)(2) exemption include a training manual for surveillance techniques[35] and a manual on the conduct of raids and searches.[36]

Other courts, however, have held that law enforcement manuals are not solely related to internal agency practices and therefore cannot be held exempt under (b)(2). These cases have concerned IRS training manuals,[37] OSHA training manuals,[38] and a Drug Enforcement Administration (DEA) manual.[39]

The matter is further muddled by differing interpretations of FOIA subsection (a)(2)(C), which states that "administrative staff manuals and instructions to staff that affect a member of the public" are supposed to be made available. (See chapter 1.) Courts differ as to whether the legislative history of this provision allows a limited exemption of law enforcement manuals.

Are rules and instructions that govern agency filing systems and procedures covered by the (b)(2) exemption?

This is another area where the courts have ruled both ways in somewhat similar cases.

Thus, filing instructions for material concerning the assassination of President Kennedy,[40] and for the FBI's COIN-TELPRO domestic surveillance program[41] were not exempt under (b)(2). However, symbols referring to FBI informants,[42] and various other kinds of filing numbers[43] were found to meet the standard of the exemption, because they had a purely internal significance.

Can the tests and examinations that the federal government uses to determine personnel qualifications be obtained?

No, not if the release would compromise the secrecy of the test questions. Such material could probably be withheld under the FOIA's (b)(2) exemption, and the Privacy Act provides an explicit exemption for them.[44]

What arguments should I consider making in an administrative appeal letter if material is withheld under a (b)(2) claim?

The first approach is to explain why this particular information is not trivial. State your purpose in asking for the data. If you know of scholarly studies, press accounts, or congressional inquiries concerning such material, you should cite these.

If the material might have investigative applications, explain uses for the interest *other* than circumventing federal regulations. For example, do you want the material so that you can determine whether the instructions to investigators take into account constitutional guarantees of personal privacy? You should also state that if the material is not released, it will amount to secret law.

The (b)(3) Exemption for Material Exempted by Other Statutes

If there are other statutes that govern the use of a particular category of information in federal records, can the FOIA be used to get that information?

Sometimes yes; sometimes no. Innumerable statutes control the flow and use of federal information, a fact that makes the FOIA's (b)(3) exemption the most legally complex of the lot. This exemption states that the FOIA does not require the disclosure of matters that are

specifically exempted from disclosure by statute, provided that such statute (A) requires that the matter be withheld from the public in such a manner as to leave no discretion on the issue, or (B) establishes particular criteria for withholding or refers to particular types of matters to be withheld.[44a]

In order for an agency's (b)(3) claim to stand up in court, the agency must cite a particular statute governing the kind of information that has been requested. The cited statute must be quite specific about controlling the material: it must either *compel* the agency to keep that material from public view, or it must make clear what the determining factors for withholding are. There is obviously a great deal of room for legal hairsplitting about whether the controls in a given statute will rise to the level of supporting a (b)(3) claim. Even if the courts do determine that the cited statute is, in fact, a valid (b)(3) statute, you can still require the government to prove in court that the records in question are actually the kind of material that is protected by that particular statute. Sometimes the situation is relatively clear, but often it is not.

Unfortunately, the FOIA's legislative history does not provide a complete list of valid (b)(3) statutes. In addition, (b)(3) is at this time the newest of the FOIA exemptions, having been amended in 1976, as part of the Government in the Sunshine Act.[45] Thus the case law has not had a chance to sift out all the changes this will bring about. The earlier (b)(3) provision had been interpreted by the courts as granting agencies very broad authority for claiming that a given statute met the criteria for a (b)(3) claim.[46] Therefore, it is presumed that many statutes that might have been valid under the 1966 version of (b)(3) would not meet the standard set out in the 1976 version.[47]

In addition, as mentioned in the Introduction, new legislation can be passed at anytime (possibly in a "rider" to an unrelated bill) which would create a (b)(3) exemption statute where one had not existed before. Proposals for such back door amendments to the FOIA have been growing in number in recent years.

What kinds of things are taken into consideration in deciding whether the agency is citing a valid (b)(3) statute in order to withhold information?

If an agency withholds information by citing the (b)(3) exemption, you should ask the agency to specify precisely what section of the cited statute they believe authorizes the withholding; also ask what other legal authorities are being relied upon. (If you end up consulting a lawyer, this will save time.)

The legal authorities that are relied on (in addition to the plain language of the statute) consist of the legislative history of the statute and of FOIA court decisions mentioning that statute. By checking the legislative history (that is, the various committee reports and floor debates for a particular act), it is usually possible to determine what kinds of controls on information the members of Congress intended. Since it is the courts that ultimately decide whether something is a (b)(3) statute, any particular cases the agency has cited should be checked out. Even when the agency cites cases that support it, the decisions may not actually apply to the precise kind of information you are requesting. In addition, there may be other cases—particularly from other circuits—that take a position different from the one that the agency has cited;[48] the agency is unlikely to tell you about these.

In short, if the statute that the agency is claiming may *not* actually be a valid (b)(3) statute, ideally, you should explain why it is not in an administrative appeal letter. (The legal research suggested here is for the ambitious. You do not, however, have to present any legal research in order to write an appeal letter; it can simply state that the statute should not be applied to a particular request and ask for an appeal review.)

But the mere fact that an agency has a valid (b)(3) does not mean that the requested records are in fact covered by that statute. This is discussed in more detail later.

What are examples of statutes that do, in fact, provide a valid basis for withholding documents under exemption (b)(3)?

As just mentioned, there is no definitive list of (b)(3) statutes. Here are a few that the courts have upheld.

13 U.S.C. Section 8(b) and 9(a) require that information collected by the U.S. Census Bureau can only be released in statistical form.[49] These data are similarly protected by an exemption in the Privacy Act.[50] (However, census records that are more than seventy-two years old are available at the National Archives; the statute presumes that, by that time, privacy interests no longer need to be protected.)

42 U.S.C. Section 2000e–8(e) directs the Equal Em-

ployment Opportunity Commission (EEOC) to withhold data dealing with charges of discrimination until formal proceedings have begun.[51]

The Atomic Energy Act, 42 U.S.C. Section 2167(a) and (d) controls "restricted data" constituting atomic secrets and certain related "safeguards information."[52] (This overlaps with the protection in the (b)(1) exemption.)

50 U.S.C. Section 403g permits the CIA to withhold information about its internal structure. Information about its functions in general cannot be withheld under this statute. 50 U.S.C. Section 403(d)(3) provides that "the Director of Central Intelligence shall be responsible for protecting intelligence sources and methods, from unauthorized disclosure." The information does not have to be classifiable (see the (b)(1) exemption above) in order to be withheld under these (b)(3) statutes.[53]

50 U.S.C. Section 402 note states that the National Security Agency (NSA) can keep information about its activities secret, as well as the names, titles, salaries, and number of persons employed.[54]

25 U.S.C. Section 122 requires that patent applications be kept secret; this includes abandoned applications.[55]

26 U.S.C. Sections 1603 and 7213 protect income tax returns. The courts are divided as to whether tax returns are available if the agency deletes information that would identify particular taxpayers.[56]

15 U.S.C. Section 2055(b)(1) of the Consumer Product Safety Act controls the release of information submitted to the Consumer Product Safety Commission (CPSC).[57]

What options are available if the information that I want is withheld under a (b)(3) claim?

If the agency has a valid (b)(3) statute, there are basically two options to be pursued in the appeal process.

First is to find out whether, if certain information were deleted (leaving only "segregable portions"), the information would still be protected by the statute. For example, if the purpose of the (b)(3) statute is to protect personal privacy, would the deletion of identifying details then take the information outside the range of protected material? Agencies should make this evaluation automatically, but they often need to be reminded.

Second, you can argue that the information in question is

not actually the kind of information that the (b)(3) statute is meant to protect. For example, if the CIA claims that the release of certain records would "jeopardize intelligence sources and methods," there is a great deal of room for argument. Does the withheld material, for example, deal with a widely circulated rumor or with something that had been treated in news accounts or scholarly studies? If so, (b)(3) is very weak; the sources and methods exemption applies only to things that are genuine secrets.

However, there is not much point in arguing that the agency should exercise its discretion and release information that is technically exempt under the (b)(3) exemption. By definition, a valid (b)(3) statute prohibits agency officials from making such discretionary release of the specified category of information.

The (b)(4) Exemption for Business Information

Can the FOIA be used to get government information about private business and commercial matters?

Yes, with certain exceptions. The FOIA does not apply to matters that are "trade secrets and commercial or financial information obtained from a person and privileged or confidential."[57a] Legally, a corporation is a "person."[58]

This exemption for confidential business records has been the subject of a great deal of ongoing congressional attention.[59] It has also produced a side effect that had been completely unanticipated when the FOIA was enacted in 1966—the "reverse FOIA lawsuit." In a reverse FOIA suit, the government may be perfectly willing to release the material to you, but the business that supplied the information sues to prevent release. (This is discussed in more detail later.)

What kinds of information are considered to be trade secrets?

The FOIA's trade secrets provision protects information if it fits four criteria: (1) the information must not be generally known within the trade or profession; (2) the corporation must in fact be maintaining the secrecy of the information; (3) the secret must be commercially valuable; and (4) the business must actually be making use of the secret.[60]

Even if the information requested is not a trade secret, it

may still be protected under (b)(4) as "commercial or financial" information.

What are examples of the kinds of information that Congress had in mind when it wrote the (b)(4) exemption for business information?

The legislative history for the fourth exemption specifically lists business sales statistics, inventories, customer lists, scientific or manufacturing processes or developments, negotiation positions in labor-management mediations, as well as material customarily protected by the doctor-patient, attorney-client, and lender-borrower privileges.[61] This list is not exhaustive, of course, but any information that falls into one of these categories can ordinarily be presumed to fall under the (b)(4) protections.

What kind of commercial or financial data are considered "confidential" and therefore protected by the (b)(4) exemption?

In order for material to fall under the (b)(4) exemption, it is not enough that the agency had promised to keep the material secret.[62] Information is considered confidential only if its release would cause some specific harm (for instance, that release would make it more difficult for the government to get similar information in the future,[63] or that it would harm the competitive position of the person who submitted the information).[64]

If an agency denies an FOIA request by citing the (b)(4) exemption, you should ask whether the person who submitted the data did in fact request that it be kept confidential. While such promises do not, by themselves, determine whether the material is actually covered by (b)(4), if there was no request for confidentiality, the lack of concern implies that the material is not really secret and the agency should release the information.

And since the passage of time often changes the importance of keeping secrets, you should ask the agency to contact the submitter of the information to find out if there is any current objection to disclosure.

What kinds of information can be withheld under (b)(4) as information that would damage a person's competitive position?

There are, of course, some fairly obvious situations where

one business competitor is asking for information about another's financial status, bids, processes, or what have you. But the fact that you are not actually a business competitor does not affect the protection of trade secrets or financial and commercial information. The courts have held that information requested by consumer groups or others studying the workings of corporations could end up causing competitive harm.

For example, one court held that data on the safety defects in television sets could be withheld. The reasoning was that a corporation that kept particularly good records because it was concerned about safety could end up looking as if it had a worse record than a company that kept poor safety records.[65]

In a reverse FOIA case, a corporation convinced the court that employment statistics that were requested in order to study possible race and sex discrimination in their employment policies would also permit competitors to determine the company's labor costs, sales volume, plans for expansion, profit margin, vulnerability to price changes, and new products. The court therefore ordered the data withheld.[66]

Does the (b)(4) exemption protect technical information and research, which might very well have some commercial application, but that has been developed in noncommercial settings, such as universities?

No. Thus far, technical data has been held protected only in the commercial, profit-oriented research situation. Research at nonprofit institutions is not protected.[67] As of this writing, Congress is considering legislative proposals to extend (b)(4) protections to include such research.

Is financial information from a nonprofit organization or a scholar without commercial goals protected under the (b)(4) exemption?

Yes. While the (b)(4) exemption does not protect information that is not "commercial," it does, however, protect any person's financial information.[68] This overlaps with the privacy protections provided in exemption (b)(6), but also applies to businesses and other organizations that have no personal privacy rights.

Can the (b)(4) exemption ever be applied to data that the government agency has itself compiled?

No. This exemption applies only to information that was submitted *to* the government *by* a person (a private business or individual). If the data was in fact generated by the agency itself, it is not covered by (b)(4).[69] The government is not considered a legal person.[70] It is possible, of course, that there may be a rather fine line between corporation-supplied and government-generated information. In addition, legislation is currently under consideration that would, if enacted, establish a system by which the government would get royalties for commercially valuable information that it had developed.[71]

(The protection for certain kinds of banking information and oil well data overlap in many ways with the (b)(4) protections, but they also provide somewhat broader coverage. For example, government-generated information relating to the banking industry may be withheld. See the discussions of (b)(8) and (b)(9) later in this chapter.

Does the agency notify the business from which it got the information that its data has been requested under the FOIA?

Generally, yes. At present there is no legal requirement in the FOIA statute or in the case law that requires that agencies notify concerned businesses or individuals when information regarding them has been requested. However, notification has apparently become nearly universal in practice. Sometimes the notice may be given informally, and with only a few days' advance warning before the release of the documents.[72]

In addition, a number of other laws require that the agencies provide notice when they intend to release certain categories of information.[73]

As of this writing, there are legislative proposals under consideration that would, if enacted, clarify the rights of the submitters of the kind of business information covered by (b)(4). For the most part, the proposals reflect the solutions that the courts have already devised and the procedures for handling business information that the agencies have already installed. In addition, it has been proposed that, where the submitter must be consulted about possible release of information, the FOIA time limits for processing the request would be extended.[74]

Do businesses pay close attention to the FOIA requests that might concern them?

Yes. In fact, one congressional committee noted that a cottage industry has grown up to monitor the flow of business information out of government files. For a fee of several hundred dollars, a private firm provides subscriptions to the FOIA logs at the Food and Drug Administration (FDA), the Environmental Protection Agency (EPA), the Federal Trade Commission (FTC), and the Consumer Product Safety Commission; in addition, subscribers can get special telephone alerts when their data is requested.[75] All of this activity has led to protests from business that the FOIA facilitates a form of industrial espionage, and there has been considerable pressure for amendments to the FOIA that would give business interests additional protection.

Can a person (including corporations) sue the agency to prevent the release of material that might be covered by the exemption for business information?

Yes. Such suits, as mentioned earlier, are generally called reverse FOIA suits. The Supreme Court has held that while the FOIA is strictly a disclosure statute, there are other federal statutes that put constraints on what can be disclosed under the FOIA. These statutes can come into play when an agency chooses to release data that the person who submitted the data believes should not be released. The agency, for its part, may not agree that the material is actually covered by the (b)(4) exemption, or it may want to make a discretionary release. If there is a disagreement, the person who submitted the data can sue to prevent the release, and argue that disclosure would be an abuse of discretion.

The Trade Secrets Act protects from unauthorized disclosure any information that "concerns or relates to the trade secrets, processes, operations, style of work, or apparatus, or to the identity, confidential statistical data, amount or source of any income, profits, losses, or expenditures of any person, firm, partnership, corporation, or association."[76] While the Supreme Court has held that neither the FOIA nor the Trade Secrets Act give a person the right to sue to prevent the disclosure of information, it has also held that another federal statute, the Administrative Procedure Act (APA), does in fact give standing to sue.[77] In other words, an agency's power to release information that might in fact fall under an FOIA exemption has certain limitations—release must not run afoul of these other federal statutes that place controls on how officials may use information.

If a reverse FOIA suit is filed to prevent the release of information that I have requested, can I protect my rights in court?

Yes. Your options in court are discussed in chapter 6.

The (b)(5) Exemption for Certain Internal Government Memorandums

Can the FOIA be used to get information about the opinions, advice, or recommendations that are offered by government officials in internal government policy deliberations?

Generally no. The FOIA does not apply to matters that are "inter-agency or intra-agency memoranda or letters which would not be available by law to a party other than an agency in litigation with the agency."[77a] Put simply, the (b)(5) exemption is meant to protect material that is either protected (1) by the attorney-client or attorney work-product privileges; or (2) by the privilege that protects internal discussion in the decision-making process.[78]

What is covered by the attorney-client and attorney work-product privileges?

Generally, these are categories of information that have been protected by the rules of discovery in lawsuits.[79] In litigation, neither side's lawyers are required to make an open book of their efforts or strategies.[80] By the same token, clients must have an assurance that their discussions with their lawyers will be confidential. Since federal agencies have lawyers, they can make use of this privilege under exemption (b)(5).

There is an exception, however: facts (as opposed to opinion, and so forth) are ordinarily discoverable in litigation and, therefore, facts are not protected by (b)(5).

Are the background discussions that lead up to an agency decision exempt under (b)(5)?

In most regards, yes. The (b)(5) exemption protects what is more commonly known as the "executive privilege," which is meant to protect the deliberations, advice, and consultations that lead up to decision-making. Without such confidentiality, it is believed that discussion would be less frank and thorough; internal debate would be dampened. Congress wanted this category of material protected because it was convinced that the "efficiency of Government would be greatly hampered if, with respect to legal and policy matters, all Government agencies were prematurely forced to operate in a fishbowl."[81]

Since the reason behind the (b)(5) exemption is to protect free internal discussions, faced with a (b)(5) claim you might ask in the appeal letter that the details that would identify particular officials be deleted and that the rest of the material be released.

Once the agency has made a decision, is background material leading up to that decision available under the FOIA?

Yes. The courts have held that the views that have been the basis of a policy that was finally adopted can be released without danger. Since it is usually a mark of prestige for employees if it is known that their advice prevailed in the decision-making process, the knowledge that the winning arguments might be made public under the FOIA will normally not cast a chill on internal discussions.[82] The views of the "losers" in the agency deliberations could still be withheld under (b)(5), however. (This is sometimes unfortunate, because these deleted views may include the most informed criticisms of the policies that the agency chose to adopt.)

And, of course, the agency's final decisions cannot be withheld under the (b)(5) exemption—the FOIA is meant to prevent such secret law. If the material that an agency is withholding under a (b)(5) claim appears to be a final decision, you should write an appeal letter to remind the agency of this. In addition, you should watch out for deletions that might be "statements of policy and interpretations which have been adopted by the agency," or "instructions to staff that affect a member of the public." Under the publications requirements of the FOIA, these are supposed to be made available.[83] (See chapter 1.)

Can an agency successfully claim the (b)(5) exemption simply by designating a given document as an "advice memorandum"?

No. If an advice memorandum is in fact a final decision (for instance, if it is sent to an agency head, who then puts it into effect by initialing it) then it is not exempt. Remember, the burden of proof is on the agency to establish that a memo is *not* a final decision. When material is denied under (b)(5) and if you suspect that the material actually reflects agency policy, it can sometimes be useful to try to find out more about the memo's history within the agency and to use this to argue for release.

Can the facts that are included in the agency deliberations be withheld under (b)(5), or do they have to be segregated and released?

The (b)(5) exemption protects opinions, but not facts. Ordinarily, "purely factual, investigative" material must be separated from the material that would reveal either attorney-privilege information or deliberations leading up to decisions.[84] (Of course, facts that could be withheld under another of the FOIA's exemptions could be withheld even if a (b)(5) claim did not apply.) As a rule of thumb, a fact is considered separable unless it is contained in the same sentence as some genuinely deliberative material.

As of this writing, the courts are divided as to whether there are certain circumstances in which facts can be withheld. Some courts have found that if the release of the facts would impair the agency's ability to get information in the future, then they can be withheld. (If the government, for example, promised confidentiality when it originally collected the data used in the deliberations, that the agency will generally be able to withhold the data.[85]

Also, in cases where the information is available through other sources or documents, but where the release of facts in a particular document would reveal the decision-making process, then the (b)(5) exemption can be claimed.[86] This means that if (b)(5) is being used to withhold facts, you may be able to get around the exemption by rewriting the request and asking for other documents, studies, or background material that might well reveal the same data.

Are expert opinions or evaluations of facts considered "facts" or "opinions" in regard to (b)(5) claims?

Expert analysis of hard facts (generally this means objective scientific data) is sometimes considered to be "fact" rather than "opinion," and cannot be successfully withheld under the (b)(5) exemption.[87]

Are the work and deliberations of consultants from outside the government protected by the (b)(5) exemption?

Various court decisions have held that, if they have formal relationships with the agency, the work of outside experts, unpaid consultants, and advisory committees can be protected by (b)(5).[88]

Is the decision-making at high-level meetings protected by the (b)(5) exemption?

If such meetings are covered by the Government in the Sunshine Act, the (b)(5) exemption cannot be used to withhold any material from the transcripts, tape recordings, or minutes of such meetings. In addition, the public may be able to sit in on such meetings. (See chapter 7.)

The (b)(6) Exemption for Private Matters

What kind of information is protected by the FOIA's (b)(6) exemption for personal matters?

This exemption protects personal privacy. It permits an agency to withhold "personnel and medical files and similar files the disclosure of which would constitute a clearly unwarranted invasion of personal privacy."[88a] There are two major factors that go into determining whether information is properly withheld under a (b)(6) claim. First, is the data actually personal and private? And second, does the public's interest in knowing the information outweigh the subject's interest in personal privacy? These will be discussed in more detail later.

Can I request records about other people?

As long as you do not request such records under false pretenses, there is nothing to prevent you from requesting such records. But except for a few categories of material, you are unlikely to get much material. The Privacy Act and the FOIA (b)(6) and (b)(7)(C) exemptions protect personal information, and ordinarily such data can be released only to the person who is the subject of the record. As discussed in chapter 2, agencies will require some sort of personal identification, usually a notarized signature, establishing that the requester is, in fact, the subject of the files.

The Privacy Act makes it a criminal offense—carrying a five-thousand-dollar fine—to try to get someone else's personal files by pretending that you are that person.[89]

Should I challenge an agency that claims it is withholding material in order to protect personal privacy?

Yes, if you think you have grounds to do so. There is not much question that the government has been overzealous at times about deleting material to protect personal privacy (for example, deleting the name of the person to whom the requester is married). There are bureaucratic reasons why (b)(6) is overinvoked—the Privacy Act provides criminal penalties (a five-thousand-dollar fine) against any government employee "who knowing that disclosure of the specific material is so prohibited [by the Privacy Act], willfully discloses the material in any manner to any person or agency not entitled to receive it."[90] On the other hand, the FOIA does not provide criminal penalties for improper withholding of material. As a result, even though it would be very hard to prove knowing and willful disclosure in all but the most egregious cases, federal employees prefer to err on the side of caution and to withhold anything that might conceivably violate personal privacy. They would much prefer to have a court order them to release material, or to have a clear administrative record that they carefully balanced privacy interests before release.

Can my files ever be withheld from me under the (b)(6) exemption claim?

An agency cannot withhold your own records from you under a (b)(6) exemption claim that it would violate *your* privacy. However, it is possible that material in which you are mentioned will have information concerning other people, and this information can be deleted using a (b)(6) claim.

Does the FOIA exemption for privacy protect entire files?

The FOIA's provision for releasing segregable portions of government records applies to personnel, medical, and similar files just as it applies to all other categories. The Supreme Court has rejected a government claim that there is a blanket exemption for personnel files.[91] As a result, if you want a category of files so that you can, for example, perform a statistical analysis of their data, the agency should remove the information that would identify the individuals, and you should get the rest.

What kind of information is protected by the exemption for privacy?

To be protected by the (b)(6) exemption, information must be of an intimate and personal nature. Courts give a broad interpretation to this exemption.[92] Generally, in handling requests from someone who is not the subject of the records, several criteria are used to determine whether data is in fact intimate and personal.

Would the release of the information in any way harm the individual(s) mentioned in the records?[93] If release would not harm the subject, you should point this out in your correspondence with the agency.

Many categories of information are considered automatically intimate and private: courts have found that marital status, legitimacy of children, medical condition, welfare payments, alcohol consumption, family fights, reputation, religious and philosophical beliefs, and so on, are private details protected by the (b)(6) exemption.[94] And of course, the Privacy Act specifically protects data about an individual's exercise of First Amendment rights, which include political and religious association, beliefs, and activities.[95]

Another important question is whether, in the process of collecting the personal information, the agency had made a promise that the data would be held confidential. However, even if the agency has promised confidentiality, the data is not automatically exempt: the balancing test is still necessary.[96] If the information has, for example, already been released in some form, this reduces the importance of a promise of confidentiality. Another situation where an agency's (b)(6) claim is weak is one where the subjects of the data are aware of the request and do not object. For example, a court ordered the release (with names and addresses included) of a federal survey of some fifteen thousand homes that had been built on uranium tailings; one justification for release was that "no householder has objected to this disclosure."[97] (In addition, of course, home ownership is not ordinarily considered an intimate personal matter.)

In deciding whether release would be an "unwarranted invasion of privacy," is the degree of risk to privacy supposed to be taken into account?

Yes. The first question in the balance is whether it is likely that any harm will actually follow release.

The Supreme Court has ruled that "Exemption 6 was directed at threats to privacy interests more palpable than mere possibilities."[98] In this case, the government argued that releasing reports dealing with honor code violations at the Air Force Academy, even with the names deleted, might jar old memories, and cause fresh embarrassment to cadets who had been in trouble years earlier. But the Court held that in order to withhold information on privacy grounds, the risk to personal privacy has to go beyond the realm of abstract possibility and have some concrete likelihood of actually happening.

In another case, however, the Court found that when the potential for risk is high, even information that is ordinarily available and not considered intimate can be withheld. Thus, records that would have indicated whether or not two members of the Revolutionary Government of Iran were U.S. citizens was held exempt under (b)(6), given the climate of political violence in that country.[99]

Therefore, in an administrative appeal letter, it will be useful to explain how it is unlikely that any harm to individuals will follow release. For instance, are the results of the study going to be published in some professional journal read by only a few specialists? (In the first case above, the material was requested for a law review article.)

Is the intended use for the information an important factor in deciding whether release would be an "unwarranted invasion of personal privacy"?

Yes. The balancing test in the privacy exemption sets up one of the few areas in which your motives for obtaining the information are important.

For example, the courts have held that having a commercial interest in the data is not a public interest that would ordinarily outweigh the privacy interest. Thus, companies cannot get mailing lists under the FOIA for promotional purposes from agency records.[100]

On the other hand, scholars, specialists, and citizens with altruistic motives are in a position to overcome some privacy interests.[101]

Can I get mailing lists under the FOIA?

Sometimes. It depends on the policy of the particular agency and on the nature of the particular list.

Some agencies will not release any lists (for instance, the Department of Defense, the Postal Service, and the Department of the Treasury). Other agencies will release a list if they believe that the list involves the business activities of people or organizations, which are not ordinarily seen as including personal privacy interests that need protection. Some agencies routinely release the names of individuals who have obtained licenses (for instance, the Federal Communications Commission (FCC) makes available its list of some nine million Citizens Band radio licenses). By contrast, one court has held that the lists of amateur winemakers who sought a tax exemption from the Bureau of Alcohol, Tobacco, and Firearms for making wine for their own use were exempt under (b)(6). Using the public airways, it seems, is not considered a private matter in the same sense that making wine at home for family consumption is.[102]

Can I get medical (including psychological) records that the federal government may have on me?

Yes. However, the agency will probably decide to release the records to you only through the intermediary of a physician whom you select.[103] Therefore, if you are asking for your medical records, the letter should include a paragraph stating that, if the agency refuses to release medical records directly to you, the records should be sent to your physician. Remember, of course, to include the physician's name and office address, and to inform your physician that you have asked the agency to send these records.

Do deceased persons have a right of privacy protected by the (b)(6) exemption?

No. These privacy rights apply only to living people. Heirs do not have a right of privacy in a deceased person.[104]

Does the exemption for personal privacy protect the privacy of persons who have been involved in historical events?

Yes and no. Depending on the event, the person's role in it, and the nature of the records, release might be considered a "warranted" invasion of privacy. It is the policy of the Department of Justice that, in situations that involve historical material or "public figure status or other notoriety of the subject," the public's interest in release might outweigh privacy concerns.[105] In regard to the Alger Hiss and the Ethel and Julius Rosenberg files, for example, Deputy Attorney General Tyler stated that the Justice Department would not claim a personal privacy exemption for material involving the principal witnesses, except where the material was "of an intimate personal nature wholly unrelated to the subject matter of the cases." Generally, "records pertaining to other persons involved in these cases are to be considered very carefully before being withheld on privacy grounds."[105a]

What are the criteria for determining whether a person is an historical figure with fewer privacy rights?

This question came up in the decision to release the bulk of the files from the Rosenberg and Hiss cases. The Department of Justice ruled that "none of these principal participants had any privacy interest at the time" that the historical events were unfolding and that, in effect, the release of the material would be simply a gloss on what had received great publicity years earlier.

The other element that led to release of the material was that "the passage of time has permitted none of these individuals [in the Rosenberg and Hiss cases] to return to obscurity." The Justice Department cited a list of recent publications, drawn from library sources, on these historical events and their participants.[106]

In other words, the FOIA's privacy protections are meant to apply only to what actually is private. The Justice Department policy recognizes the fact that the process of becoming an historical figure removes much of a person's privacy, and there is no point in protecting what has already been lost.

Can records concerning government employees be withheld under exemption (b)(6)?

In regard to their employment, government personnel are subject to a different standard of privacy. The rules of the

Office of Personnel Management (OPM) for example, (formerly called the U.S. Civil Service Commission) provide that the name, present and past positions, titles, grades, salaries, and duty stations of most present and former federal employees are to be available to the public.[107] Similarly, the legislative history of the 1966 FOIA stated that (b)(6) is not intended to cover "the facts concerning the award of a pension or benefit."[108] And Veterans' Administration (VA) information concerning the amount of a veteran's compensation is supposed to be released to any person requesting it.[109] The Ethics in Government Act of 1978, requires that high-ranking executive branch personnel (generally, GS–16 and above) file detailed financial disclosure reports, which, along with a copy of their official job descriptions, will be made available for public examination.[110]

In situations where a federal employee has been accused of a crime or impropriety, the courts have concluded that the public's interest will be especially important and release will ordinarily be warranted. (Of course, purely personal details and subjective evaluations that do not have anything to do with the possible impropriety will be deleted.) Thus, courts have ordered the release of personnel records of former meat inspectors convicted of taking bribes;[111] the arrest record of a witness accused of cutting an improper deal with a prosecutor, (but not the names of those people receiving them);[112] and the drugs prescribed by the Attending Physician to Congress for congressional members, families, and staffs.[113]

In other instances, however, agency officials may not be suspected of crime or impropriety, but of ineptitude. In a case brought under the Government in the Sunshine Act, the influential D.C. Circuit held that the protected privacy interests don't extend to sheltering "substandard performance" by officials with executive responsibilities.[114] Since the wording of the FOIA and the Sunshine privacy exemptions is virtually identical in meaning, this decision should apply to FOIA cases as well (see chapter 8).

All this is not to say that records on federal employees are an open book. The FBI, for example, can withhold the names of its agents and informants under the (b)(6) exemption.[115]

Are organizations, such as businesses or political and religious groups, protected by the FOIA privacy exemptions?

No. While such organizations are legal "persons" [see the earlier discussion of exemption (b)(4)], only individuals (the flesh-and-blood variety) have "personal privacy" interests that are protected by the FOIA or the Privacy Act. Therefore, an organization's files cannot be withheld because of personal privacy. However, anywhere that the records mention individual people, those personal references may be deleted according to the (b)(6) and (b)(7)(C) standards for protecting personal privacy.

If you are requesting records on behalf of an organization, you may find that there are extensive deletions to protect personal privacy. If so, you should consider asking likely members of that organization if they would be willing to write a letter waiving their privacy rights with regard to those particular documents. Or, members could be asked to request the documents themselves and then pass along any personal references they did not mind making public. (See sample letter in Appendix A.)

Are agencies required to keep a record of their FOIA releases that involve what might be considered personal information?

No. While the Privacy Act ordinarily requires agencies to keep records of their dissemination of personal information, there is a special exemption from this record-keeping requirement for material released under the FOIA.[116]

If personal information is released under the FOIA, is an agency required under the Privacy Act to make certain that the material is accurate?

No. The Privacy Act exempts FOIA releases from the Privacy Act requirements that personal information be accurate.[117] You should be aware that records may very well contain half-truths, distortions, inaccuracies, and falsehoods. As mentioned earlier, the FOIA provides access to government files; it does not provide any quality control on what is found in those files. The personal data found in files should not be taken as proving anything.

Can agencies make discretionary releases of personal information that is otherwise protected by the FOIA's (b)(6) exemption?

No. The Privacy Act prohibits agencies from releasing personal information without the written consent of the subject *unless* release is *required* by the FOIA.[118] This "interface" between the FOIA and the Privacy Act means that the (b)(6) exemption of the FOIA is mandatory; the agency may not make discretionary releases of any personal information if that release would be an "unwarranted invasion of personal privacy."[119] [By contrast, the FOIA does not restrict an agency's discretion to release, say, national security information that would be covered by the (b)(1) exemption.]

If I am the subject of a file that the agency intends to release and feel that release would be a clearly unwarranted invasion of my privacy, what can I do to prevent release of the file?

Just as the exemption for trade secrets and financial or commercial information unexpectedly spawned the reverse FOIA suits, if you feel that a release of some federal records would be an "unwarranted" violation of your privacy, you could also sue under the Administrative Procedure Act to stop release. However, since there is no requirement that individuals be given prior notice when material concerning them is going to be released under the FOIA, the subject has no guarantee of advance warning.[120]

If I file suit against an agency to contest whether documents are properly withheld under an exemption for personal privacy, does the subject of those records have to be notified?

Yes. Under the provisions of the Privacy Act, agencies are required to "make reasonable efforts to serve notice on an individual when any record on such individual is made available to any person under compulsory legal process when such process becomes a matter of public record."[121] The filing of an FOIA suit would be an example of what is covered by this provision. This is imperfect protection, however. Individuals move around, and may not be readily found, even with "reasonable efforts." If people do find out about a lawsuit for files that they believe contain personal information about them, they may wish to have their own lawyer, in addition to Department of Justice lawyers, represent them in the litigation.[122]

The (b)(7) Exemption for Certain Records of Law Enforcement Investigations

Can the FOIA be used to get records concerning federal law enforcement investigations?

Yes, law enforcement records can be obtained under the FOIA—unless one or more of six specific harms would follow the release of the information. The FOIA permits agencies to withhold.

> investigatory records compiled for law enforcement purposes, but only to the extent that such records would (A) interfere with enforcement proceedings, (B) deprive a person of a right to a fair trial or an impartial adjudication, (C) constitute an unwarranted invasion of personal privacy, (D) disclose the identity of a confidential source and, in the case of a record compiled by a criminal law enforcement authority in the course of a criminal investigation, or by an agency conducting a lawful national security intelligence investigation, confidential information furnished only by the confidential source, (E) disclose investigative techniques and procedures, or (F) endanger the life or physical safety of law enforcement personnel.[122a]

This section goes over each of these exempted categories separately and sketches out the scope of investigatory records.

Are law enforcement records available under the Privacy Act?

No, only the FOIA provides access to law enforcement records. The Privacy Act provides sweeping exemptions for law enforcement records.[123] Because investigatory records are subject to review under the FOIA, agencies have adopted a policy of processing such requests under *both* acts. This dual processing is strictly optional for the agencies—since you must sue under the FOIA if you wish to contest withholding of material in law enforcement records.

These peculiarities have some unexpected side effects. Ordinarily, if you request your own personal files you can avoid being charged search fees for locating the records by making the request under the Privacy Act alone. But since law enforcement investigatory records are effectively exempted from the Privacy Act access provisions, law enforcement agencies will ordinarily process Privacy Act requests under the FOIA provisions, which permit them to charge search fees.[124]

Not all of the records of law enforcement agencies are exempt from disclosure under the Privacy Act—the exemptions apply only to *investigatory* records. For requests for the noninvestigatory personal records of such agencies, it is business as usual under the Privacy Act. For example, as with all other federal employees, FBI employees can gain access under the Privacy Act to their own personnel files (which are, of course, *administrative* rather than investigatory records).

The broad Privacy Act exemption for investigatory materials also contains an exemption of its own. If an investigation is not for the purpose of enforcing the criminal laws, and if the material is used to deny an individual a benefit, then the disclosure provisions of the Privacy Act *are* enforceable, and the only exempted information is that which protects the identity of a confidential source.[125]

What kinds of records are considered "law enforcement records" for purposes of a (b)(7) claim?

According to the legislative history of this exemption, (b)(7) protects both investigations leading to enforcement of the criminal laws and investigations that enforce the laws by means of civil suits. (Antitrust violations, for example, are enforced by civil lawsuits.) In addition, (b)(7) protects records of investigations that may end up being enforced through various administrative proceedings that are conducted by government agencies rather than in federal court.[126] An investigation that may result in a sanction, such as a cutoff of federal funds, may also create an investigatory record protected by (b)(7).[127]

This means that the (b)(7) exemption is claimed not just by those agencies that have well-known law enforcement roles—such as the FBI, the Drug Enforcement Administration (DEA), the Internal Revenue Service (IRS), the Immigration and Naturalization Service, the Customs Service, the Department of Justice, and the Bureau of Alcohol, Tobacco, and Firearms. The (b)(7) exemption also can be claimed by an agency with a regulatory role, such as the Food and Drug Administration (FDA), the Securities and Exchange Commission (SEC), the National Labor Relations Board (NLRB), the National Highway Traffic Safety Administration, the Department of Agriculture, the Department of Health and Human Services, and so on.

But the mere fact that an agency has a law enforcement role of some kind does not automatically make a (b)(7) claim valid. Sometimes an investigation may be carried out not for law enforcement purposes but, say, to monitor employee performance, or to enforce personnel policies; such purposes are not ordinarily covered by exemption (b)(7).[128] The particular *record* must relate to a law enforcement investigation. If records are being withheld under a doubtful (b)(7) claim, you should ask the agency to state what specific law its investigation was aimed at enforcing.[129]

In addition, even if the information in question is very useful for some legitimate law enforcement purpose, it cannot be withheld unless it was actually compiled as part of an investigation.

Finally, even though the records may in fact be considered law enforcement records, they are only exempt if they *also* fall under one of the six subsections of the (b)(7) exemption. These will be discussed shortly.

Since the FOIA exemptions are not intended to protect material that has already been released, does dissemination of investigatory records to state and local police departments mean that such records must be released under the FOIA?

No.[130] Giving records to other law enforcement agencies is not considered a release to the public.

Does exemption (b)(7) protect discredited political surveillance programs (such as COINTELPRO) that the FBI conducted against the civil rights, antiwar, and other movements?

Yes. The courts have held that even where the FBI's claims that an investigation was for law enforcement purposes seemed "little more than self-serving declarations," the records of those investigations qualify as law enforcement records that may be covered by the (b)(7) exemption. And although the Privacy Act protects First-Amendment privacy matters,[131] the Privacy Act does not require that such improperly acquired information be released.[132] (And as just mentioned, the Privacy Act exempts law enforcement agencies from its disclosure provisions.)

Even where the information collected in such questionable law enforcement investigations is then summarized in documents that are compiled for political purposes (such as when "name check" summaries on prominent liberals were sent to the Nixon White House), the summaries are covered by exemption (b)(7).[133]

Is the Central Intelligence Agency able to claim that it is conducting a law enforcement investigation and thereby entitled to use the (b)(7) exemption?

Since the statute setting up the CIA prohibited it from having any domestic law enforcement functions, it is not ordinarily able to use a (b)(7) claim to protect data collected from its domestic intelligence operations.[134] (Some internal personnel investigations may qualify, however.)

However, as discussed later, the CIA can use (b)(7)(D) —one of several subsidiary provisions in this exemption—to protect its sources in "a lawful national security intelligence investigation."

Can the FOIA be used to get records of ongoing investigations?

Generally, no. If an investigation has not yet been closed, most or all of the material will be withheld under a (b)(7)(A) claim that release would "interfere with enforcement proceedings."[135]

Sometimes the definition of an *ongoing* investigation is extremely loose. The FBI, for example, initially stated that their investigation of the death of Karen Silkwood was closed. But, following an FOIA request, the FBI stated that the Silkwood investigation was actually "dormant," and therefore records could be withheld under (b)(7)(A) as long as the possibility of law enforcement action remained.[136]

However, (b)(7)(A) does not automatically exempt an entire investigatory file; it permits withholding only that part that would *interfere* with the ongoing investigation. Any other information that can be separated out must be released. In practice, released material consists mostly of public record information (arrests, subpoenas, and so on), which you would probably already know about.

In situations where the FBI does not want to acknowledge that you are the subject of an ongoing investigation, the Bureau's backlog of unanswered FOIA/PA requests (the Bureau takes more than a year to process routine requests) is apparently used as an effective cover to avoid revealing the fact that an investigation is underway.[137]

If the FOIA request is made by someone *other* than the subject of the investigation, and if the target of the investigation already has access to the records, then the agency will have difficulty showing that release would interfere with an investigation. For example, the Environmental Protection Agency was not able to convince a court that disclosing the identities of those responsible for cleaning up hazardous wastes would "interfere with law enforcement proceedings" by interfering with cooperation voluntary cleanup programs.[138]

Can information be withheld from investigatory records in order to protect a person from unfavorable publicity relating to a law enforcement proceeding?

Yes. Subsection (b)(7)(B) permits a law enforcement agency to withhold information if release would "deprive a person of a right to a fair trial or an impartial adjudication." This applies to criminal trials and to administrative proceedings conducted by an agency.[139] However, the exemption cannot be invoked merely on the basis of speculation about possible publicity.[140]

Can material be withheld from investigatory records in order to protect privacy?

Yes. Subsection (b)(7)(C) states that material may be withheld if release would "constitute an unwarranted invasion of personal privacy." This overlaps with (b)(6), which also protects personal privacy. Here, too, there is a balancing test—if there is a legitimate reason for the release of the information, this may override an individual's right of personal privacy. (This means that your appeal letter might explain either that the information is not actually of a personal nature, or that there are overriding public concerns that would be served by release.)

Information that shows that someone has been investigated for suspected criminal violations or for other wrongful activities is covered by the (b)(7)(C)[141] exemption for privacy. However, the mere mention of someone's name within the context of an investigation is not enough to justify withholding; a balancing test must be made. For example, one court held that where the area under investigation related to business conduct, such as the handling of hazardous wastes, which is of great concern to the public, the material should be released.[142]

Similarly, public figures, particularly candidates for public office, have fewer privacy rights, especially for records on their campaign contributions.[143] As already discussed, FBI agents and other officials who don't make policy will ordinarily have their names deleted; courts have found that this intrusion may be warranted when there is a question about the performance of a particular agent.[144]

Courts have held that the law enforcement privacy exemption applies to confidential sources, who are also protected by (b)(7)(D). There is however some confusion about the status of witnesses. Some courts have held that, in order to encourage candor, witnesses must be covered by (b)(7)(C) as well.[145] Other courts have held that since witnesses expect to testify, their identities and information are not covered by this privacy exemption.[146]

Can the FOIA be used to find out the identity of informants, infiltrators, or other government sources of information?

No. Agencies maintain that both the (b)(7)(C) privacy exemption and the (b)(7)(D) exemption for concealing the identities of confidential sources protect informants. Exemption (b)(7)(D) states that an agency can withhold information if its release would reveal

> the identity of a confidential source and, in the case of a record compiled by a criminal law enforcement authority in the course of a criminal investigation, or by an agency conducting a lawful national security intelligence investigation, confidential information furnished only by the confidential source.

The protection of confidential sources is to be total. At the time that the 1974 amendments were enacted, Senator Phillip Hart stated that

> the [FOIA] amendment protects without exception and without limitation the identity of informers. It protects both the identity of informers and information which may reasonably be found to lead to such disclosure. These may be paid informers or simply concerned citizens who give information to enforcement agencies and desire their identity to be kept confidential.[147]

A few grounds do exist for challenging a (b)(7)(D) claim. First, the source must actually be a "confidential" source (see below). And second, if information is being withheld to prevent its being traced back to a confidential source, the agency must be able to establish that the data would permit such a trace. In addition, this exemption for material that might be traceable can be used only by agencies that enforce criminal laws or conduct "lawful national security intelligence investigations"; it does not apply to agencies (such as the National Labor Relations Board (NLRB)) which enforce only civil or administrative laws.

One other word of caution seems in order: namely, that it is not a good idea to try to use FOIA releases—especially from highly censored files to piece together the identity of an informer. Not only are agencies entitled to delete anything that might suggest the identity of an informer, but even if some information that looked like a "clue" were released, it is highly probable that it would be just another example of inaccurate and unverifiable information contained in the agency's files. And finally, the FBI used "snitch jackets" to discredit its COINTELPRO targets by planting false evidence that someone was an informer, or snitch. Although the FBI is apparently no longer doing this, people should be aware that instigating witch hunts for informers is an established tactic for disruption, and they should therefore be avoided.[148] There is also congressional testimony indicating that, at least in some cases, the government concocts what might be called a reverse snitch jacket. Former Deputy Attorney General Laurence Silberman has testified that in order to protect an informer's identity, the government will sometimes "make up a phony file in order to protect his identity."[149]

All in all, the prospects for correctly identifying an informer are exceedingly low, and the chances of misidentifying an innocent person are very high.

What is a "confidential source"?

A confidential source may be an institution as well as an individual.[150] And the assurance of confidentiality may have been implied, rather than explicit, and the courts have been quite liberal in inferring an implied promise of confidentiality.[151] In addition, in criminal investigations and in national security intelligence investigations there is an extra layer of protection for the source: if the information came from only one source, then the FOIA assumes that the release of that information could allow a knowledgeable party to deduce the identity of the source from the information. Therefore, the information provided, as well as the source, is exempt under (b)(7)(D).

In practice, the definition of a *confidential source* varies from agency to agency.

According to the FBI's guidelines, for example, confidential sources include informants (tipsters, codefendants, paid or unpaid informers), state and local government agencies (such as state or local police, but not another federal agency), foreign governments, schools, and commercial organizations (such as corporations and credit bureaus). Other agencies, such as the Drug Enforcement Administration (DEA), have somewhat different rules, however; the DEA does not consider credit companies or drug companies to be confidential sources.[152] The FBI maintains that all categories of sources on its list have received either an express or implied promise of confidentiality.[153]

It is possible to get material released if you can establish that it was not really given to the agency under an express or implied promise of confidentiality. As mentioned earlier, it is assumed that witnesses expect to come forward and give public testimony, and do not expect to remain unknown.

Can the (b)(7) exemption be used to conceal evidence of illegal activities undertaken by law enforcement agencies?

It is the stated policy of the Department of Justice that the (b)(7) exemption should not be used to conceal unlawful activities.[154] However, this does not mean that agencies are required to release information showing illegal activities if they can find some other grounds for withholding the information; indeed, many researchers have been complaining that records that are released seem stripped clean of information suggesting illegal or improper activities.

There seems to be a time lag in getting agencies to implement this principle. For example, for at least a year after this policy directive that prohibits concealing unlawful activities came down, the FBI continued its policy of using exemption (b)(7)(D) to conceal information that was provided by a federal employee who was acting either beyond his or her authority, or in violation of agency regulations. However, according to Justice Department policy, the FBI should not withhold information showing that, say, a Selective Service

System staffer had given the Bureau information in violation of the Selective Service System's own regulations protecting confidentiality.[155] Neither should information about the errant staffer's identity and actions be protected under (b)(7)(C), because the public has an interest in knowing about misdeeds of officials, and therefore release would not be a "clearly unwarranted" invasion of privacy. [See the preceding discussion of (b)(6).]

Can electronic surveillance devices (wiretaps and bugs) ever be considered a "confidential source" under (b)(7)(D)?

No. In spite of the fact that internal agency jargon has often referred to such investigative techniques as confidential sources, the FOIA's legislative history makes it clear that they are not supposed to be protected by (b)(7)(D).[156]

Can the FOIA be used to get information about the techniques that law enforcement agencies use in carrying out investigations?

Exemption (b)(7)(E) permits information to be withheld if its release would "disclose investigative techniques and procedures." The legislative history makes it clear that this is supposed to apply only to *secret* techniques, and that material indicating well-known tests, such as fingerprinting or spectrographic analysis, should be released.[157] In addition, the FBI manual states that ballistics tests and "bait money" are also well-known techniques that should not be withheld under (b)(7)(E); some of the programs used to target "subversives," such as the Administrative Index and the Security Index, are likewise supposed to be released, as are illegal techniques, such as warrantless wiretaps and "black bag" jobs (FBI burglaries). Courts have held, though, that the layout and security devices of a bank can be withheld under this exemption.[158]

But there is also plenty of room for debate about whether or not a great many other techniques are well known. The FBI, for example, withholds information indicating such seemingly well-known investigative techniques as mail covers, pretext phone calls and interviews, trash covers, stop notices, photo albums, pretext contracts, and photosurveillance.[159] Since virtually everyone who reads the newspapers has heard of these FBI techniques, such information would presumably be released if a lawsuit were filed. (By contrast, the Drug

Enforcement Administration uses (b)(7)(E) to withhold information about more technological sorts of investigatory devices, such as flash rolls, body transmitters, drug field tests, tracking devices, and surveillance aircraft.)[160]

Can the FOIA be used to get information about the federal agents who have been involved in the investigation of a particular case?

The (b)(7)(F) exemption permits law enforcement agencies to withhold information if release would "endanger the life or physical safety of law enforcement personnel." Agencies such as the FBI seem to be interested in using both this exemption and the (b)(7)(C) exemption for protecting personal privacy to prevent the release of its agents' names. At times, the enthusiasm for deleting names of agents has clearly been carried to the point of logical absurdity. For example, one political activist received the FBI file copy of an appeals court decision concerning him. Such court records are, of course, a matter of open public record, and this particular one had actually been published in West's *Federal Reporter*. Nevertheless, the FBI had carefully deleted the names of all the agents mentioned in the published court records.[161]

As just mentioned, court decisions allow the FBI to delete agents' names.

When denied material because of a (b)(7)(F) claim, you should argue (if true) that the subjects of the investigation have no record of violence or criminal activity, or that they already know, from various contacts during the investigation and/or trial, who the agents were, and that all they want is to know which agent wrote which file memo.

What are the government's filing systems like?

They are all different, which makes it necessary—and difficult—to tailor an FOIA request to fit a particular agency. The contrast between the FBI and CIA filing systems give a sense of the diversity that exists. This should also give you an example of the kinds of things you might want to find out about when you are drafting your request letter. (See chapter 2.)

The FBI has a central records system in its Washington D.C. headquarters, consisting of two components. First, it has approximately 20 million subject-matter files that are grouped into 191 different categories of file topics, each with its own number (for example, it has categories for "Training Schools," "Neutrality Matters," "Overthrow or Destruction of the Government," and "National Firearms Act").[162] In order to find material in these numerical files, there is an alphabetical index, known as the "general index." This contains approximately 59 million 3″ × 5″ index cards, and it is organized primarily according to the names of individuals (there are approximately 20 million such names).[163] These cards typically contain such data as name, file numbers, birth place, birth date, sex, race, address, and Social Security number. Since index cards are supposed to be created and placed in the general index only if the data they contain is material that the FBI may want to retrieve, this means that the general index may not include references to data that you might consider significant, but that the FBI would not.

The FBI opens subject files under the names of particular persons either if that person was the subject of an investigation, or if sufficient information was collected during an investigation on that person to warrant a separate file.

Many people who have been politically active will have their names cropping up in a variety of subject files without the FBI ever having actually opened up a separate subject file on them. Such people may not be properly indexed, and therefore an FOIA/PA search under their names turns up negative. For example, someone may appear in the files on a given organization, but unless there is an index card with the correct name on it, such records couldn't be located through a general index check.

Often the general index card under a given name will not list that person as the subject of a file, but will instead provide See Reference notations. This means that, while there may not be a main subject file for that person, the name appears in various subject files on other people or on organizations. If the FBI writes back and says that it has no file on you, it is a good idea to inquire whether it has in fact checked out the See References that might be in the general index. Since tracking down the various See References is of course more expensive than simply pulling out one named file, you should also ask for a cost estimate. For people who do have their own subject file, it is probably not worth the cost of searching the See References listed on the index card, because this material, if at all significant, should be duplicated in their own files.

In addition to the material at headquarters, FBI records are also kept by the 59 field offices and 13 foreign liaison offices.[164] Typically, the field offices contain material that was not sent to headquarters but that may be of considerable interest. You should be forewarned that the FBI field offices (but not headquarters) have started a program of destroying their records 5 years after a particular investigation is closed.[165] It is a good idea to request files as soon as you know that you might want them. Even if field office records are older than five years, an FOIA request should still be made, because (as of this writing) the FBI only had time to *begin* to destroy the records before a court order protecting the records was issued. The files in the local office will be organized under a different system than the central records system, and you may want to find out about this system if you are having difficulties retrieving information. For example, according to a General Accounting Office (GAO) report, "Some field offices do not catalog this information in alphabetical order. They may use other identifying means, such as telephone number, race, height, date of birth, or chronological order."[166]

Many kinds of records, in addition to the working files of the FBI field offices, are not, and never were, in the Bureau's main index. For example, the "Do Not File" files of the Hoover era and the ELSUR (Electronic Surveillance) Index are not cross-referenced in the general index. (Field offices may also have separate ELSUR indexes of their own). If you think that the kinds of records that you want may not be in the general index, you can specify in the request letter that these other systems (or agents' records or divisions or what have you) should also be checked.[167]

In contrast to the FBI, the CIA's filing system is highly decentralized, or compartmented, as the agency calls it. The records are set up this way so as to maintain greater secrecy even within the CIA itself.[168] It might take several days for a diligent agency employee to collect all the available personal information on someone. The employee would have to figure out every country that person had been in, and would then have to check the records of the "desk" for each of those countries. You can make the search much easier by specifying what countries you have visited, and when.

The various security programs likewise have filing systems of their own.

Americans who have traveled abroad, particularly if they

were not strictly tourists (for example, journalists, business people, or professors), may have records in the files of the Domestic Contact Service. It's not generally known that the CIA conducts background investigations on such people returning from overseas when the agency is considering whether to debrief them about what they saw and with whom they talked. (Of course, people who know they were debriefed by the CIA may be very interested in what the background check found out about them. These background checks, incidentally, have been conducted without the permission or knowledge of the subject.)

The CIA's domestic political operations would be in the agency's Counterintelligence Division under such titles as "Operation Chaos."[169]

Analytical material, rather than personal files, will be found in the CIA's scholarly wing, the Directorate for Intelligence. Records dealing with covert operations, including espionage and covert action, are found in the Directorate for Operations.[170]

Is Congress considering whether to make changes in the (b)(7) exemption for certain law enforcement records?

Yes. However, the proposals thus far seem to be rather technical, and are aimed primarily at codifying the case law that already exists. The one major difference would be to allow the withholding of law enforcement manuals. [See the discussion under (b)(2).][171]

The (b)(8) Exemption for Regulation of Financial Institutions

Does the FOIA provide access to records about banks and financial institutions?

No. The (b)(8) exemption to the FOIA allows agencies to withhold matters that are "contained in, or related to, examination, operating, or condition reports prepared by, on behalf of, or for the use of an agency responsible for the regulation or supervision of financial institutions."

Exemption (b)(8) overlaps in many ways with the protections provided in the (b)(4) exemption for financial information; it is ordinarily thought merely to add extra emphasis to the protection of banking records.[172] But while (b)(4) limits its scope to financial information obtained from outside the agencies (that is "from a person"), (b)(8) includes material that the agency itself may generate.[173]

Agencies that can use the (b)(8) exemption include the Comptroller of the Currency, the Federal Reserve System, and the Federal Home Loan Bank Board.

What kinds of financial institutions are covered by the (b)(8) exemption?

Financial institutions covered by the (b)(8) exemption are banks, trust companies, investment bankers, banking associations or firms, bank holding companies, and similar organizations.[174] It does not, however, include records on organizations such as the New York Stock Exchange.[175]

The (b)(9) Exemption for Oil Wells

Does the FOIA provide access to information about oil wells?

No. The (b)(9) exemption allows the government to withhold information concerning "geological and geophysical information and data, including maps, concerning wells." Like exemption (b)(8), the oil well exemption also overlaps with the (b)(4) exemption, and is thought by many to be redundant. But while it gives a double layer of protection to "confidential commercial information," it also provides a blanket exemption to this category of records contained in the files of the Bureau of Land Management (within the Department of the Interior) and of the Federal Power Commission (FPC) (now within the Department of Energy).[176]

This exemption is rarely called into play.

NOTES

1. 5 U.S.C. Section 552(a)(6)(A)(i).
2. *Halperin v. Dept. of State,* Civ. Action No. 75–0674 (Deposition of George Vest, Director, Bureau of Politico-Military Affairs, U.S. Department of State, July 29, 1975) (D.D.C.); Comptroller General of the United States, *Government Field Offices Should Better Implement the Freedom of Information Act,* GAO Report LCD 78–120 (Washington, D.C.: General Accounting Office, July 25, 1978); *Continuing Problems in DOD's Classification of National*

2. Security Information, GAO Report LCD–80–16 (Washington, D.C.: General Accounting Office, 1979).

3. 5 U.S.C. Section 552(b).

4. Attorney General's 1974 FOI Amendments Memorandum, pp. 14–15.

5. *Chilivis v. SEC*, 673 F.2d 1205 (11th Cir. 1982).

6. *Gulf & Western Industries v. U.S.*, 615 F.2d 527 (D.C. Cir. 1979).

7. *Exxon Corp. v. FTC*, 384 F. Supp. 755 (D.D.C. 1974); *Holy Spirit Assn. v. CIA*, Civ. No. 79–0151 (D.D.C., order of July 27, 1979) ("Congressional authority and control extend over documents exchanged directly with an agency in pursuit of Congress's originating intent.") *See also* James T. O'Reilly, *Federal Information Disclosure* (Colorado Springs: McGraw-Hill, Shepards, 1977), sec. 17.14 chap. 17, p. 38.

8. 5 U.S.C. Section 552a(k).

9. 5 U.S.C. Section 552a(i).

9a. 5 U.S.C. Section 552(b)(1).

10. 5 U.S.C. Section 552a(k)(1).

11. *EPA v. Mink*, 410 U.S. 73 (1973) (Stewart, J., concurring).

12. Comptroller General of the United States, *Improved Executive Branch Oversight Needed for the Government's National Security Information Program*, GAO Report LCD–78–125 (Washington, D.C.: General Accounting Office, Mar. 9, 1979), pp. i–vi and generally; Comptroller General, *DOD's Classification*, *supra* note 2.

13. 47 Fed. Reg. 14874 (Apr. 6, 1982). The executive order went into effect Aug. 1, 1982, 47 Fed. Reg. 14884.

14. U.S., Congress, House, Committee on Government Operations, *Security Classification Policy and Executive Order 12356*, Ho. Rept. 97–731, 97th Cong., 2d sess., 1982. *See also First Principles*, Sept./Oct. 1982, pp. 14–15. *First Principles* is available from the Center for National Security Studies, 122 Maryland Ave., N.E., Washington, DC 20002.

15. *See* Christine M. Marwick, "The Freedom of Information Act and National Security Secrecy: How It's Working After Two Years," *First Principles*, (Dec. 1976), reprinted in U.S., Congress, Senate, Committee on the Judiciary, Subcommittee on Administrative Practice and Procedure, *Freedom of Information Act: Hearings on Oversight of the Freedom of Information Act* [hereafter cited as *Oversight Hearings*], 95th Cong., 1st sess., 1977, pp. 629–39. *See also Former Secrets: Government Records Made Public Through the Freedom of Information Act* (500 case studies) available from the Campaign for Political Rights, 201 Massachusetts Ave., N.E., Washington, D.C. 20002; "From Official Files: Abstracts of Documents on National Security and Civil Liberties," available from the Center for National Security Studies (CNSS) 122 Maryland Ave., N.E., Washington, DC 20002 (the list is updated regularly, and the documents listed may be ordered from the CNSS).

16. For an alternative classification system, *see* Morton H. Halperin and Daniel N. Hoffman, *Top Secret: National Security and the Right to Know* (Washington: New Republic Press, 1976), chap. 5. (*Top Secret* is available from the CNSS, *see supra* note 14).

  If Congress were to enact a classification system over the objections of the President, it would most likely have to override a veto. In such a case, the executive might challenge in court the constitutionality of such a legislated system. Indeed, it is possible that the executive might yet choose to challenge the constitutionality of the FOIA's provisions for national security information.

  Up until the Truman executive order establishing the classification system, the individual military services and various government agencies dealing with national security information had their own regulations for protecting secrets. For a history of these policy developments, *see* U.S., Congress, House, Committee on Government Operations, Subcommittee on Foreign Operations and Government Information, *Security Classification Reform: Hearings*, 93d Cong., 2d sess., 1974, pp. 505–98.

17. Halperin and Hoffman, *supra*, 26, 108–110; Christine M. Marwick, "The Espionage Laws: In Need of Reform," *First Principles* (May 1976): 3–9.

17a. E.O. 12356, Section 1.1(a)(3).

18. The Carter standard required "identifiable damage"; the Reagan order returns to the standard of Nixon's E.O. 11652.

19. However, the government does have means for classifying information without the permission of a researcher or inventor. *See* Halperin and Hoffman, *Freedom vs. National Security* (New York: Chelsea House, 1977), pp. 120–121, for background on withholding a patent for national security reasons. The chapter on "Control of Government Information," pp. 99–235, provides an excellent background on national security secrecy claims generally.

20. During the court case over whether the government has the power to censor an article about hydrogen bombs written for the *Progressive* magazine, the government reclassified some documents in the Los Alamos Library that had been declassified and made available to the public some four years earlier. This reclassification was done under the provisions of the Atomic Energy Act (NEA). *See* Morton Mintz, "AEC Error Exposed Secrets of H-Bomb," *Washington Post*, May 24, 1979, p. A2; Christine M. Marwick, "The Growing Power to Censor," *First Principles* (June 1979): p. 2.

21. E.O. 12065, Section 3–400.

22. *See* Editor's Note, in "New Developments in National Security Secrecy: Greater Public Access through FOIA," *First Principles* (Sept. 1978): 5–7, which describes how the Carter balancing test was to have worked.

23. U.S., Congress, Senate, *Conference Report: Freedom of Information Act Amendments*, 93 Cong., 2d sess., Oct. 1, 1974, S. Rept. 93–1200; U.S., Congress, House, H.Rept. 93–1380, 93 Cong., 2d

sess., Oct. 1, 1974, p. 12, reprinted in U.S., Congress, House, Committee on Government Operations, Subcommittee on Information and Individual Rights, and Senate, Committee on the Judiciary, Subcommittee on Administrative Practice and Procedure (Joint Committee Print), *Freedom of Information Act and Amendments of 1974 (P.L. 93–502): Sourcebook: Legislative History, Texts, and Other Documents*, 94th Cong., 1st sess., Mar. 1975 [hereafter cited as *1974 FOIA Sourcebook*].

24. *Halperin v. Dept. of State*, 565 F.2d 699 (D.C. Cir. 1977); *Lesar v. Dept. of Justice*, 636 F.2d 472 (D.C. Cir. 1980); *Taylor v. Dept. of the Army*, 684 F.2d 99 (D.C. Cir. 1982).

25. 5 U.S.C. Section 552(a)(4)(B).

26. *Ray v. Turner*, 587 F.2d 1187 (D.C. Cir. 1978). *But see Salisbury v. U.S.*, 690 F.2d 966 (D.C. Cir. 1982); *Gardels v. CIA*, 689 F.2d 1100 (D.C. Cir. 1982).

27. *See Conference Report, supra* note 23, at 12.

27a. 5 U.S.C. Section 552(b)(2).

28. *Vaughn v. Rosen* (II), 523 F.2d 1136, 1142 (D.C. Cir. 1975).

29. *Dept. of the Air Force v. Rose*, 425 U.S. 352, 369 (1976).

30. *Id.*

31. *Vaughn, supra* note 28.

32. *Stokes v. Brennan*, 476 F.2d 699 (5th Cir. 1973).

33. *Benson v. GSA*, 289 F. Supp. 590 (W.D. Wash. 1968), aff'd, 415 F.2d 878 (9th Cir. 1969).

34. *Crooker v. BATF*, 670 F.2d 1051 (D.C. Cir. 1981) (*en banc*).

35. *Id.*

36. *Caplan v. BATF*, 587 F.2d 544 (2d Cir. 1978); *Hardy v. BATF*, 631 F.2d 653 (9th Cir. 1980).

37. *Hawkes v. IRS*, 467 F.2d 787 (6th Cir. 1972).

38. *Stokes, supra* note 32.

39. *Cox v. Dept. of Justice*, 576 F.2d 1302 (8th Cir. 1978).

40. *Allen v. CIA*, 636 F.2d 1287 (D.C. Cir. 1980).

41. *Stern v. Richardson*, 367 F. Supp. 1316 (D.D.C. 1973).

42. *Lesar, supra* note 24.

43. *Scherer v. Kelly*, 584 F.2d 170 (7th Cir. 1978); *Nix v. U.S.*, 572 F.2d 998 (4th Cir. 1978); *Maroscia v. Levi*, 569 F.2d 1000 (7th Cir. 1977).

44. 5 U.S.C. Section 552a(k)(6).

44a. 5 U.S.C. Section 552(b)(3).

45. *See* Public Law 94–409 Section 5(b) (1976), 90 STAT. 1241.

46. The Supreme Court had held that the only thing that the 1966 version of (b)(3) had permitted the courts to review was "the factual existence of such a statute, regardless of how unwise, self-protective, or inadvertent the enactment might be." *Administrator, FAA v. Robertson*, 422 U.S. 255, 270 (1975).

47. The Legislative history of the 1966 FOIA suggests that there were "nearly 100 statutes or parts of statutes which restrict public access to specific Government records." U.S., Congress, House, H. Rept.

89–1497, 89th Cong., 2d sess., 1966, p. 10, reprinted in U.S., Congress, Senate, Committee on the Judiciary, Subcommittee on Administrative Practices and Procedures, *Freedom of Information Act Sourcebook: Legislative Materials, Cases, Articles*, 93d Cong., 2d sess., 1974 [hereafter cited as the *1966 FOIA Sourcebook*].

48. The Department of Justice publishes a list of FOIA cases that have been decided; the list also indicates which exemptions were involved in each particular suit. *See* "Freedom of Information Case List," published by the Office of Information Law and Policy, U.S. Department of Justice, Washington, DC 20530. This list is regularly updated.

49. *Baldridge v. Shapiro*, 455 U.S. 345 (1982).

50. 5 U.S.C. Section 552a(k)(4).

51. *United Technologies Corp. v. Marshall*, 464 F. Supp. 845 (D. Conn. 1979).

52. *Virginia Sunshine Alliance v. NRC*, 509 F. Supp. 863 (D.D.C., aff'd, 669 F.2d 788 (D.C. Cir. 1981). *See also* Halperin and Hoffman, *supra* note 19, at 221–25.

53. U.S., Congress, *Congressional Record*, Aug. 31, 1976, p. H9260; *Goland v. CIA*, 607 F.2d 339 (D.C. Cir. 1978), *cert. denied*, 445 U.S. 927 (1980); *Afshar v. Dept. of State*, 702 F.2d 1125 (D.C. Cir. 1983).

54. *Founding Church of Scientology v. NSA*, 610 F.2d 824 (D.C. Cir. 1979); *Hayden v. NSA*, 608 F.2d 1381 (D.C. Cir. 1979).

55. *Irons & Sears v. Dann*, 606 F.2d 1215 (D.C. Cir. 1979); *cert. denied*, 444 U.S. 1075 (1980); *Lee Pharmaceuticals v. Kreps*, 577 F.2d 610 (9th Cir.), *cert. denied*, 439 U.S. 1073 (1979).

56. Allowing release of income tax returns with deletions: *Long v. IRS*, 596 F.2d 362 (9th Cir. 1979), *cert. denied*, 446 U.S. 917 (1980); *Willamette Industries v. U.S.*, 689 F.2d 865 (9th Cir. 1982); *Neufeld v. IRS*, 646 F.2d 661 (D.C. Cir. 1981). Not allowing release with deletions: *King v. IRS*, 688 F.2d 488 (7th Cir. 1982).

57. *Consumer Product Safety Commission v. GTE Sylvania*, 447 U.S. 102 (1980).

57a. 5 U.S.C. Section 552(b)(4).

58. 5 U.S.C. Section 551(2).

59. *See e.g.*, U.S., Congress, House, Committee on Government Operations, *Business Record Exemption of the Freedom of Information Act: Hearings*, 95th Cong., 1st sess., Oct. 3, 4, 1977; U.S., Congress, Senate, *Freedom of Information Reform Act*, S 774, S. Rept. 98–221, 98th Cong., 1st sess., 1983, pp. 14–17.

60. The precise definition of a *trade secret* is still in flux. See Restatement of Torts, 757, comment b at 5 (1939); *Consumers Union v. Veterans' Admin.*, 301 F. Supp. 796, 801 (S.D.N.Y. 1969), *appeal dismissed as moot*, 436 F.2d 1363 (2d Cir. 1971); *Public Citizen Health Research Group v. FDA*, 704 F.2d 1280 (D.C. Cir. 1983).

61. H. Rept. 89–1497, *supra* note 47, at 32.

62. *Ackerly v. Ley*, 420 F.2d 1336, 1139–40 n. 3 (D.C. Cir. 1969).

63. *National Parks & Conservation Assn. v. Morton*, 498 F.2d 765, 770 (D.C. Cir. 1974).

64. *Id.* at 767.

65. *GTE Sylvania, Inc. v. Consumer Product Safety Commission*, 404 F. Supp. 352 (D. Del. 1975).

66. *Westinghouse Electric Corp. v. Schlesinger*, 392 F. Supp. 1246 (E.D. Va. 1974), aff'd, 542 F.2d 1190 (4th Cir. 1976), *cert. denied, sub nom Brown v. Westinghouse Electric Corp.*, 431 U.S. 924 (1977); *Sears, Roebuck & Co. v. GSA (II)*, 553 F.2d 1378 (D.C. Cir. 1977).

67. *Washington Research Project Inc., v. Dept of HEW*, 504 F.2d 238 (D.C. Cir. 1974), *cert. denied*, 421 U.S. 963 (1975). *See Business Record Exemption, supra* note 59, at 21.

68. In *Rural Housing Alliance v. U.S. Dept. of Agriculture*, 498 F.2d 73 (D.C. Cir. 1974), the (b)(4) exemption as well as the (b)(6) privacy exemption, was available to protect financial data of welfare recipients.

69. *Consumers Union, supra* note 60, 301 F. Supp. at 803; *Grumman Aircraft Engineering Corp. v. Renegotiation Board*, 425 F.2d 578, 582 (D.C. Cir. 1970).

70. *See* 5 U.S.C. Section 551(2).

71. *See, e.g.,* S. Rept. 98–221, *supra* note 59, at 8–9.

72. *Business Record Exemption, supra* note 9, at Appendix 6.

73. *See, e.g.*, the Federal Insecticide, Fungicide, and Rodenticide Act, 7 U.S.C. Section 136h (1976); the Toxic Substances Control Act of 1976, 15 U.S.C. Section 2613 (1976); the Tax Reform Act of 1976, 26 U.S.C. Section 6110; the Consumer Product Safety Commission Act of 1972, 15 U.S.C. Section 2055.

74. *E.g.*, S. Rept. 98–221, *supra* note 59, at 14–17.

75. U.S., Congress, House, Committee on Government Operations, *Freedom of Information Act Requests for Business Data and Reverse-FOIA Lawsuits*, H. Rept. 95–1382, 95 Cong., 2d sess., July 20, 1978, p. 6. The company is FOI Services, Inc., Rockville, Maryland. It will also file FOIA requests without revealing its clients' identities.

76. 18 U.S.C. Section 1905.

77. *Chrysler v. Brown*, 441 U.S. 281 (1979). The Administrative Procedure Act, 5 U.S.C. Section 702 (1976), provides in Section 10(a) that "A person suffering legal wrong because of agency action, or adversely affected or aggrieved by agency action, . . . is entitled to judicial review thereof." In Section 10(e) of the APA the courts are given power to

(2) hold unlawful and set aside agency action, findings, and conclusions found to be—

(A) arbitrary, capricious, an abuse of discretion, or otherwise not in accordance with law; . . .

(F) unwarranted by the facts to the extent that the facts are subject to trial de novo by the reviewing court.

77a. 5 U.S.C. Section 552(b)(5).

78. U.S., Congress, House, H. Rept. 89–1497, 89th Cong., 2d sess., 1966, p. 10; U.S., Congress, Senate, S. Rept. 89–813, 89th Cong., 1st sess., 1965, pp. 2, 9, reprinted in *1966 FOIA Sourcebook, supra* note 47.

79. The rules of discovery are supposed to be applied "by way of rough analogies." *Mink, supra* note 11, at 73, 86.

80. *F.T.C. v. Grolier, Inc.*, 76 L.Ed.2d 387, 103 S.Ct. 2209 (1983).

81. S. Rept. 89–813, *supra* note 78 p. 9.

82. *NLRB v. Sears, Roebuck & Co.*, 421 U.S. 132, 161 (1975).

83. 5 U.S.C. Section 552(a)(2)(B) and (C). "Exemption 5, properly construed, calls for the disclosure of all 'opinions and interpretations' which embody the agency's *effective law and policy*, and the withholding of all papers which reflect the agency's group thinking in the process of working out its policy and determining what its law shall be." *Sears, Roebuck & Co., supra* note 82, at 153.

84. *Mink, supra* note 11, at 89; *Bristol Myers Co. v. FTC*, 424 F.2d 935, 939 (D.C. Cir. 1970), *cert. denied*, 400 U.S. 824 (1970) (Exemption 5 "does not authorize an agency to throw a protective blanket over all information by casting it in the form of an internal memorandum. Purely factual reports and scientific studies cannot be cloaked in secrecy by an exemption designed to protect only those internal working papers in which opinions are expressed and policies formulated and recommended."); *Coastal States Gas Corp. v. Dept. of Energy*, 617 F.2d 854 (D.C. Cir. 1980); *ITT World Communications, Inc. v. FCC*, 699 F.2d 1219 (D.C. Cir. 1983).

85. *Cooper v. Dept. of the Navy*, 558 F.2d 274 (5th Cir. 1977); *Weber Aircraft Corp. v. U.S.*, 79 L.Ed.2d 814 (1984).

86. *Russell v. Dept. of the Air Force*, 682 F.2d 1045 (D.C. Cir. 1982); *Lead Industries Assn. Inc. v. OSHA*, 610 F.2d 70 (2d Cir. 1979).

87. *Moore-McCormack Lines, Inc., v. ITO Corp. of Baltimore*, 508 F.2d 945 (4th Cir. 1974); *Union of Concerned Scientists v. Nuclear Regulatory Commission*, 2 Med. L. Reptr. 1458 (D.D.C. 1977).

88. *Soucie v. David*, 448 F.2d 1067 (D.C. Cir. 1971); *Wu v. National Endowment for the Humanities*, 460 F.2d 1030 (5th Cir. 1972); *Washington Research Project, supra* note 67.

88a. 5 U.S.C. Section 552 (b)(6).

89. 5 U.S.C. Section 552a(i)(3) of the Privacy Act states, "Any person who knowingly and willfully requests or obtains any record concerning an individual from an agency under false pretenses shall be guilty of a misdemeanor and fined not more than $5,000." *See* statement of Representative Moorhead, U.S., Congress, 120 *Congressional Record*, 36,655, Nov. 20, 1974.

90. 5 U.S.C. Section 552a(i)(1). Section(i)(2) of the Privacy Act also provides for criminal penalties against government employees who "willfully maintain a system of records without meeting the notice requirements" found in Section (e)(4) of the Privacy Act. This is to prevent secret systems of records about individuals, of which an FOIA/PA Office might not be aware.

91. *Supra* note 29, at 352. "[W]e find nothing in the wording of Exemption 6 or its legislative history to support the agency's claim that Congress created a blanket exemption for personnel files." *Arieff v. Dept. of the Navy*, 712 F.2d 1462 (D.C. Cir. 1983).

92. *Dept. of State v. Washington Post Co.*, 456 U.S. 595 (1982).

93. H. Rept. 89–1497, *supra* note 78., p. 11.

94. *See Rural Housing Alliance, supra* note 68, at 77.

95. 5 U.S.C. Section 552(e)(7).

96. *See Ackerley, supra* note 62; *Washington Post Co. v. Dept. of H.H.S.*, 690 F.2d 252 (D.C. Cir. 1982).

97. *Robles v. Environmental Protection Agency*, 484 F.2d 843, 846 (4th Cir. 1973).

98. *Rose, supra* note 91.

99. *Washington Post, supra* note 92.

100. *Wine Hobby v. IRS*, 502 F.2d 133, 137 (3d Cir. 1974) (the company attempted to get a list of amateur winemakers from the tax records).

101. *Getman v. NLRB*, 450 F.2d 670 (D.C. Cir. 1971) (the National Labor Relations Board had to give law professors specializing in labor relations the names of voting union members because such professors were "properly and directly concerned"); *Disabled Officers' Assn. v. Rumsfeld*, 428 F. Supp. 454 (D.C. 1977); *aff'd without opinion sub. nom. Disabled Officers' Assn. v. Brown*, 574 F.2d 636 (D.C. Cir. 1978).

102. *See* Letter Report from the Acting Comptroller General of the United States to the Honorable Charles A. Vanik, U.S. House of Representatives, Aug. 25, 1977 (GAO Report LCD–77–112); OMB Guidelines, 40 *Fed. Reg.* 28,951, July 9, 1975; *Wine Hobby, supra* note 100.

103. The Privacy Act, 5 U.S.C. Section 552a(f)(3), allows agencies to set up special procedures for providing access to these records.

104. *Diamond v. FBI*, 707 F.2d 75 (2d Cir. 1983); *Sims v. CIA*, 642 F.2d 562 (D.C. Cir. 1980); *Providence Journal Co. v. FBI*, 470 F. Supp. 778 (D.R.I. 1978); *rev'd on other grounds*, 602 F.2d 1010 (1st Cir. 1979).

105. Memorandum from Quinlan J. Shea, Jr., Director, Office of Privacy and Information Appeals, Department of Justice, May 25, 1977, Re: Privacy Exemptions 6 and 7(C), reprinted in *Oversight Hearings, supra* note 15, at 663, Exhibit 77.

105a. Statement of Harold R. Tyler, Jr., Deputy Attorney General, August 17, 1975. This particular letter dealt with the (b)(7)(C) exemption for protecting personal privacy in investigatory records. The policy would presumably carry over to other categories of historical documents.

106. Justice Department Guidelines on Release of Third Party Information in Files of Historical Interest, reprinted in *Oversight Hearings, supra* note 15, at 668, Exhibit 79. "Public figures" ordinarily have less in the way of privacy rights than others. Some individuals occupy "positions of such persuasive power and influence that they

are deemed public figures for all purposes." In other instances, the nature of someone's involvement in a particular controversy is important. An attorney with a well-known case, for example, may not, in fact, be a public figure. *See Gertz v. Robert Welch, Inc.*, 418 U.S. 323 (1974); *New York Times v. Sullivan*, 376 U.S. 254 (1964); *Nixon v. Administrator, GSA*, 433 U.S. 425 (1977); *Time, Inc. v. Firestone*, 424 U.S. 448 (1976); *Hutchinson v. Proxmire*, 443 U.S. 111, (1979); *Providence Journal v. FBI*, 460 F. Supp. 778 (D.R.I. 1978), *rev'd*. 603 F.2d 1010 (1st Cir. 1979). Another reason why public figures need less privacy protection is that they can resort to effective "self-help." *Wolston v. Reader's Digest Assn.*, 443 U.S. 157 (1979). In FOIA cases, *see Fund for Constitutional Government v. Natl. Archives*, 656 F.2d 856 (D.C. Cir. 1981); *Common Cause v. National Archives*, 628 F.2d 179 (D.C. Cir. 1980); *Congressional News Syndicate v. Dept. of Justice*, 438 F. Supp. 538 (D.D.C. 1977).

107. 5 C.F.R. 294.702.

108. H. Rept. 89–1497, *supra* note 78.

109. Comptroller General, *Government Field Offices*, *supra* note 2, at 16.

110. The Ethics in Government Act, P.L. 95–521.

111. *Columbia Packing Co., v. Dept. of Agriculture*, 563 F.2d 495 (1st Cir. 1977).

112. *Ferri v. Bell*, 645 F.2d 1213 (3d Cir. 1981).

113. *Arieff*, *supra* note 91.

114. *Common Cause v. Nuclear Regulatory Commission*, 674 F.2d 921 (D.C. Cir. 1982).

115. *Providence Journal v. FBI*, 602 F.2d 1010 (1st Cir. 1979), *cert. denied*, 444 U.S. 1071 (1980).

116. 5 U.S.C. Section 552a(c)(1).

117. 5 U.S.C. Section 552a(c)(6).

118. 5 U.S.C. Section 552a(b)(2).

119. *See* U.S. Privacy Protection Study Commission (Linowes Commission), *Personal Privacy in an Information Society*, GPO Stock No. 052–003–00395–3 (Washington, D.C.: Government Printing Office, 1977).

120. *See* Ronald L. Plesser, "The Reverse Privacy Case: Beginning a Trend," *Legal Times of Washington*, Dec. 18, 1978, pp. 9, 11; *Chrysler Corp. supra* note 77.

121. 5 U.S.C. Section 552a(e)(8).

122. *Providence Journal v. FBI*, 460 F. Supp. 778 (D.R.I. 1978), *rev'd on other grounds*, 603 F.2d 1010 (1st Cir. 1979); *cert. denied*, 444 U.S. 1071 (1980) (subject of the files had been investigated by the FBI and convicted of criminal activities; the Court held that the subject therefore had interests separate from those of the Justice Department, which was representing the FBI.

122a. 5 U.S.C. Section 552(b)(7).

123. 5 U.S.C. Sections 552a(j)(2) and (k)(2).

124. The regulations of the Department of Justice concerning the Privacy Act and law enforcement records are published at 28 *C.F.R.* Section 16.96 (1976). The department insists that its decision to process personal records under both the FOIA and the PA is strictly discretionary.

125. 5 U.S.C. Section 552a(k)(2) provides that the head of any agency may put into effect rules under the Privacy Act that would exempt any system of records that consist of

Investigatory material compiled for law enforcement purposes, other than material within the scope of subsection (j)(2) of this section: *Provided, however,* That if any individual is denied any right, privilege, or benefit that he would otherwise be entitled by Federal law, or for which he would otherwise be eligible, as a result of the maintenance of such material, such material shall be provided to such individual, except to the extent that the disclosure of such material would reveal the identity of a source who furnished information to the Government under an express promise that the identity of the source would be held in confidence, or prior to the effective date of this section, under an implied promise that the identity of the source would be held in confidence.

Subsection (j)(2) exempts material maintained by law-enforcement agencies for the purpose of enforcing the *criminal* laws, and subsection (k)(2) refers to *civil* laws and administrative sanctions.

126. H. Rept. 89–1497, *supra* note 78, p. 11.

127. U.S., Congress, *Congressional Record* S.9337 (daily ed., May 30, 1974).

128. *Rural Housing Alliance, supra* note 68, at 81–82; *Sears, Roebuck & Co. v. GSA*, 509 F.2d 527 (D.C. Cir. 1974).

129. *Holy Spirit Assn. v. FBI*, 683 F.2d 562 (D.C. Cir. 1982).

130. *Committee to Investigate Assassinations v. Dept. of Justice*, Civ. No. 71–1829 (D.C. Cir., Oct. 24, 1973).

131. 5 U.S.C. Section 552a(e)(7).

132. *Irons v. Bell*, 596 F.2d 468 (1st Cir. 1979).

133. *FBI v. Abramson*, 456 U.S. 615 (1982). *See also, Pratt v. Webster*, 673 F.2d 408 (D.C. Cir. 1982); *Lesar v. Dept. of Justice*, 636 F.2d 472 (D.C. Cir. 1980).

134. *Weissman v. CIA*, 565 F.2d 692 (D.C. Cir. 1977). *See also Church of Scientology v. Dept. of the Army*, 611 F.2d 738 (9th Cir. 1979).

135. *See* U.S., Congress, House, *Conference Report*, 93d Cong., 2d sess., 1974, H. Rpt. 93–1380, p. 11; U.S., Congress, Senate, 120 *Congressional Record*, S9329 (May 30, 1974), reprinted in *1974 FOIA Sourcebook, supra* note 23. *See also NLRB v. Robbins Tire & Rubber Co.*, 437 U.S. 214 (1978); *Coastal States Gas Corp. v. Dept. of Energy*, 617 F.2d 854 (D.C. Cir. 1980).

136. *National Public Radio v. Bell*, 431 F. Supp. 509 (D.D.C. 1977), *vacated as moot*, No. 77–1419 (D.C. Cir., Sept. 29, 1977).

137. U.S., Congress, House, Committee on Government Operations, *FBI Compliance with the Freedom of Information Act: Hearings before the Subcommittee on Government Information and Individual Rights*, 95th Cong., 2d sess., 1978. p. 8.

138. *Cohen v. EPA*, 575 F. Supp. 425 (D.D.C. 1983).

139. *Attorney General's Memorandum on the 1974 Amendments to the Freedom of Information Act (Feb. 1975)*, pp. 8–9; *Education/Instruction, Inc. v. HUD*, 471 F. Supp. 1074 (D. Mass. 1979).

140. *Playboy Enterprises v. Dept. of Justice*, 516 F. Supp. 233 (D.D.C. 1981), *aff'd with directions to modify order*, 677 F.2d 931 (D.C.Cir. 1982).

141. *Fund for Constitutional Government v. National Archives*, 656 F.2d 856 (D.C. Cir. 1981); *Baez v. Dept. of Justice*, 647 F.2d 1328 (D.C. Cir. 1980).

142. *Cohen, supra* note 138.

143. *Common Cause, supra* note 106. *But see Bast v. Dept. of Justice*, 665 F.2d 1251 (D.C. Cir. 1981).

144. *Lesar, supra* note 24; *Baez, supra* note 141.

145. *Forrester v. Dept. of Labor*, 433 F. Supp. 987 (S.D.N.Y.), *aff'd*, 591 F. 2d 1330 (2d Cir. 1978).

146. *Associated Dry Goods Corp, v. NLRB*, 455 F. Supp. 802 (S.D.N.Y. 1978); *Title Guarantee Co. v. NLRB*, 534 F.2d 484 (2d Cir.), *cert. denied*, 429 U.S. 834 (1976); *Poss v. NLRB*, 565 F.2d 654 (10th Cir. 1977).

147. Senate Debate and Votes of May 30, 1974, *reprinted in 1974 FOIA Sourcebook, supra* note 23, at 333–34.

148. For background on the informer problem, *see* Christine M. Marwick, "The Government Informer: A Threat to Political Freedom," *First Principles* (March 1977).

149. U.S., Congress, Senate, Committee on the Judiciary, *The Erosion of Law Enforcement Intelligence—Capabilities—Public Security: Hearings before the Subcommittee on Criminal Laws and Procedures*, 95th Cong., 1st sess., 1977, p. 16.

150. *Founding Church of Scientology v. Regan*, 670 F.2d 1158 (D.C. Cir. 1981); *Lesar v. Dept. of Justice*, 636 F.2d 472 (D.C. Cir. 1980); *Baez v. Dept. of Justice, supra* note 141; *Founding Church of Scientology v. Dept. of Justice*, 612 F.2d 417 (9th Cir. 1979); *Nix, supra* note 43; *Keeney v. FBI*, 630 F.2d 114 (2d Cir. 1980).

151. *Miller v. Bell*, 661 F.2d 623 (7th Cir. 1981), *cert. denied sub nom.*, *Miller v. Webster*, 456 U.S. 960 (1982); *Dunaway v. Webster*, 519 F. Supp. 1059 (N.D. Cal. 1981).

152. Comptroller General, *Timeliness and Completeness of FBI Responses to Requests Under Freedom of Information and Privacy Acts Have Improved*, GAO Report No. GGD–78–51 (Washington, D.C., General Accounting Office, Apr. 10, 1978) pp. 61–63.

153. *FBI Compliance, supra* note 137, at 71–74.

154. Memorandum to Quin Shea, Director, Office of Information and Privacy Appeals, Department of Justice, from Peter F. Flaherty, Deputy Attorney General, June 2, 1977, reads in its entirety:

"The protections of 5 U.S.C. 552(b)(7)(A)—intended to preclude interference with law enforcement activities—should not be used to conceal unlawful activities, regardless of the intent with which those activities were conducted. Similarly, just as this Department will not obtain information directly by means of unlawful activities, we will not shield with 5 U.S.C. 552(b)(7)(D) information which was initially obtained through the use of such means by other persons or law enforcement organizations. Neither the use nor methodology of unlawful investigative techniques or procedures is to be protected by reliance on 5 U.S.C. 552(b)(7)(E)."

155. Comptroller General, *FBI Responses Have Improved, supra* note 152, at 62–63.
156. H. Rpt. 93–1380, *supra* note 135, at 12.
157. *Id.*
158. *Malloy v. Dept. of Justice,* 457 F. Supp. 543 (D.D.C. 1978).
159. Comptroller General, *FBI Responses Have Improved, supra* note 152, at 64–65.
160. *Id.*, p. 65.
161. *Guild Notes* (National Lawyers Guild), Oct. 1978, p. 25.
162. 42 *Fed. Reg.* 26,479, May 24, 1977.
163. Comptroller General, *FBI Taking Actions to Comply Fully with the Privacy Act,* GAO Report GGD–77–93) (Washington, D.C. General Accounting Office. December 26, 1977) pp. 2, 7.
164. *Id.* at 1.
165. Agencies can institute routine policies for destroying records that are no longer being used. For example, in 1976 the FBI instructed its field offices to destroy records on cases that had been closed for more than ten years. In October 1977, this was changed to include cases that had been closed for five years or more. Certain categories of files are exempt—those that have historical interest or that are involved in an unresolved FOIA/PA request—but critics contended that such material was in fact being destroyed. A lawsuit resulted in an injunction against the destruction and ordered the creation of a systemic review to protect historical materials. *American Friends Service Committe v. Webster,* 485 F. Supp. 222 (D.D.C. 1980). *See also* Jonathan Kwitny, "Hot Issue: FBI Agents Rap Policy of Burning Files, Link It to Public Access Acts," *Wall Street Journal,* Sept. 27, 1978, pp. 1, 21; *FBI Compliance, supra* note 137, at 22, 31.
166. Comptroller General, *FBI Taking Actions, supra* note 163, at 3.
167. For a detailed explanation of getting FBI files, *see* Ann Mari Buitrago and Leon Andrew Immerman, *Are You Now or Have You Ever Been in the FBI Files: How to Secure and Interpret Your FBI Files* (New York: Grove Press, 1980); The General Accounting Office (*supra* note 152) also describes FBI search procedures, p. 8.
168. Statement of Frank Carlucci, Deputy Director of Central Intelligence, before U.S., Congress, House, Permanent Select Committee on Intelligence, Subcommittee on Legislation, Apr. 5, 1979.

169. *See* Morton H. Halperin, et al., *The Lawless State: The Crimes of the U.S. Intelligence Agencies* (New York: Penquin, 1976), for a discussion of various improper CIA operations.

170. For an exhaustive explanation of the peculiarities of the filing systems of the FBI and the CIA, *see* Athan G. Theoharis, "The FBI and the FOIA," *First Principles*, Sept/Oct. 1981, vol. 7, no. 1, pp. 1 ff.

171. S. Rept. 98–221, *supra* note 59, at 23–35. The most substantial change in the law enforcement area seems to be that if informant records are sought by a third party, asking for them according to the informant's name or personal identifier, the agency would not have to acknowledge the existence of such records.

172. "Attorney General's Memorandum on the Public Information Section of the Administrative Procedure Act" (1967), p. 38, reprinted in *1966 FOIA Sourcebook*, *supra* note 47, at 237. Commentators have argued that (b)(8) is "in keeping with banking tradition, although that tradition rests heavily on facts of a former day such as uninsured bank accounts and runs on banks." Kenneth Culp Davis, 34 *U.Chi. L. Rev.* 761, 800–801 (1967), reprinted in *1966 FOIA Sourcebook*, *supra* note 47.

173. *See Kaye v. Burns*, 411 F. Supp. 897 (S.D.N.Y., 1976); *Consumers Union v. Heimann*, 589 F.2d 531 (D.C. Cir. 1978).

174. *Kay*, *supra* note 173.

175. *M. A. Schapiro & Co. v. Securities & Exchange Commission*, 339 F. Supp. 467 (D.D.C. 1972).

176. *See Pennzoil Co. v. FPC*, 534 F.2d 627 (5th Cir. 1976).

V

Writing an Appeal

If an agency has denied part or all of my request for information, what can I do?

You should write an administrative appeal letter, asking the agency to reconsider. FOIA requesters who have received a denial of some or all of the material requested, and are considering going to court to compel release of material (see chapter 6), are required to first write an appeal letter. Privacy Act requesters can go to court immediately if the denial letter does not indicate that appeals procedures are available; if the denial letter does indicate appeals procedures, you should make use of these before going to court.

While going to court is often difficult, time-consuming, and expensive, writing an administrative appeal letter is easy and cheap. Yet the figures show that relatively few requesters are making use of this right. For example, in 1977, the Agriculture Department made 1,230 initial denials, but only 116 of these were appealed. Of these 116, 57 requests ended up being granted in full, 30 were granted in part, and only 29 were withheld in full. During the same period, the Department of Defense made 8,174 initial denials, received 462 appeals, granted 47 appeals in full and 187 in part, and denied 228 appeals in full. Such figures vary from agency to agency (with the Department of Energy and the State Department being perhaps the least forthcoming with new data upon appeal—only around 10 percent of appeals get more material), but even at these odds, it is ordinarily worth writing an appeal, whether or not you have any intention of suing.[1]

What kinds of agency decisions can I write an administrative appeal about?

You can appeal

1. if the agency denies your request in full or in part;
2. if the agency does not respond to your request within the time limits set by the FOIA;
3. if the fees that the agency wants to charge seem excessive; or
4. if you feel that you should be getting a reduction or waiver of fees because the release of the information would benefit the public.

While you may not have a case that you could win in court, remember that the FOIA exemptions are not mandatory. Even if no other grounds exist, you can always ask for a discretionary release. The agencies can decide, that as a member of the public, you deserve a favor and release what you want at a cost that you can afford and in time so that it will do you some good.

Should I write an administrative appeal letter even if I am unsure whether I am entitled to the material?

Yes, definitely. If you are unfamiliar with the ways of bureaucracies you might be intimidated by the appeals process, but it is really a very simple, routine administrative procedure. Appendix A includes a sample appeal letter that can be either simplified and shortened, or made more sophisticated and adapted to a particular case. If you are at a loss as to what your grounds are for contesting the denial, follow the simple form—there is no requirement that you must give detailed, technical arguments why material should be released. On the other hand, if you have an educated guess about how to argue that the exemptions have been improperly claimed, you can pull out the stops and give the agency every reason you can think of to support release of the requested information.

Sometimes the sophisticated and detailed appeal letters get better results than the simple ones; sometimes the sophistication of the appeal letter seems to make no difference. Policies in handling appeal letters differ from agency to agency, and from FOIA official to FOIA official. Some agencies have a very conscientious approach to reviewing appeal requests; other agencies end up giving them back to the same person who refused the request in the first place, which is never a very promising review.

But—in spite of the fact that the appeal procedure is less than perfect—it is well worth your time to write an appeal. Very often some or all the withheld material does in fact end up being released. One reason for this is that, in most agencies, the appeal letters go to higher officials who are aware of their own authority and less anxious about making decisions. Sometimes, in fact, it looks as if the request letter never got serious consideration at the initial request level.

If you are unsure what details to bring up in your appeal letter, *do not* let that stop you from writing a letter. Although this book provides examples of the kinds of detailed arguments that can be included in appeal letters and may help dislodge additional information, many requesters have gotten good results from using simple form letters, without any elaboration. After all, the officials handling the appeals are supposed to be knowledgeable about agency policy; likewise, they are supposed to check up on whether material has been properly processed at the initial request level.

Can I write more than one appeal letter for any given request?

Yes. You should not be appealing precisely the same point twice, but you can appeal different legal points concerning the same request at different times. There are many different grounds for appeal.

For instance, if the agency is slow in responding to your initial request, you might want to write an appeal letter asking the agency to respond within the time limits set out by the FOIA. When the agency does respond to your request, it may then quote you search and copying fees that are higher than you expected. You may be able to get the official handling the initial request to reduce or waive the fees if you make a good case that the charges are exorbitant or that release would benefit the public, but if you are denied on that level you can write an appeal letter on the amount of fees charged. When the agency finally processes the material, it may claim that everything requested is exempt. You would then write an appeal letter insisting that "segregable portions" be released.

If you then get some documents released with deletions, you may be able to make an educated guess from the context that the deletions were improper—and you would want to write still another appeal letter requesting the material that was deleted. Even after all this, the agency might release a report or declassify some related material or submit evidence in a court proceeding. Any of these actions may change the legal status of the material you requested; agencies are not supposed to conceal the documentation for what is already public information. In such case, you would want to write another appeal letter asking the agency to reconsider its earlier decision to withold in light of the more recent releases.

Sometimes, particularly with requests for large quantities of documents, the material will be reviewed and/or released in separate stages. You can write the appropriate appeal letters in separate stages as well.

Does an agency have to tell me about my appeal rights if it denies my request?

According to the FOIA, when an agency denies some or all of your request for information, it must tell you three things:[2]

1. It must specify what exemptions it relied on when it claimed the authority to withhold the information that you have requested. This is required so that you don't have to shadowbox when making an appeal. If you want to write a detailed appeal, you should scrutinize such claims carefully. A close reading of chapter 4 will help you decide whether there is a reasonable basis for their making a particular claim. For instance, if your request was under the FOIA, the agencies do not have the right to withhold information from you under an exemption that applies only to the Privacy Act. Or it may seem that the specific exemption being claimed makes little sense when applied to the particular material that you've asked for.

2. The denial must also tell you the name and title of anyone responsible for denying your request. These names should be mentioned in your appeal letters and will be useful if you end up taking the agency to court.

3. The denial must inform you that you have the right to appeal that denial. It should tell you to whom and by what date you should write an appeal letter.

Should I consider sending an appeal letter to other offi-

cials within the agency, in addition to the person mentioned
in the denial letter?

All that is necessary is that you send your administrative
appeal letter to the person mentioned in the denial letter.
However, some commentators also advise sending copies to
an agency's general counsel (the agency's chief in-house lawyer)
or to the agency head.[3] Certainly this can do no harm, and it
might produce results.

What information should be included in *all* appeal letters?

1. Every appeal letter should state that it is an appeal
under the FOIA.[3a] Since the Privacy Act does not explicitly give you the right of appeal, the frustrated requester
of personal files would not ordinarily want to cite the
Privacy Act. However, most agencies have in fact issued
regulations permitting appeals under the Privacy Act, and
you may be informed that your request is being handled
under Privacy Act regulations. The agencies have the right
to do this as long as it does not reduce your rights under
the FOIA.

2. All appeal letters should state that you expect a reply
within twenty working days, as specified by the FOIA.

3. All appeals should of course include your name and
address and a telephone number where you can be contacted during the day.

4. All appeal letters should, if possible, identify your request by the date of your initial request letter; describe the
material requested; give the names and positions of other
officials who have had a part in the processing of the
request; and provide any and all bureaucratic numbers or
designations that have been assigned to the request.

I didn't get the material I requested, and I think the agency claimed some exemptions improperly. What information should I include in my appeal letter?

If the agency has withheld all or most of the requested
material, you should remind the agency that segregable portions must, by law, be released.[3b]

You should try to include arguments explaining why some
or all of the deletions are improper. Compare the specific
exemptions the agency cites in its denial letter to the discussions of exemptions in chapter 4. If you think the exemptions

claimed by the agency don't apply to the specific material you have requested, say so in your appeal letter and explain why. As you will realize by now, different arguments apply to different kinds of information, but some arguments are useful across the board. If these arguments apply in your case, you should use them.

For instance, if the requested material is very old, argue that the material should be released because release would no longer cause any harm. What was a trade secret in the 1930s, may today be little more than grist for the historian's mill. If the subject of the files is dead, argue that release can no longer violate that person's personal privacy. If the request is for a national security secret of some distant vintage, argue that its release could have no plausible effect on today's security issues. And so on.

If the material has already been released in other forms—through reports to Congress, news accounts, leaks, and so on—say so, and include what you can to document this fact. The fact that the information is no longer really confidential is a strong point in favor of release. (There is a caveat here, however. Something may be public knowledge without ever having been officially released. Common sense might dictate releasing the backup documentation, but you may not have a legal case.)

You should ask that the agency exercise its discretion and release the information even though it may technically be exempt. Then state that, even if the requested material is technically exempt, release would not actually cause any harm and/or that release would actually be beneficial to the general public.

State that, if the agency decides not to release the information you are appealing, you want a more specific justification for the withholding. State that you want an index of the withheld material, an indication of the specific exemptions that are claimed for each portion, and an explanation of what harms would follow release. (Of course, you may not get such an index.)

State that if the agency does not release the requested material or provide a satisfactory explanation of why the information should be withheld, you intend to file suit to compel disclosure. (You can say that you intend to file suit if that is your intention at the time you write your appeal. Later on, of course, after you have consulted a lawyer, you can always decide not to file.) Sometimes, a credible threat that you will, in fact, put the agency to the inconvenience of a suit is enough to get the agency to rethink things. Other times, agencies seem relieved by the prospect of a lawsuit, because a suit means the agency can pass the buck to the FOIA lawyers at the Department of Justice or in the U.S. Attorney's Office.

This list of possible arguments to use in an appeal letter cannot cover every situation. If you can think of other reasonable arguments that might persuade the agency, you should by all means try them.

And finally, think about the tone of your letters. The idea is to persuade a reasonable person. Be businesslike; don't come across like an irritable crank no matter how foolishly you think the agency has behaved.

How quickly must I send a letter appealing an agency denial?

The FOIA does not specify how soon you must send out an appeal letter, but most agencies have issued regulations stating that administrative appeal letters should be received within thirty days after a denial has been sent. If you discover that an agency time limit has elapsed, write your appeal letter anyhow. If the agency refuses to process it, you always have the option of beginning the process over again with a new FOIA request for the same material. Or you could construe the refusal to process it as a denial and take the agency to court.

Should I hire a lawyer to write an appeal letter?

Probably not, although there are possible advantages to having a lawyer write an appeal letter. Since some agencies pay more attention to an appeal if it looks like it might be backed up by a lawsuit, and since a letter signed by a lawyer makes the possibility of a lawsuit more credible, it is sometimes a good idea to have a lawyer write the appeal letter. On the other hand, it will probably cost about a hundred dollars, and many agencies are not swayed by legal arguments contained in the appeal letter or by threats of a lawsuit. A nonlawyer can ordinarily write a perfectly good appeal letter by adapting the form letters in Appendix A and adding relevant arguments taken from chapter 4.

Can I telephone the agency to check on the status of my appeal letter?

Yes. Just as it is a good idea to establish direct contact with the people handling the initial request, it is often a good idea to establish direct contact with the people handling the appeal. If you don't know whom to call, ask the agency's Office of the General Counsel for the name of the person handling FOIA/PA appeals.

I wrote the FBI in 1975 for my file, and I never received it. Is there any point in writing another request later for the same material?

Policies have liberalized considerably since 1975, when the FOIA first went into effect. According to a General Accounting Office (GAO) report, the FBI became far more cooperative in 1977.[4] Therefore, if it is extremely important to you, and if you are willing to pay the necessary fees again, you might consider writing an appeal letter asking that your request be processed under the improved procedures. Of course administrative policies may be changed again.

In an administrative appeal letter for personal records that have been denied under an FOIA/PA request, do I have to include identification again?

No. If you provided satisfactory identification in the initial request, you will not have to resubmit it in later communication with the agency. (You must, of course, make sure that the appeal identifies the original request.)

What kinds of responses to an appeal letter do the agencies give?

There are several possible agency responses. An agency may decide to grant you all the material that was initially withheld, or only some of it. Or it may stick with its earlier decision to withhold information.

If the agency denies your appeal or part of your appeal, it must inform you that you have the right to seek judicial review of its decision.[5] This means that you have the right to sue the agency and to ask the judge to order the agency to release the information you have requested. You also have the right to go to court if the agency does not respond to the appeal letter within the time limits the FOIA provides—twenty working days, with ten additional days sometimes allowable in special circumstances. (See chapter 3.) The basics of an FOIA/PA lawsuit are described in chapter 6.

Can I get help from my representatives in Congress?

Yes. (See chapter 1). It is sometimes quite helpful to write a letter to your congressional representatives, carefully explaining any problems that you have encountered with a particular agency. Be sure to enclose copies of your correspondence with the agency so that your representative's office can determine precisely what has occurred. The address for Senators is

> Honorable _____
> United States Senate
> Washington, DC 20510

and the address for all Representatives is

> Honorable _____
> House of Representatives
> Washington, DC 20515

The telephone number for the congressional switchboard, which can connect callers with the House, the Senate, and all congressional committees and subcommittees, is (202)224–3121.

Bear in mind, however, that individual members of Congress have no greater right to federal information than any other person. But they do have influence they can bring to bear. Do not expect miracles, however.[6] To date, for example, congressional pressure has produced some results with the CIA, but not with the FBI. The influence varies greatly from agency to agency.

Even if your effort to get congressional help does not produce the information you want, it will have one good effect—it will let Capitol Hill know that access to government information is very important to constituents, and therefore Congress should continue to take an active interest in making sure that the information statutes work, and if necessary, that they are strengthened rather than weakened.

You should also be aware that there are congressional committees that have the responsibility of overseeing how the executive branch is implementing the various laws—including, of course, the statutes that govern access to government information. As of this writing relevant oversight committees are

The Subcommittee on Government Information, Justice, and Agriculture
Committee on Government Operations
U.S. House of Representatives
Washington, DC 20515
(202)225-3741
and

The Subcommittee on The Constitution
The Committee on the Judiciary
U.S. Senate
Washington, DC 20510
(202)224-8191

Finally, citizens should be aware that Congress also provides an avenue outside the FOIA for getting records into the open. Although the individual member of Congress has no greater right to information than any other citizen, congressional committees have subpoena power to obtain documents (and testimony as well), whether or not such material might be exempt under a federal information statute.[6a] If you fail to get your material, you should consider whether that information would in fact be of interest to one of the innumerable committees and subcommittees in the House or Senate. If so, write a letter to the relevant committees (or better yet, to a particular member of Congress who is known to be already working on the problem that you are trying to track down). An informed letter might well provide an energetic committee with a useful investigative lead concerning possible misconduct, cost overruns, bad judgment, or what have you. And while it is a long shot that such a letter will get a snowball rolling, if a committee does follow through, you may ultimately have the satisfaction of reading the information you were after in the report of a congressional investigation.

If my appeal letters have failed, are there any other government offices that I can ask to review my request before I decide whether to file a lawsuit?
Yes. There is another possibility, short of going to court, for dislodging material that you believe is improperly withheld. The Civil Service Reform Act of 1978, set up the Office of the Special Counsel, which is empowered to investigate allegations of "arbitrary and capricious" withholding of material

that should have been released under the access statutes. (One category of information, however, is effectively exempt from this review—intelligence and counterintelligence information is given a special exclusion.)

You should not automatically forward your complaints to this office. Not every error in judgment or difference in opinion is an example of arbitrary and capricious decision-making, and the Office of the Special Counsel is intended only for such extreme cases. (The courts, by contrast, have the far greater power of *de novo* review and have the power to decide whether a decision to withhold is actually correct, and not just reasonable. (See chapter 6.) Even a court decision that concludes that material was incorrectly withheld does not necessarily mean that the withholding was arbitrary or capricious.) If the agency can make some plausible arguments that there is a legal basis for withholding, even a rather thin legal basis that most people would not agree with, the withholding would not be considered arbitrary and capricious.

But if you have reason to believe that the withholding is in fact arbitrary and capricious, without any reasonable basis—if the agency seems to be trying to use exemptions that don't exist or to be disregarding the law in some particular instance—perhaps you should allege "arbitrary and capricious withholding" and ask the Office of Special Counsel to investigate.

Such allegations should be addressed to the Office of the Special Counsel, 1717 H St., N.W., Washington, DC 20419. Your letter should include the following information, together with copies of relevant documentation that would support your charge:

1. State what specific information you requested and from whom, at which agency, and under what agency regulations. (You can find agency regulations with the help of a librarian in a law library, or you can ask the agency's FOIA/PA Office for a copy of its FOIA regulations.) Give the address of the agency. Provide a copy of your request letter.

2. State the agency's response to the request and provide a copy.

3. State your understanding of what information was withheld. (Even if there is a partial release, the deletions may be alleged to have been arbitrary or capricious.)

4. State when and to whom you wrote an administrative

appeal letter and what the agency's response to the appeal was. Provide a copy of the appeal and reply letters.

5. Explain why you believe the withholding was arbitrary or capricious.

The Office of the Speical Counsel will review this information and inform you of any actions taken. Bear in mind, however, that this office does not have the power to order release—the aim of Congress in enacting this provision was that the office would provide another arena for review, and that a finding of arbitrary and capricious withholding would convince an agency official to reconsider his earlier decision. You should also be aware that the act setting up the Office of the Special Counsel does not establish the same sorts of procedural requirements that the access statutes do. It does not, for example, put any time limits on how long the office has to respond to such requests for an investigation.[7] And finally, the diligence of this office in following through on FOIA complaints will depend strongly on the interests of whoever is in charge at the time. The office has numerous other functions, such as protecting whistle-blowers, and may have little time left-over for examining FOIA problems.

You do not need to ask for an investigation from the Office of the Special Counsel before you can file suit in federal court; indeed, if you have the resources to sue it is probably better, as a practical matter, to bypass this option than to see what might come of it.

NOTES

1. For a statistical summary of agency appeals, *See* Harold C. Relyea, "The Administration of the Freedom of Information Act: A Brief Overview of Executive Branch Annual Reports for 1977," Congressional Research Service, Library of Congress, Nov. 15, 1978 (JC 660).
2. 5 U.S.C. Section 552(a)(6)(A)(i).
3. James T. O'Reilly, *Federal Information Disclosure: Procedures, Forms, and the Law* (Colorado Springs: McGraw-Hill, Shepards, 1977), Chapter 7.04, pp. 7–18.
3a. 5 U.S.C. Section 552(a)(6).
3b. 5 U.S.C. Section 552(b).

4. Comptroller General of the United States, *Timeliness and Completeness of FBI Responses to Requests under Freedom of Information
   and Privacy Acts Have Improved*, GAO Report No. GGD–78–51
   (Washington, D.C.: General Accounting Office, Apr. 10, 1978) p.
   59.
5. 5 U.S.C. Section 552(a)(6)(A)(ii).
6. For an example of the problems that members of Congress can
   have, *See* "Senator Abourezk's FOIA Request," U.S., Congress,
   Senate, Committee on the Judiciary, Subcommittee on Administrative Practice and Procedures, *Freedom of Information Act: Hearings on Oversight of the Freedom of Information Act*, 95th Cong.,
   1st sess., Sept. 15, 16, Oct. 6, and Nov. 10, 1977, pp. 876–86. In
   spite of the fact that Senator Abourezk was then the chairman of the
   Senate subcommittee with responsibility for overseeing the operations of the FOIA, it took him a year to get his FBI files, and
   even then there were substantial deletions.
6a. 5 U.S.C. Section 552(c).
7. The Civil Service Reform Act of 1978 (P.L. 95–454), 5 U.S.C
   Section 1206(e)(1)(C) establishes a Special Counsel having authority
   to

> conduct an investigation of any allegation concerning . . . arbi-
> trary and capricious withholding of information prohibited under
> section 552 of this title, except that the Special Counsel shall
> make no investigation under this subsection of any withholding
> of foreign intelligence or counterintelligence information the dis-
> closure of which is specifically prohibited by law or Executive
> order.

> Office of the Special Counsel regulations appear at 44 *Federal
> Register (Fed. Reg.)* 75,917, Dec. 21, 1979. For a description of
> special counsel functions in regard to the FOIA, *see* Letter
> (9–442) to Lawrence Ostrovsky, Center for National Security
> Studies, Washington, D.C., from Lynn R. Collins, Assistant
> Legal Counsel for Prosecution and Legal Division, Office of the
> Special Counsel, dated Dec. 5, 1979.

> The author is grateful to Louis Clark, Director, Government
> Accountability Project, Institute for Policy Studies, Washington,
> D.C., for his help in deciphering the special counsel's role.

VI

Going to Court

What can I do if the agency never processes my request, or if, even after an appeal, it does not release the material I have requested?

Both the FOIA and the Privacy Act give you the right to sue in federal court for the release of information you have been denied in full or in part. The discussion in this chapter will provide you with the necessary legal background so that you can knowledgeably discuss your case and options with lawyers. It will also provide some background for deciding whether it is a good idea to pursue the case in court.[1] And, finally, it includes a few ideas on getting legal representation.

What things should I consider in deciding whether to go to court to enforce my right to government information?

The first thing to consider is whether you have done everything, short of filing suit, that the FOIA requires in order to obtain release. The courts do not have "jurisdiction" over the case unless there has been an "exhaustion of administrative remedies." For the most part this means that all time limits must have elapsed and all necessary appeals must have been written. (See chapter 5.) Remember, also, lawsuits are expensive and time-consuming, and therefore are to be avoided. Even if you are quite sure you have grounds for going to court quickly, it is often wiser to be patient and to try to negotiate with the agency.

The next step is to ask how important the material really is to you. Is it worth the risk that, even after investing time, energy, and money, you might still lose in court? Is it worth the risk that, even after the government has fought tooth and nail to withhold the material, it may nevertheless turn out to be very dull reading indeed? If you decide to consult a lawyer, you should discuss these risks before filing suit.

If you think the records are worth a fight, you should make sure that all your records are in good order: nothing missing, everything in logical order, everything labeled, and everything *important* set out in a streamlined cover memo.

After my request for records has been turned down and my administrative appeal has been exhausted, how much time do I have in which to decide to file a lawsuit?

The FOIA does not establish a time limit for filing suit, and there is no case law on the issue. If a problem were to come up, it could be easily resolved by writing another request letter and creating a fresh right of access to government information. As of this writing, there is proposed legislation before Congress that would, if enacted, require that you file suit within 180 days of the agency's final administrative action. Even if this change were made, you would still be able to file an identical FOIA request to give yourself a fresh cause of action after the statute of limitations elapsed.[2]

The Privacy Act does have a time limit—lawsuits must be filed within 2 years of the denial of information, unless the agency has misrepresented the situation, in which case the lawsuit must be filed within 2 years after the discovery of the misrepresentation.[3]

On the other hand, it is sometimes possible to file suit too quickly. Courts like to see signs of reasonableness and patience, even if you have the legal right to move into the courtroom as soon as the statutory time limits have elapsed. For example, a court may decide not to award attorney fees if the agency was trying to comply quickly but the plaintiff made a "rush to the courthouse door" as soon as the time limits had passed.[4]

What are the chances for success in an FOIA lawsuit?

Statistically, the chances are fairly good. A General Accounting Office study shows that in better than half the lawsuits filed, the requesters obtained some or all of the information they were after. But precise statistics have not been available because cases cannot be easily categorized into win and lose. Often a case concludes with each side winning some points and losing others. In addition, cases are often settled out of court by negotiated agreement between the plaintiff and the government.[5]

But general statistics, of course, are not going to control what happens in a particular case. The chances for success or failure depend on the individual case. This is one of the risks that should be discussed forthrightly with any lawyer you consult. Success depends on both human and legal factors.

On the human side, the skill of the lawyers—both yours and the government's—the attitudes of the agency and of the Department of Justice, and the perspective of the judge or judges who hear the case will all be important.

On the legal side, some cases are simply better than others. The courts treat some exemptions—such as the national security exemption—with a great deal of deference, even though the FOIA gives judges the authority to overrule an agency's classification decisions. Other categories of material are probably not worth the effort of taking to a lawyer, much less taking to court. For example, there is ordinarily no point in trying to sue under the FOIA for the names of informers deleted from law enforcement records. Check the discussion of exemptions in chapter 4 to help you to make an educated guess whether the material is clearly exempt, and whether there might well be a basis for a legal argument that could convince a judge. Bear in mind, of course, that chapter 4 is not an exhaustive study of the FOIA exemptions. It is entirely possible that there may be some unexpected precedents that would make your success (or failure) in court likely. It is possible that since chapter 4 was written, higher courts have reversed the lower court decisions that were described, or even that the higher courts have reversed themselves. It is also possible that the material you want may fall into what is currently a legal gray area—the courts may never have ruled on your particular question. And finally, much of a lawyer's work turns on the ability to persuade a court that two seemingly similar situations are really different—that in considering a particular bowl of fruit, it is necessary to separate the apples from the oranges.

The next step is to consult a lawyer who, ideally, knows something about FOIA/PA law. If the material is important to you, you may want to do this even if you are fairly certain that it is exempt.

Some suggestions about getting legal counsel appear at the end of this chapter.

What are the different stages of an FOIA/PA lawsuit?

The first stage of a lawsuit takes place when you file a "complaint" (actually when your lawyer does this in your name) in a U.S. District Court; after the case is filed, you are called a plaintiff or complainant. The government agency then becomes the "defendant," and will be represented by lawyers from the U.S. Department of Justice.

The lawyers for both sides will file various "motions" for the district court judge to decide upon.

For example, both sides may file "motions" and "cross motions" asking the judge to find that the law supports their side. Legal "briefs" will be written to persuade the judge as to what the law is and how and why it should be applied in the given circumstances. The plaintiff, for instance, might file a motion asking the judge to find that the statute that the agency claims authorizes withholding information under the (b)(3) exemption does not really fit the legal definition of a valid (b)(3) statute. The agency, of course, will be working hard to convince the judge that it is indeed a (b)(3) statute. If the judge finds that it is not a valid (b)(3) statute (and if the higher courts agree), then the agency would have to release the material or find other grounds for withholding. If the judge rules that the cited statute is valid for a (b)(3) withholding, then more motions and briefs would be filed by each side to prove that the specific documents are or are not actually covered by the statute.

The lawyers for both sides will also be marshaling evidence to support their respective claims. Evidence includes "affidavits" from knowledgeable people explaining why a given piece of information does or does not fall under a particular exemption; these are commonly submitted by ranking agency officials. The judge will also be asked to grant various "discovery" motions, thus ordering the parties to produce various kinds of evidence. Since the government has control of the material that is being disputed, discovery in FOIA/PA cases is one-way, with the plaintiff's side trying to find out more about the material in order to establish that it isn't covered by an exemption. And since the FOIA/PA establish procedures for agencies to follow, the plaintiff may want to take discovery about how the agency went about processing the request. The government may routinely oppose discovery motions, and it is up to the judge to decide whether to grant them. The plaintiff's discovery will consist primarily of requests from sworn statements from agency officials to support the claim that the material is in fact being properly withheld. Sometimes people outside the government will also have some expertise to contribute. The questions may be put in the form of "interrogatories" (requiring written answers) or "depositions" (requiring oral answers that are transcribed by a court reporter).

A few examples of the kinds of questions that may be asked in discovery should give you an idea of how an FOIA/PA suit proceeds. The purpose of all the court action, of course, is to gather together the evidence and arguments that will convince the judge to order the release of the information. You will probably want to file a *Vaughn* motion, asking for a detailed index and description of the withheld material, together with an explanation of the legal grounds for withholding. (This will be discussed in more detail later on in this chapter.) The plaintiff might want to ask the agency what standards it uses for deciding whether information is exempt; if the standards don't fit the legal requirements laid out in the statute, the legislative history of the statute, or the legal precedents set by earlier FOIA/PA cases, the judge should decide that the withholding is improper. The plaintiff might also want to find out whether any similar material has been released to anyone else, and, if so, why this particular case is supposedly different. If an agency has claimed that it hasn't had time to find the requested documents, the discovery process would ask about the agency's backlog of FOIA/PA requests, and whether the agency is making a "good faith" effort to respond to requests as quickly as possible. If the agency claims that it could find little or none of the material that had been requested your lawyers will try to find out about the agency's search procedures; if the search procedures look inadequate, the judge may order the agency to go back and look harder.

In addition to questions about how the agency has gone about carrying out its FOIA/PA responsibilities, there will also be many questions asking how specific exemption claims have been used.

And finally, since FOIA/PA suits are not decided by juries, the district court judge will make a decision as to whether the requested material should be withheld or released. The decisions are seldom all-or-nothing verdicts; frequently, a court will decide that both the plaintiff and the government are right on different legal points and in claims for different documents and deletions. One side will always be unhappy about the decision; often both sides are.

And one or both sides may then file an appeal in a U.S. Court of Appeals (these appeals courts are also called circuit courts), which is the next rung up the ladder in the federal judicial system. These appeals will ask the higher court to find that the lower court made errors in its procedures, findings of law, or interpretations of the evidence. The appeals court may then "reverse" some or all of the earlier determinations, and "remand" the case (that is, send it back) for consideration in light of its findings. Or the appeals court may uphold the lower court's findings.

Circuit court decisions are made by a vote of a panel of three judges. If either or both sides of the lawsuit disagree with the decision of the panel, a petition can be filed for a "rehearing *en banc.*" If the judges on the circuit decide to rehear the case (this happens infrequently), all the judges in that circuit (rather than the usual three-judge panel) gather together for a rehearing *en banc* and ultimately hand down a new decision.

If either or both sides believe that the court of appeals made an error, they have the option of petitioning the U.S. Supreme Court for a "writ of *certiorari.*" Like rehearings *en banc*, it is up to the Supreme Court justices to decide whether to hear the case (to grant *certiorari*). Since the Supreme Court can take only 260 cases per year, the odds for a "*cert.* petition" being granted are less than one case in seven. Cases are chosen either because the Justices believe that they present legal issues of national importance, or because different circuit courts around the country have created legal confusion by coming to different conclusions about what the law is on the same legal point. Supreme Court decisions, then, set out the definitive interpretation of the law regarding a particular issue.

After reading briefs submitted by both sides and hearing oral arguments, the nine Supreme Court Justices decide the case by voting. Again, since every case ordinarily presents a number of legal issues, the Court may find both for and against each of the parties. And, as with the decisions of the courts of appeals, the Supreme Court will either "affirm" the various points, or "reverse and remand" to let the district court work out the details and issue the court orders necessary to implement the holdings of the High Court.

And finally, this entire process may be cut short at any point by your decision to drop the case. Or both parties may decide to settle the matter out of court; often it is possible to make a deal with the government that if you get some material, you will drop the suit for the remainder.

How long do FOIA lawsuits typically take?

In amending the FOIA in 1974, Congress took note of two facts—that much information is of interest to the public for only a limited time, and that lawsuits ordinarily are a very lengthy process. As a result, the FOIA specifies that the government must answer a complaint within 30 days (rather than the usual 60 days) after it is filed.[6] In addition, the act instructs the district and appeals courts that FOIA cases should be "expedited in every way." And, while the act gives the court the discretion to decide that some cases may be of "greater importance," it also states that FOIA cases are otherwise supposed to "take precedence" over other pending legal actions.

In practice, this means that a typical FOIA case will take a year or more, particularly if it is appealed. The government generally does appeal decisions that are not in its favor, and about 80 percent of FOIA cases take 2 to 3 years.

However, every case is different, and there is actually no such thing as a "typical" case; there are quite a few different scenarios that may be played. For instance, the Justice Department lawyers may decide at the outset that the agency made a mistake and that none of its exemption claims should be defended; in this situation, the lawsuit may be over in a month or two. Or the government might release some of the contested material shortly after the suit is filed and then go on to fight vigorously to withhold the rest. Or the government may want to settle the case out of court by striking a bargain; you may be offered some material if you agree to drop the suit for the remainder. Or, if the legal and factual issues are fairly clear, the judge may grant "summary judgment," without taking time for any discovery, within a few months—in this situation, the judge will issue a finding on behalf of one side or the other (or possibly for both sides, ordering the release of some material but authorizing withholding other records). Since summary judgments can be appealed, the lawsuit may nonetheless drag on through the appeals process. An FOIA lawsuit for a huge volume of records (the records in the Rosenberg espionage case, for instance, numbered well over a hundred thousand pages) should ordinarily take longer than one that seeks only a few pages. And, of course, the government may decide to fight tooth and nail and to use every delaying tactic in the book, and the suit may go on for years.

How can FOIA plaintiffs argue effectively for the release of documents that they have never seen?

There are several provisions in the statute and some procedures that have sprung up in the FOIA case law that help even up a contest where the plaintiff is not permitted to look at the material being fought over. The judge has the power to order a "*Vaughn* showing," to conduct an "*in camera* inspection" and to conduct a "*de novo* review." In addition, the FOIA specifies that the "burden of proof" is on the agency.

What is a "*Vaughn* showing"?

One unique feature of FOIA litigation is the *Vaughn* showing, which is part of the discovery process. This is a procedure that has been established by the courts to allow litigation to proceed even though your lawyers have never been able to look at the specific information. An early FOIA lawsuit, *Vaughn v. Rosen* established a precedent when the court ordered the government to provide the plaintiff with enough information so that the litigation could proceed.[7] Generally, when a judge issues a *Vaughn* order the government is required to itemize the material that is being withheld, to provide a detailed justification as to why each item is properly exempt and to provide an index that cross-references the itemizations and the justifications. With this information, the plaintiff is in a better position to make concrete arguments that the agency has not followed procedures or has improperly invoked the exemptions.

What is "*in camera* inspection"?

The FOIA gives the court the power to conduct *in camera* inspection.[8] This means that the district court judge may, if he or she chooses, examine in the secrecy of the judicial chambers, the records that are in dispute. This permits judges to determine for themselves the accuracy of the agency's claims about the withheld material, and it is an important option if the judge is going to exercise the power of *de novo* review.

A plaintiff, particularly one who is paying legal fees, may wonder whether any time-consuming discovery is necessary when the whole matter might, by means of a motion requesting *in camera* inspection, be settled promptly by the judge. Unfortunately, *in camera* inspection is not a cure-all, and discovery is usually worthwhile. A judge may decide not to conduct *in camera* inspection, or a busy judge who is wading through a pile of bureaucratic paper may not have enough background to second-guess the agency's claims—unless the discovery process has carefully developed arguments and explanations why withholding is improper. And sometimes it will be necessary to conduct discovery in order to have evidence to back up the lower court's decision if it is appealed.

What is "*de novo* review"?

Since the FOIA gives the courts the power of *de novo* review,[9] judges are required by law to decide anew whether to withhold or release the material. In other words, judges are to substitute their judgment for that of the agency. The agency's prior decisions bear no special weight when the matter reaches the courts. By contrast, without the power of *de novo* review, the courts would have the power only to determine whether the agency's decision had been arbitrary, capricious, an abuse of discretion, or otherwise not reasonable and not to go on to inquire whether they would agree that the agency's decision to withhold information also happens to be correct.

What does it mean when the burden of proof is on the agency in an FOIA lawsuit?

When the FOIA places the burden of proof on the agency,[10] it means that the court is supposed to assume that the documents should be released until the agency proves otherwise. Essentially, it means that if the judge has doubts about whether something is properly withheld, the material should be released.

In what districts courts can an FOIA/PA lawsuit be filed?

The FOIA permits requesters several choices in deciding where to file suit (this is known as choosing venue). This choice of venue means that it might be reasonable to consider choosing a lawyer in a city *other* than where you live. Under the FOIA or the Privacy Act, you may file suit in the district court (1) where you live; (2) where you have your principal place of business; (3) where the documents are located; or (4) in the District of Columbia.[11] (There is one exception to this: the place where prisoners are incarcerated is not considered their legal residence; prisoners cannot enforce their right to sue where they are, in fact, involuntarily living.[12])

There are ninety-one U.S. District Courts in the fifty states, Puerto Rico, the District of Columbia, Guam, and the Virgin Islands. (Some states have more than one district court—for example, California has a northern, a central, and a southern district court.) The U.S. District Courts feed into the following U.S. Courts of Appeals:

First Circuit—Maine, Massachusetts, New Hampshire, Puerto Rico, and Rhode Island

Second Circuit—Connecticut, New York, and Vermont

Third Circuit—Delaware, New Jersey, Pennsylvania, and the Virgin Islands

Fourth Circuit—Maryland, North Carolina, South Carolina, Virginia, and West Virginia

Fifth Circuit—Alabama, Florida, and Georgia (formerly also had Louisiana, Mississippi, and Texas, which in 1980 were split off to form the Eleventh Circuit)

Sixth Circuit—Kentucky, Michigan, Ohio, and Tennessee

Seventh Circuit—Illinois, Indiana, and Wisconsin

Eighth Circuit—Arkansas, Iowa, Minnesota, Missouri, Nebraska, North Dakota, and South Dakota

Ninth Circuit—Alaska, Arizona, California, Hawaii, Idaho, Montana, Nevada, Oregon, Guam, and Washington (state)

Tenth Circuit—Colorado, Kansas, New Mexico, Oklahoma, Utah, and Wyoming

Eleventh Circuit—Louisiana, Mississippi, and Texas (formerly part of the Fifth Circuit)

District of Columbia Circuit—Washington, D.C.

In choosing venue, it is sometimes useful to consider which circuit court the lower court decisions will be appealed to. Unless the Supreme Court has already handed down a decision settling some particular point, the circuits may be divided in their interpretations of a law. The case law in one circuit may be more favorable to your case than it would be in another. For example, the District of Columbia Circuit has decided that FBI delays in processing FOIA requests are justified because of the large volume of requests and the backlog at that agency. Other circuits are not required to follow the D.C. Circuit's lead. The Ninth Circuit, for example, found that there are circumstances in which an FOIA request should be processed ahead of others in the backlog.[13] Similarly, the Seventh Circuit has held that tax return information may not be released to third parties even if material that would identify the taxpayer is deleted; the Ninth Circuit has held otherwise.[14]

The District of Columbia Circuit has, by far, the heaviest caseload of FOIA lawsuits, and therefore it has the most experience. It is not necessarily advantageous, however, for you to file suit there, depending on what aspect of the existing case law is most important to the particular situation. For instance, if you have *very* modest means, you should be aware that in some circumstances court costs may be assessed against a losing requester.[15] This would add perhaps two hundred to four hundred dollars to the other costs of a suit. (Unless that would be a financial burden, it would probably be wiser to choose venue because of other legal considerations.)

Does the FOIA provide that the government should sometimes pay for attorney fees and the cost of the lawsuit if the court decides that the agency mistakenly withheld information?

Yes. The FOIA and the Privacy Act state that the court *may* decide to order the government to pay a successful plaintiff reasonable attorney fees and other litigation costs, if the plaintiff has "substantially prevailed."[16] This award of fees is not automatic, however. It is up to the judge to decide if the release of some, but not all, of the contested records amounts to the plaintiff's having "substantially prevailed." This has ordinarily been interpreted rather broadly by the courts—plaintiffs can win litigation costs, for example, even if the government releases the records shortly after the suit is filed, and without having been ordered to do so by the court.[17]

The legislative history of this provision includes some additional factors that a court should consider in deciding whether to award attorney fees. Fees should be awarded if release serves some "public benefit"; for instance, that the material will be published or is sought by a public interest organization or will be used in scholarly research.[18] Even if the government had a reasonable basis in law, and if its motive for withholding the material was not an apparent effort to avoid embarrassment or to frustrate the requester, courts are supposed to award fees if the release benefits the public.[19] However, if the information was sought for commercial reasons, particularly on behalf of a "large corporate interest," then an award of attorney fees is unlikely, unless there had been no "reasonable basis" in law for the agency to withhold the information.[20]

Obviously, a prospective client will want to discuss the possibility of fee awards with any lawyers who are consulted. One thing to consider is that once a lawyer takes a case on the chance that fee awards will come along later, he or she has in effect a financial investment in pursuing the case in court. The client cannot lightly drop the case. And the time to think about alternative, informal routes that might dislodge some or all of the information is *before* filing suit.

Does the FOIA provide any sanctions to discourage officials from withholding information improperly?

Yes. In addition to the fact that the government might have to pay your costs in bringing the case to court, the FOIA also provides that a successful litigant can ask the Merit System Protection Board's Office of Special Counsel to consider disciplinary action against the official "primarily responsible" for arbitrary or capricious withholding.[21] Most commentators believe, however, that the sanctions provisions are not likely to be used, and they are not a promising deterrent.[22]

It remains to be seen whether filing allegations with the Office of the Special Counsel (see chapter 5) will have much effect.

What special difficulties are presented when a reverse FOIA suit is filed to prevent the release of requested material?

As discussed in chapter 4, "reverse FOIA" suits may be filed to prevent the release of information that might be covered by the (b)(4) exemption for trade secrets and for commercial and financial information. These cases will present numerous difficulties.

First, while the FOIA explicitly states that the courts must place FOIA lawsuits on an expedited schedule (this means that FOIA suits may take only half as long as most suits), reverse FOIA suits enjoy no such clear privilege under current law. Although they can sometimes be moved along swiftly, they can also sometimes proceed through the clogged and backlogged courts as slowly as other cases.[23] In addition, reverse FOIA suits can be particularly complex, with corporations submitting great quantities of expert testimony, statistical data, and other kinds of evidence with which you may be totally unfamiliar, and it is an awkward situation to have to rely totally on the agency to fight the reverse suit for the release of the data.

If you can find legal counsel to represent your interests, you have the option of "intervening" in the reverse FOIA lawsuit.[24] However, you are not required to do so.

Confronted with a reverse FOIA suit, you also have the option of filing your own separate lawsuits under the FOIA, filed in the court of your own choosing. However, a Supreme Court decision has held that if the submitter of the information obtains a court injunction prohibiting the agency from releasing the contested material, a second court in another jurisdiction cannot then order the agency to release that same material.[25] Therefore, faced with the possibility of getting involved in a reverse FOIA suit, you should ordinarily go to court as quickly as possible.

In a reverse FOIA suit, when can the submitter of the information file suit to prevent the release of the information?

The reverse FOIA suit can be filed at any time after the initial request has been made but before the documents are actually released to you. This means that a lawsuit to prevent disclosure may begin even before the FOIA time limits (discussed in chapter 1) have had a chance to run and before the agency has decided whether to release the material. It also means that the submitters of the information can launch a reverse FOIA suit before you can file an FOIA suit to compel release, selecting which district court you want to file suit in. If the district court is not nearby, the choice of venue may make it more difficult and expensive for you to intervene in the reverse FOIA lawsuit. The Supreme Court decision discussed in the preceding question, which held in essence that the first suit with a valid court order determines the judicial forum in which the dispute must be handled, seems to turn reverse FOIA cases into not only a race to the courthouse, but into a race for the first court order. The submitters of the information so far would seem to have an advantage over the FOIA requesters.[26]

Can an individual file suit to challenge the release of personal information?

Yes, the Privacy Act permits individuals to object to agency plans for disclosure of information that has been requested from "systems of records" (see the earlier discussion of the Privacy Act), but there have been few cases so far.[27] In addition, (b)(6) also provides a basis for filing a suit in order to protect personal privacy.[28] (See chapter 4.)

What should I consider, find out and discuss when consulting a lawyer about filing suit?

Dealing with a lawyer is a two-way street; the information flows in both directions, and there is a good deal that you should have carefully prepared before taking your case to a lawyer you are considering working with.

You should have in good order *your* records of *your* efforts to get the information. A busy lawyer may well decide that a potential client is too disorganized to be worth the trouble of trying to figure out what his or her case is all about. Picking lawyers is a two-way proposition: the lawyers convince you that they would in fact do a good job, while you convince them that you would be a good client. This is particularly true if you are going to ask for favors; for instance, asking that the case be taken in the expectation that you will substantially prevail and that the court will award attorney fees. If you pay the full rate as the case progresses, your disorganization will cost a good deal of money. And if you are going to try to fight an exemption claim or try to get a waiver of fees by arguing, say, that release is in the public interest, you should be able to present coherent arguments—and, if possible, documentation as well—to that effect. If for example, you want the material for scholarly or journalistic purposes, you should be able to show convincing credentials to a judge. And, of course, it doesn't hurt to explain to a lawyer why your case may be an *interesting* one; for instance, that it's newsworthy, of historical importance, or discusses major issues.

In addition to preparing what you will tell your prospective lawyer, there is a good deal of information that you will want to get from him. You want to find out about professional competence, legal fees, and the chances for winning your particular case.

First, you should find out about his or her experience in federal practice (law involving the federal government) and particularly the FOIA. Ask what other FOIA cases he or she may have handled and how they turned out. All other things being equal, the more experience the better. But there is a trade-off. The more experienced lawyers with established reputations are going to cost more. (Indeed, some may not even be willing, depending on the nature of their practice, to take the case of an individual plaintiff.) An experienced lawyer who has done little FOIA work, but who is a competent generalist, may produce very good work, but if new to FOIA practice, the hourly rate should be lower than for areas of special competence.

The subject of fees is something that should be discussed at the outset, so that there are no unpleasant surprises. Make no mistake, legal representation is expensive. Depending on the area of the country, and subject to inflation, rates may run from $30 to $75 per hour for FOIA work. (And there are court costs on top of that.) When you first contact a lawyer, do not be afraid to ask explicit questions about what is going to cost how much, and when it is supposed to be paid. Happily, it is sometimes possible to bargain about fees, particularly with lawyers who are not yet established or who find the issue an exciting departure from what they usually do. Some private law firms will ask for an initial fee when the case is filed (generally $500 to $1,000) and will ask for the rest as an award of fees from the court if you win your case. You may have to agree to pay costs (secretarial help, copying, court costs, court reporters' fees, and so forth) as you go along. Ordinarily, you will have to agree to pay the fees yourself if you don't get a court award. Obviously, then, your prospective lawyer will have the right to ask in some detail about your ability to pay.

And you should be prepared for a serious discussion of whether it is worthwhile for you to take the case to court: whether you can afford it, how good the chances for success are, and what the risks are. But remember, no lawyer can guarantee how a case will turn out; what you are talking about are risks.

During this discussion, you will need to gauge how much confidence you have in the lawyer you have consulted. Having read this book, you should have enough background to decide whether what is being said makes sense, or whether what is being said is uncomfortably vague and full of generalizations, instead of specific and aggressive. You want someone who, even if not currently an FOIA expert, picks up on things quickly, comes up with concrete ideas about how to proceed and discusses fees openly.

And if you are going to be investing a great deal of money, you will want to take the time to think before making a decision to go ahead with the case.

Can I get free legal representation for an FOIA/PA suit?

There are some public interest groups (such as the ACLU) and law-school clinics that may be willing to take some FOIA cases for free. (A short list is printed in Appendix C.) In addition, there are some public interest law firms that may be willing to take cases for a low fee. And although the costs may be nothing or very low, the quality of the representation is good to excellent.

Since such groups do not charge the going rate, they inevitably have more requests for help than they can possibly handle, and so they can pick and choose. All the suggestions for the responsibilities of the prospective client just discussed apply equally, if not more so, when asking for free or low-cost legal help. These groups choose cases that they believe will be of value to a great many people. Generally, this means that the documents in question involve important policy issues, have important historical value or present some technical legal question that the courts haven't decided yet.

All requests for help from public interest organizations should be in writing, and you should include carefully organized copies of all the relevant correspondence and notes, as well as a succinct explanation of why the release of these documents is important to the public interest. Keep it brief and don't expect immediate attention, and don't be disappointed if you are turned down.

If public interest groups cannot take the case, they are a good source of names of reputable private lawyers who might be interested in the case.

Can I file a lawsuit on my own behalf, without hiring a lawyer?

Yes. This is known as being attorney *pro se* and litigating in

your own behalf. The FOIA does permit this, but a few
words of warning are in order. Generally, if you are not a
lawyer, it is a difficult road to file a *pro se* FOIA suit.
Government lawyers are likely to take advantage of a *pro se*
litigant's inexperience and succeed in getting away with things
that an experienced lawyer would know to object to. Lacking
experience, *pro se* litigants do not know how to build a
record in the lower court that will stand up on appeal; there
is some indication that government lawyers are taking advantage of this to make what is known as "bad case law," which
will set unfortunate precedents for others and that might well
have been avoided if the litigator had understood legal strategy.
And finally, if *pro se* litigants do get into trouble with their
cases, it can be very hard to get an experienced lawyer who
will be willing to take over and try to salvage the situation.

If you are trying to cut your costs, it is a wiser choice to
offer to do some of the legwork, paralegal work, research, or
secretarial work in order to reduce the fees. Most lawyers
will turn down such an offer, however. You may have no
choice but to represent yourself if you are to have your day in
court.

NOTES

1. For a detailed treatment of FOIA/PA litigation, *see* Morton H.
   Halperin, ed., *The 1984 Edition of Litigation Under the Federal
   Freedom of Information and Privacy Acts* (Washington, D.C. Cen
   ter for National Security Studies, 1983) A descriptive brochure and
   order blank are available from the

   Center for National Security Studies
   122 Maryland Avenue, N.E.
   Washington, DC 20002.

2. U.S., Congress, Senate, S. Rept. 98–221, 98th Cong. 1st sess.,
   1983, pp. 17–18.
3. 5 U.S.C. Section 552a(g)(5).
4. *Vermont Low Income Advocacy Council v. Usery*, 546 F.2d 509,
   513 (2d Cir. 1976); *Cunoo v. Rumsfeld*, 553 F.2d 1360 (D.C. Cir.
   1977).
5. Comptroller General of the United States, *An Informed Public
   Assures that Federal Agencies Will Better Comply with Freedom of
   Information/Privacy Laws*, GAO Report LCD–80–8 (Washington,
   D.C.: General Accounting Office, Oct. 24, 1979) Appendix p. 3.
6. 5 U.S.C. Section 552(a)(4)(C).

7. *Vaughn v. Rosen* (I), 484, F.2d 820 (D.C. Cir. 1973), *cert. denied*, 415 U.S. 977 (1974).

8. 5 U.S.C. Section 552(a)(4)(B).

9. *Id.*

10. *Id.*

11. *Id.*; and 5 U.S.C. Section 552a(g)(5).

12. *Turner v. Kelley*, 411 F. Supp. 1331 (D. Kan. 1976).

13. *Open America v. Watergate Special Prosecution Force*, 547 F.2d 605 (D.C. Cir. 1976); *Exner v. FBI*, 542 F.2d 1121 (9th Cir. 1976).

14. *King v. IRS*, 688 F.2d 488 (7th Cir. 1982); *Williamette Industries Inc. v. U.S.*, 689 F.2d 865 (9th Cir. 1982), *cert. denied*, 51 U.S.L.W. 3703 (U.S. Mar. 28, 1983).

15. *Baez v. Dept. of Justice*, 684 F.2d 999 (D.C. Cir. 1982) (*en banc*).

16. 5 U.S.C. Sections 552(a)(4)(E) and 552a(g)(2)(B).

17. *Cuneo v. Rumsfeld*, 553 F.2d 1360 (D.C. Cir. 1977); *Kaye v. Burns*, 411 F. Supp. 897 (S.D.N.Y. 1976); *Vermont Low Income, supra* note 4.

18. U.S., Congress, House, Committee on Government Operations, Subcommittee on Information and Individual Rights, and U.S., Congress, Senate, Committee on the Judiciary, Subcommittee on Administrative Practice and Procedure (Joint Committee Print), *Freedom of Information Act and Amendment of 1974 (P.L. 93–502: Sourcebook: Legislative History, Texts, and Other Documents*, 94th Cong., 1st sess. Mar. 1975, p. 171.

19. *Id.* at 192.

20. *Id.* at 171.

21. 5 U.S.C. Section 552(a)(4)(F).

22. *See* Vaughn, "The Sanctions Provision of the Freedom of Information Act Amendments," 25 *Amer. U.L. Rev.* 7 (1975).

23. U.S., Congress, House, Committee on Government Operations, Subcommittee, *Business Record Exemption of the Freedom of Information Act: Hearings*, 95th Cong., 1st sess., Oct. 3, 4, 1977, Appendix 8.

24. *See* Nancy Duff Campbell, "Reverse FOIA Litigation," in Halperin, *supra* note 1.

25. *GTE Sylvania, Inc. v. Consumers Union*, 445 U.S. 375 (1980). For background, *see Freedom of Information Act Requests for Business Data: Reverse FOIA Lawsuits*, U.S., Congress, House, Committee on Government Operations, 25th Report, 95th Cong., 2d sess., H. Rept. 95–1382, July 20, 1978, pp. 64–65.

26. Nancy Duff Campbell, Center for Law and Social Policy, cited in *Access Reports* (Apr. 1, 1980): 5.

27. 5 U.S.C. Section 552a(g). *See Reverse-FOIA Lawsuits, supra* note 25, at 54, n. 186; *Metropolitan Life Insurance Co. v. Usery*, 426 F. Supp. 150 (D.D.C. 1976); *Sonderegger v. Dep't. of Interior*, 424 F.

Supp. 847 (D. Idaho 1976); *Sears, Roebuck and Co. v. GSA*, 402 F.
Supp. 378 (D.D.C. 1975); *rev'd on other grounds*, 553 F.2d 1378
(D.C. Cir. 1977).
28. Id. at 54, n. 188.

II

Access to Government Meetings

In some cases, you have the legal right to attend meetings of government officials and advisors. The Government in the Sunshine Act[1] and the Federal Advisory Committee Act (FACA)[2] give the public the right to attend certain kinds of meetings held by federal officials. The Sunshine Act and the FACA are access statutes that are paired in much the same way that the FOIA and the Privacy Act may be said to be paired. While most of their provisions are quite different—since they set out to serve quite different purposes—some of their provisions do overlap. With the FOIA and Privacy Act, both provide a legal right of access to one category of identical material, namely personal records, but the other details are quite different. The Sunshine Act and the FACA each provide access to a similar kind of information, namely, the right to attend certain official meetings, but each puts very different procedural constraints on the process of conducting such meetings.

Neither the Sunshine Act nor the FACA has proved as popular with the public or with litigators as the FOIA and the Privacy Act. A meeting, it seems, might be staged, and it is, after all, often inconvenient to attend. On the other hand, documents, including transcripts of meetings, often provide real content with little inconvenience.

As a matter of practice, the Sunshine Act has proved less important than the FOIA, but more usable than the FACA. As a result, this book gives the Sunshine Act less coverage than the FOIA, but more coverage than the FACA. The primary purpose of the Government in the Sunshine Act is to open up to the public the meetings of agency governing boards (also called collegial bodies). And if procedures for closing meetings are not followed, or if exemptions that permit the closing of meetings are not properly invoked, the Sunshine Act gives members of the public the right to sue in federal court. The Sunshine Act is also notable because, while it carries over the language of most of the FOIA exemptions, it eliminates the privilege for "predecisional" and "advice" materials (the FOIA's (b)(5) exemption), an important departure in the law concerning "executive privilege."

The Federal Advisory Committee Act, enacted in 1972, establishes the right of the public to attend the meetings of federal advisory committees and provides some procedural requirements for conducting meetings. Initially, the FACA had its exemptions pegged to those of the FOIA—a situation that worked out poorly in practice. Consequently, when Congress enacted the Sunshine Act in 1976, it included an amendment to the FACA, stating that the operative FACA exemptions would no longer be those of the FOIA but those of the Sunshine Act.[3] Both statutes controlling access to federal government meetings now establish identical categories of information as the basis for closing meetings.

The FACA has had less impact than the Sunshine Act for a number of reasons. For a start, its access provisions are weaker. It was not designed to be primarily an access statute; most of the statute in fact deals with procedures for setting up federal advisory committees, conducting their business and terminating them, rather than with providing public access. (In this sense, the FACA parallels the Privacy Act, which sets out first to create operating principles to protect privacy; the Privacy Act provisions for the release of personal documents are a secondary interest and weaker than those of the FOIA.) One measure of this inattention is that the FACA does not explicitly provide mechanisms for suing in federal court to require the agencies to follow provisions of the act.

Chapter 7 discusses the Government in the Sunshine Act, in general, while chapter 8 covers the Sunshine/FACA exemptions that provide the grounds for closing meetings. Chapter 9 discusses the FACA generally, and points out major differences between it and the Sunshine Act—particularly in the ways that the FACA fails to mandate the extensive procedural details of the Sunshine Act and provides for only limited judicial review of the closing of meetings.

Much of what is described in chapters 7, 8, and 9 assumes that the reader has some knowledge about the ways in which the federal FOIA and the Privacy Act work. This familiarity is particularly important where the Sunshine Act and the FACA exemptions are identical to FOIA exemptions, and the case law of one will apply to the case law of the other. We will also try to point out some of the major differences among the FOIA, the Privacy Act, the Sunshine Act, and the FACA.

NOTES

1. The Government in the Sunshine Act is codified at 5 U.S.C Section 552b. The Sunshine Act and its Conference Report (U.S., Congress, House, H. Rept. 94–1441, 94th Cong., 2d sess., Aug. 26, 1976) are printed in Christine M. Marwick, ed., *The 1981 Edition of Litigation Under the Federal Freedom of Information and Privacy Acts* (Washington, D.C.: Center for National Security Studies, 1980). As mentioned earlier, the Sunshine Act also contained an amendment to the (b)(3) exemption of the FOIA. The Sunshine Act is largely the result of the work of Senator Lawton Chiles (D.-Fla.), and was inspired by a successful Sunshine Act in Florida.

    This discussion of the Sunshine Act is indebted to the work of Richard K. Berg and Stephen N. Klitzman, *An Interpretive Guide to the Government in the Sunshine Act* (Washington, D.C.: Administrative Conference of the U.S., June 1978).

    The Committee on Adjudication of the Administrative Conference of the United States is preparing a report on the implementation and effects of the federal Government in the Sunshine Act. As of this writing, it is available in draft form.

2. 5 U.S.C, Appendix I.

3. P.L. 94–409, Section 5(c).

VII

The Government in the Sunshine Act

How effective has the Government in the Sunshine Act been in opening government meetings to the public?

Common cause, a citizen-lobbying organization, has conducted a study of the effects of the Sunshine Act. They found that of a total of 2,242 meetings held between March 1977 and March 1978, 36 percent (or 813 meetings covered by the Sunshine Act) were entirely closed; 26 percent (583 meetings) were partially closed; and 38 percent (846 meetings) were fully open.[1]

As with the FOIA, agencies show different attitudes toward openness. The Interstate Commerce Commission (ICC) and the Tennessee Valley Authority (TVA) were cited for excellent records of Sunshine openness. At the other end of the spectrum, the Export-Import Bank, the National Labor Relations Board (NLRB), the Commodity Futures Trading Commission, the Occupational Safety and Health Review Commission, the U.S. Parole Commission, the Federal Reserve Board, and the Federal Home Loan Bank Board closed all or almost all of their meetings.[2]

If I choose to attend a meeting that is being held "in the Sunshine," can I participate in the meeting?

No. The Sunshine Act only gives you an enforceable legal right to attend meetings.[3] However, a few agencies have provisions for allowing members of the public to speak at some meetings, but only by prearrangement.

If I attend a meeting being held "in the Sunshine," can I use a camera, take notes or make a tape recording?

Agencies have different policies on such questions. Either check with agency officials, or check the *Code of Federal Regulations (CFR)* to determine what limitations an agency will enforce. The Equal Employment Opportunity Commission (EEOC) will, for example, permit photographs to be taken without flashbulbs at the beginning of the meeting, and permit the use of tape recorders; the Board of Governors of the Federal Reserve System (FRS), the U.S. Parole Commission, the Nuclear Regulatory Commission (NRC), and the Securities and Exchange Commission (SEC), however, require an attendee to get permission in advance. Others, such as the Federal Energy Regulatory Commission, prohibit cameras and tape recorders.[4]

What federal agencies are covered by the Sunshine Act?
Sunshine covers certain high-level meetings of agencies and major subdivisions of agencies. The act reads:

(1) the term "agency" means any agency, as defined in section 552(e) of this title, headed by a collegial body composed of two or more individual members, a majority of whom are appointed to such position by the President with the advice and consent of the Senate, and any subdivision thereof authorized to act on behalf of the agency.[4a]

As of this writing, some fifty agencies fit this description.

Board for International Broadcasting (BIB)
Civil Aeronautics Board (CAB)
Commodity Credit Corporation (CCC) (Board of Directors)
Commodity Futures Trading Commission (CFTC)
Consumer Product Safety Commission (CPSC)
Copyright Royalty Tribunal
Council on Environmental Quality (CEQ)
Depository Institutions Deregulation Committee
Equal Employment Opportunity Commission (EEOC)
Export-Import Bank of the United States (EIB) (Board of Directors)
Federal Communications Commission (FCC)
Federal Deposit Insurance Corporation (FDIC) (Board of Directors)
Federal Election Commission (FEC)
Federal Energy Regulatory Commission (FERC)

Federal Farm Credit Board (FFCB) within the Farm Credit Administration

Federal Home Loan Bank Board (FHLBB)

Federal Home Loan Mortgage Corporation (FHLMC)

Federal Maritime Commission (FMC)

Federal Reserve Board (FRB)

Federal Trade Commission (FTC)

Harry S Truman Scholarship Foundation (HSTSF) (Board of Directors)

Indian Claims Commission (ICC 20)

Inter-American Foundation (IAF)

Interstate Commerce Commission (ICC 22)

Legal Services Corporation

Mississippi River Commission (MRC)

National Center for Productivity and the Quality of Working Life (NCPQWL)

National Commission on Libraries and Information Science (NCLIS)

National Council on Educational Research (NCER)

National Labor Relations Board (NLRB)

National Mediation Board (NMB)

National Museum Services Board

National Railroad Passenger Corporation (NRPC)

National Science Board (NSB) of the National Science Foundation

National Transportation Safety Board (NTSB)

Nuclear Regulatory Commission (NRC)

Occupational Safety and Health Review Commission (OSHRC)

Overseas Private Investment Corporation (OPIC) (Board of Directors)

Postal Rate Commission (PRC)

Railroad Retirement Board (RRB)

Renegotiation Board (RB)

Securities and Exchange Commission (SEC)

Tennessee Valley Authority (TVA) (Board of Directors)

Uniformed Services University of the Health Sciences (USUHS) (Board of Regents)

U.S. Commission on Civil Rights (USCCR)

U.S. Foreign Claims Settlement Commission (USFCSC)

U.S. International Trade Commission (USITC)

U.S. Parole Commission (USPC)

U.S. Postal Service (USPS) (Board of Governors)

U.S. Railway Association (USRA)[5]

This list is limited because, generally speaking, the Sunshine Act applies to federal commissions rather than what is more commonly thought of as an "agency." With this confusion in mind, some technical discussion of what a "Sunshine agency" is, is in order. These definitions are important if you want to sue in court (see the discussion later) and argue that some agency is not actually exempt from the Sunshine Act provisions.

The Sunshine Act begins by using the FOIA's definition of a *government agency*[6] (see chapter 1). But it then limits Sunshine Act meetings to those that are held by officials who are sitting as members of a "collegial body"—roughly speaking, this means the governing board of the agency. Not only must the agency have such a collegial body (most don't), but in order to qualify for Sunshine Act meetings, the majority of the members of this collegial body must be presidential appointees who are confirmed by the Senate. Furthermore, the members must have been specifically appointed to, and confirmed for, the post on that particular collegial body if it is to be considered a Sunshine Act agency. A board that is staffed wholly by people who happen to be presidential appointees to other positions (such as the cabinet secretaries, the Chairman of the Federal Reserve Board, and the Comptroller General who were assigned by Congress the duty of sitting on the board handling the loan guarantees made to the Chrysler Corporation) would not be an agency covered by the Sunshine Act.[7]

A subdivision of an agency is covered by the Sunshine Act if it is authorized to act on behalf of the agency. For example, a panel or board is covered if it is "authorized to submit recommendations, preliminary decisions, or the like to the full commission, or to conduct hearings on behalf of the agency."[8] This subdivision must consist of people who are, again, appointees to the panel or board. Thus, a Nuclear Regulatory Commission (NRC) licensing board is not a Sunshine Act agency because no NRC commissioner serves on it.[9]

However, the fact that a Sunshine Act agency does not follow proper procedures when it delegates authority to a subdivision is not enough to take that subdivision out of the Sunshine. The D.C. Circuit, for example, found that the consultative process gatherings (CP's) set up by the Federal Communications Commission (FCC) for reaching agreements with their counterparts in foreign governments qualified as Sunshine Act meetings.[10]

In addition, the fact that a Sunshine Act agency also happens to have the function of advising the President does not take those meetings where advice is formulated out of the Sunshine[11]

However, Sunshine Act agencies and meetings never include the deliberations of an informal working group; the group must have a specified membership and fixed responsibilities. If it has no clear authority, it is not covered by the Sunshine Act, although it might fall under the FACA.

What kinds of agency meetings are covered by the Sunshine Act?

A Sunshine Act meeting takes place when a quorum of members of an agency that fits the Sunshine Act definition gets together to deliberate or to take care of agency business.[11a] If the meeting is called in order to deliberate some point, without intending to reach a decision by casting votes, it is nonetheless a Sunshine Act meeting.[12] If the members choose to get together at, say, a restaurant, they would still be covered by the Sunshine Act, as long as they are conducting business that the act covers. By the same token, the meeting could be a conference telephone call. However, there must be "some degree of formality" to the meeting, since the bill is not supposed to prevent agency members "from engaging in informal background discussions." Agency officials are supposed to make certain that they do not use such informal sessions to make decisions that they then merely approve "in the Sunshine."[13]

Is a meeting that is held in order to decide whether to close another meeting(s) supposed to be held in the Sunshine?

No. Meetings that are held either to determine whether to close a meeting, or to decide how, when, and where to set up a given meeting, are not covered by the Sunshine Act provisions.[13a]

Does the Sunshine Act permit agencies to make decisions by circulating papers (which would lay out options and so on) among the agency members?

Yes. The Sunshine Act restrictions apply only to agency meetings. Such notational voting, voting by noting a choice among the options on the papers, has withstood court challenge.[14]

If some portion of a given meeting covered by the Sunshine Act is covered by one of the exemptions, does that mean that the entire meeting is exempt?

No. Although there is no clear definition of how agencies are to differentiate open and closed portions of meetings, the legislative history of the Sunshine Act makes it clear that this should be done.[15] Loosely speaking, the Sunshine Act has a parallel to the "segregable portions" provision in the FOIA. Agencies may, for example, set the meeting's agenda so that the topics that are exempt are clustered at the end; the first part of the meeting would then be open to the public, while for the second part the public would be asked to leave.

Is an agency *required* to close meetings if there are grounds for doing so?

No. As with the FOIA, an agency may choose to exercise its discretion and to open a meeting that it could have closed.[16]

Sunshine Act Requirements for Informing the Public of Meetings

Does the Sunshine Act require that agencies publish certain categories of information?

Like the FOIA and the Privacy Act, the Sunshine Act requires agencies to publish regulations on how the act will be implemented. These will be found in the *Code of Federal Regulations (CFR).* [16a]

And as discussed later, agencies are also required to make the transcripts, recordings, minutes, or other records of Sunshine Act meetings "promptly available." In many cases this means that agencies put such records on file in their public reading room (see the discussion of such reading rooms in the earlier section on the FOIA).

Does the Sunshine Act require agencies to give the public notice of their meetings before they can be closed?

Yes, except in pressing circumstances, agencies are required to make a public announcement at least a week ahead of each meeting. This announcement must state the time, place, and subject matter of the meeting and whether it will be open or closed to the public. In addition, the public announcement must provide the name and phone number of an agency official to contact concerning the meeting.[16b]

If a majority of the members vote that the agency business is so pressing that the meeting cannot be delayed seven days, the meeting can take place on shorter notice; in such cases, notice must be provided "at the earliest practicable time," and all the required information must be provided. In unusual circumstances, however, it is possible that the announcement might have to be issued at the same time that the meeting is convened.[17]

When meetings are called on short notice, many agencies provide for such steps as posting notices on bulletin boards, and mailing or phoning notices to interested parties.[18]

Failure to follow notice procedures can be reviewed in court.[19]

Can an agency change the time, place, subject matter, or its decision to open or close a meeting after the required public announcements have been made?

Yes. After the public announcements have been made, a majority of the members of an agency can vote to change the time, place, subject matter, or Sunshine Act status of the meeting if they determine that pressing agency business so requires and they then provide public notice of such changes "at the earliest practicable time."[19a]

What are the means by which an agency should issue its public announcements that a meeting is to take place?

The primary means of announcing meetings is through the publication of a notice in the *Federal Register (Fed. Reg.)*. Congress also recommended that agencies post notices on agency bulletin boards and in their Public Affairs offices, send a calendar of meetings to mailing lists of interested persons, issue press releases and make use of recorded phone announcements.[20] Agency regulations may spell out the announcement procedures more explicitly.

Sunshine Procedures for Closing Meetings

What voting procedures must an agency go through in order to legally close a meeting or part of it.

Meetings covered by the Sunshine Act cannot be closed unless a majority of the membership of the collegial body votes to close the particular meeting or part of it.[20a] While the votes cannot be cast by proxy, the votes can be taken by circulating ballots or tally sheets to the members or by holding a meeting. The record of the votes must be publicly available within a day, and if a meeting or part of it is closed, the agency must also provide a "full written explanation" of the reasons for doing so.[20b]

If the members of the collegial body vote to close a meeting or a part of it, the General Counsel or chief legal officer for the agency must file a certification with the agency stating the grounds for closing the meeting.[20c]

Can the agency members vote once to close an entire series of meetings?

Yes, but only if the entire series of meetings covers the same subject, and is, essentially, "the same discussion which stretches over more than one meeting."[21] The Sunshine Act specifies that such meetings have to be held within thirty days of the first meeting on the subject.[21a]

Does the agency have to state who will in fact be attending a meeting that is closed?

Yes. The Sunshine Act requires agencies to make public the names and the affiliations of the people who will be attending a particular meeting, or part of a meeting, which is closed to the public.[21b] Agencies have adopted different policies about listing the names of staff people who will attend.

This provision is intended to allow you to question if favoritism—certain persons improperly granted access while others are excluded—is being practiced.

Can a person request that an agency close a meeting or a portion thereof?

Yes, a person (this includes, of course, corporations) who may be directly affected by something under discussion at a proposed meeting, can cite the Sunshine Act's exemptions (c)(5), (c)(6), or (c)(7) and ask that the relevant portion be closed. (These are the exemptions protecting personal privacy, possible official accusations, and investigatory records, which are discussed in chapter 8.) The affected person can ask any member of the agency for a recorded vote on closing the meeting[21c]

If the members vote that the meeting remain open, the person affected can probably sue in federal court to close the meeting. It is assumed that a reverse Sunshine Act lawsuit could be carried out under the provisions of the Administrative Procedure Act (APA), just as reverse FOIA suits can be.[22]

Although the statute does not explicitly say so, persons should also be able to ask that meetings be closed where exemption (c)(4) (business information) interests may be involved.[23]

Are agencies ever entitled to use shortcut procedures for closing their meetings?

Yes. Agencies can simplify their procedures if a majority of their meetings can be closed under the exemption for discussions of trade secrets, sensitive financial reports, financial information that might lead to speculation, or agency involvement in adversary proceedings (see chapter 8).[23a] (Agencies that make use of these procedures must be able to document the fact that a majority of their meetings are closed.) The Federal Reserve Board, the Securities and Exchange Commission, and the National Labor Relations Board are examples of such agencies.

Under the simplified procedures, the agency—

1. does not have to give notice of the meeting seven days in advance, but simply "at the earliest practicable time";

2. can wait until the meeting itself to vote whether to close that meeting;

3. does not have to publish with its announcement in the *Federal Register* the "full written explanation" for closing the meeting, the list of the attendees, or the name and phone of an agency "contact" concerning the meeting;

4. can change the subject of a meeting without the usual procedures for doing so.

Even if a meeting is closed under these procedures, a majority of the members must still vote to close the meeting, a record of this vote must be available to the public, and the General Counsel of the agency must certify that the meeting is properly closed.[24]

Access to Sunshine Act Records

Do agencies have to keep a record of what went on at their meetings?

Yes. This Sunshine Act record, in most cases, can be in the form of a verbatim transcript or tape recording of the meeting.[24a] If the agency makes use of a tape recorder, it must make provisions "adequate to identify each speaker."[25]

However, for meetings that are closed under the exemptions for bank reports, financial speculation, and adversary proceedings (discussed in chapter 8), an agency can choose to use minutes as its Sunshine Act record.

While these Sunshine Act transcripts, tapes, and minutes may contain a great deal of information that could be put to effective use, they have, to date, an ambiguous legal status in one regard. The act does not consider whether or not these Sunshine Act records are part of what is called the official *administrative record* of the agency. Only if records of Sunshine Act deliberations are included in the legal definition of the *administrative record* can they be used as evidence in court to try to challenge some agency decision.[26]

How long does an agency have to keep the Sunshine Act record of a particular meeting on file?

Agencies have to keep the records of meetings on file for at least two years. If the meeting was part of an ongoing agency proceeding, the record must be kept for at least a year after the proceeding has concluded, even if this is longer than two years after the meeting itself.[27] If the meeting concerns an investigation, the record must be kept at least until final agency action has been taken.[28]

Are the records of closed meetings or portions of closed meetings available to the public after the meeting has taken place?

Yes, unless otherwise exempt. The Sunshine Act requires agencies to make nonexempt portions of such records "promptly available" to the public. In most situations this will mean that the record will be on file in an agency's public document room.[29] Some agencies automatically place such records on file, whether there has been a request for them or not. Others as a matter of policy will sometimes wait for a member of the public to request access to the record.

The agencies have the authority to edit these records prior to release and to withhold material that would be covered by the Sunshine Act's exemptions.[29a] Such transcripts can be requested under FOIA procedures. In many cases, information that may be properly exempt at the time of the meeting will no longer be covered by exemptions as time goes on, and you should remember to say so in an access request.

Appendix A contains a sample letter asking for Sunshine Act records.

What is the relationship between the FOIA and the Sunshine Act?

The Sunshine Act states that it neither "expands nor limits" the rights given by the FOIA, except that the exemptions that allow an agency to withhold transcripts, recordings, or minutes of agency meetings will be those in the Sunshine Act, rather than in the FOIA.[29b] Any documents that are discussed or distributed at a meeting (rather than the record of what was *said* at the meeting) will be processed under the FOIA.[30] This means that if you want a copy of the actual record of what was said at a Sunshine Act meeting, those portions that would otherwise have been unavailable because of the FOIA's exemption (b)(5) will be available under the Sunshine Act, which doesn't contain a comparable exemption. But any background material that is not incorporated into the oral record of the meeting (say, a position paper mentioned at the meeting but never actually incorporated into the record of the meeting) would be processed under FOIA exemptions instead of under Sunshine Act exemptions.

Since the exemptions of the FOIA and the Sunshine Act are not always identical, the kind of information available for agency meetings is somewhat different.

As mentioned earlier, the Sunshine Act has no exemption comparable to the FOIA's (b)(5) exemption for certain kinds of internal memoranda and internal decision-making. In fact, the Sunshine Act was designed to remove some of that traditional confidentiality. This means that if you want a copy of the Sunshine Act record of a meeting, those portions that would have been unavailable under FOIA's (b)(5) exemption will be available.

What can the agency charge for a copy of the record of a meeting?

The Sunshine Act states that "copies of such transcript, or minutes, or a transcription of such recording disclosing the identity of each speaker, shall be furnished to any person at the actual cost of duplication or transcription."[30a] Unlike the FOIA, the Sunshine Act does not permit search fees.

Since it might be expensive to pay the cost of having a recording transcribed, the Sunshine Act legislative history makes it clear that you can ask for (and pay for only) a copy of a tape recording of a meeting, rather than a transcription.[31] Therefore, you should try to find out how to cut costs. (See the earlier discussion on cutting FOIA fees.)

Does the Sunshine Act permit agencies to waive fees for providing copies of the official records?

Yes.[32] You should make the same kinds of arguments as when asking for a waiver of fees under the FOIA.

Sunshine Act Rights in Court

Does the Sunshine Act give me the right to sue in federal court in order to enforce the provisions of the act?

Yes. The Sunshine Act gives "any person" the right to sue in court for alleged violations of the act.[32a] (See chapter 6 for a description of litigation in the federal courts.) The suit can be filed any time before a particular meeting, but not later than 60 days after the meeting under dispute. However, if the agency has not provided a proper public announcement of the particular meeting, the 60 days count from the time that the required announcement was in fact made. And if no announcement was made, the 60-day limit does not apply.[33] (Even if 60 days have passed, you can still sue for a Sunshine Act record under the FOIA as discussed later.[34])

If the provisions of the Sunshine Act have been violated, judges have the authority to order an agency to open a meeting or portion of a meeting, to order release of the record or part of the record, to prohibit a meeting or portion of a meeting from taking place, or to declare some agency practice or decision unlawful.[35]

If the agency loses a Sunshine Act lawsuit, can I win attorney fees and other litigation costs?

Yes. The Sunshine Act provides that the judge may assess

attorney fees and court costs against an agency if you "substantially prevail."[35a] (See chapter 6 for the comparable provision in the FOIA and the Privacy Act).

Are there any risks involved in filing a lawsuit under the Sunshine Act?

Yes. Unlike the FOIA and the Privacy Act, the government's attorney fees and litigation costs may be assessed against you if you lose and if the judge also finds that the suit was filed "primarily for frivolous or dilatory purposes."[35b]

Obviously, no one should be taking any case to court— whether under the Sunshine Act, the FOIA, or what have you—without a serious reason for doing so, but this provision in the Sunshine Act is something that you should discuss and weigh with your lawyer before deciding to file suit. If the suit is for release of a transcript, you might prefer to sue for those records under the FOIA.

If I want to sue for a Sunshine Act violation first, do I have to go through special appeal procedures, like those in the FOIA?

There is no requirement to "exhaust administrative remedies" in the Sunshine Act, but it is always a good idea to try to resolve problems before going to court. When the bill was under consideration, Congress recommended that potential plaintiffs make use of informal channels to set matters straight.[36] Many agencies have issued regulations that set up channels for reviewing complaints and for handling appeals. Ordinarily these regulations will explain to whom an appeal should be written, and so on.[37] For the most part, the principles used for FOIA appeals can be adapted to Sunshine Act appeals.

In what courts can a Sunshine Act lawsuit be filed?

You can sue in the federal district court in the district "where the meeting was or is to be held, where the agency has its headquarters, or in the District of Columbia."[37a] Unlike the FOIA or the Privacy Act, the Sunshine Act fails to give you the right to file suit in the district where you live or have your principal place of business.

Are Sunshine Act suits handled by the courts on an expedited schedule?

Yes and no. For Sunshine Act cases, the defendant agency

must respond to the initial complaint within thirty days rather than the usual sixty days.[37b] However, Sunshine Act suits, unlike FOIA suits, do not by law take precedence over most of the other cases on the court's docket.

Is the burden of proof on the agency, as it is with the FOIA?

Yes. The Sunshine Act specifies that, "The burden is on the defendant to sustain his action."[37c]

In Sunshine Act lawsuits, can judges examine the record of meetings *in camera*, as with FOIA documents?

Yes.[37d] (See the discussion in chapter 6 of *in camera* inspection in FOIA lawsuits.)

In Sunshine Act lawsuits, can judges choose to allow my lawyers to examine the records of meetings and make *in camera* arguments for release?

Yes.[38]

NOTES

1. Robert Rodriguez, *The First Year of Sunshine: Federal Agency Compliance with the Government in the Sunshine Act of 1976*, (Washington, D.C.: Common Cause, Aug. 1978), p. 7.
2. *Id.* at 10–12. For additional information on the record of the agencies in implementing the Sunshine Act requirements, *see*, U.S., Congress, Senate, Committee on Governmental Affairs, Subcommittee on Federal Spending Practices and Open Government, *Oversight of the Government in the Sunshine Act (Public Law 94–409)*, 95th Cong., 1st and 2d sess. (Nov. 29, 1977; June 13 and Aug. 4, 1978).
3. U.S., Congress, Senate, S. Rept. 94–354, 94th Cong., 1st sess., 1975, p. 19.
4. Richard K. Berg and Stephen N. Klitzman, *An Interpretive Guide to the Government in the Sunshine Act* (Washington, D.C.: Administrative Conference of the U.S., June 1978).
4a. 5 U.S.C. Section 552b(a)(1).
5. *Id.* Berg & Klitzman, *supra* note 4, at 112–115. The U.S. Civil Service Commission was formerly on this list; this agency has been restructured into the Office of Personnel Management (OPM), which is not headed by a collegial body and is not, therefore, a Sunshine Act agency. *See also Symons v. Chrysler Corp. Loan Guarantee Board*, 670 F.2d 238 (D.C. Cir. 1981).

6. 5 U.S.C. Section 552(e).

7. *Symons, supra* note 5, at 336.

8. U.S., Congress, House, Government Operations Committee, 94th Cong., 2d sess., 1976, H. Rept. 94–880 (Part 1), p. 7, cited in Berg and Klitzman, *supra* note 4, at 2.

9. *Hunt v. Nuclear Regulatory Commission*, 468 F. Supp. 817 (N.D. Okla. 1979), *aff'd*, 611 F.2d 332 (10th Cir. 1979).

10. *ITT World Communications, Inc. v. Federal Communications Commission*, 699 F.2d 1219 (D.C. Cir. 1983).

11. *Pacific Legal Foundation v. Council on Environmental Quality*, 636 F.2d 1259 (D.C. Cir. 1980).

11a. 5 U.S.C. §552b(a)(2).

12. *Pacific Legal Foundation, supra* note 11.

13. S. Rept. 94–354, *supra* note 3, at 18–19; Berg and Klitzman, *supra* note 4, at 5–6; *ITT World Communications v. FCC, supra* note 10, at 1243–44.

13a. 5 U.S.C. Sections 552b(d) and (e).

14. *Communications Systems Inc. v. Federal Communications Commission*, 595 F.2d 797 (D.C. Cir. 1978); U.S., Congress, House, H. Rept. 94–1441 (Conference Report on the Government in the Sunshine Act), 94th Cong., 2d sess., Aug. 26, 1976, p. 11.

15. 5 U.S.C. Section 552b(d)(1); Conference Report, *supra* note 14, at 17.

16. S. Rept. 94–354, *supra* note 3, at 20; Berg and Klitzman, *supra* note 14, at 17. "Closing a meeting on these grounds is permissive, not mandatory. The agency should not automatically close a meeting because it falls within an exception."

16a. 5 U.S.C. Section 552b(g).

16b. 5 U.S.C. Section 552b(e)(1).

17. S. Rept. 94–354, *supra* note 3, at 30.

18. Berg and Klitzman, *supra* note 4, at 48–49. *See also* Conference Report, *supra* note 14, at 19.

19. *A.G. Becker v. Board of Governors of the Federal Reserve System*, 502 F. Supp. 378 (D.D.C. 1980); *Northwest Airlines, Inc. v. EEOC*, 24 FEP Cases 255 (D.D.C. 1980).

19a. 5 U.S.C. Section 552b(e)(2).

20. Conference Report, *supra* note 14, at 19.

20a. 5 U.S.C. Section 552b(d)(1).

20b. 5 U.S.C. Section 552b(d)(3).

20c. 5 U.S.C. Section 552b(f)(1).

21. S. Rept. 94–354, *supra* note 3, at 27.

21a. 5 U.S.C. Section 552b(d)(1).

21b. 5 U.S.C. Section 552b(d)(3).

21c. 5 U.S.C. Section 552b(d)(2).

22. *See generally* Berg and Klitzman, note 4, at 89–90.

23. *Id.* at 32-34. For a sample letter requesting closing a Sunshine Act meeting, *see* James T. O'Reilly, *Federal Information Disclosure: Procedures, Forms, and the Law* (Colorado Springs: McGraw-Hill, Shepards, 1977), p. F–14.

23a. 5 U.S.C. Section 552b(d)(4).

24. Berg and Klitzman, *supra* note 4, at 38–42.

24a. 5 U.S.C. Section 552b(f)(1).

25. S. Rept. 94–354, *supra* note 3, at 31.

26. Berg and Klitzman, *supra* 4, at 92–94.

27. 5 U.S.C. Section 552b(f)(2); Conference Report, *supra* note 14, at 20.

28. S. Rept. 94–354, *supra* note 3, at 32.

29. *Id*.

29a. 5 U.S.C. Section 552b(f)(2).

29b. 5 U.S.C. Section 552b(k).

30. S. Rept. 94–354, *supra* note 3, at 39; Berg and Klitzman, *supra* note 4, at 97–102.

30a. 5 U.S.C. Section 552b(f)(2).

31. "[I]f a person requests a copy of a tape, rather than a transcription of it, this should also be provided at the actual cost of copying." S. Rept. 94–354, *supra* note 3, at 32.

32. Berg and Klitzman, *supra* note 4, at 78–79.

32a. 5 U.S.C. Section, 552b(h).

33. S. Rept. 94–354, *supra*, note 3, at 33.

34. 5 U.S.C. Section 552b(k); Berg and Klitzman, *supra*, note 4, at 88.

35. 5 U.S.C. Section 552b(h)(1); H. Rept. 94–880, *supra* note 9, at p. 17; S. Rept. 94–354, *supra* note 3, at 33–34; *Pan American World Airways v. Civil Aeronautics Board*, 684 F.2d 31 (D.C. Cir. 1982); *Braniff Master Executive Council, Inc. v. CAB*, 693 F.2d 220 (D.C. Cir. 1982).

35a. 5 U.S.C. Section 552b(i).

35b. 5 U.S.C. Section 552b(i).

36. Conference Report, *supra* note 14, at 22.

37. Berg and Klitzman, *supra* note 4, at 76–78.

37a. 5 U.S.C. Section 552b(h)(1).

37b. *Id*.

37c. *Id*.

37d. *Id*.

38. S. Rept. 94–354, *supra* note 3, at 33, says, "In appropriate cases, [the court] may also permit attorneys for all parties to examine the record of the meeting and argue the case in camera."

VIII

Open Meeting Exemptions

As explained earlier, the Government in the Sunshine Act of 1976 amended the Federal Advisory Committee Act (FACA) so that FACA meetings may be closed to the public only if they meet the Sunshine Act's standards for closing meetings. Therefore, the Sunshine Act exemptions for closing meetings and the FACA exemptions for closing meetings are identical. This discussion on open meeting exemptions will not be repeated in chapter 9, which explains the Federal Advisory Committee Act. In all other respects (for instance, the kinds of meetings covered, the procedures for closing meetings, and redress in court) the Sunshine Act and the FACA are very different and should not be confused. In addition, Sunshine Act documents may be withheld under the Sunshine Act exemptions, but FACA documents may be withheld under the FOIA exemptions instead.

When can a Sunshine Act agency or an advisory committee close a meeting?
An agency may choose to close a meeting or a portion of one if the discussion would be likely to disclose information that falls into one of ten categories of exempt information. But, in order to close the meeting, the agency must also determine that the public's interest does not require that the meeting be open even though some or all of the discussion might touch upon topics that are technically exempt.[1] This explicit balancing test has no parallel in the FOIA or the Privacy Act.

The reader will see that Sunshine Act and FACA exemptions (c)(1), (c)(2), (c)(3), (c)(4), (c)(6), (c)(7), and (c)(8) are identical or virtually identical to corresponding FOIA exemptions. In these instances, the discussions in chapter 4, dealing with the FOIA exemptions, carry over to the Sunshine Act/FACA, and should be referred to.

In practice, however, even identical Sunshine Act/FACA exemptions are broader than those of the FOIA—for the simple reason that agencies are permitted to make plausible guesses about needing to protect some topic that *may* come up, but with the FOIA, you are dealing with information that is already frozen on paper. The protected material is either there or it is not, and deletions of bits and pieces of exempt material can easily be made.

Do the Sunshine Act and the FACA permit agencies to close meetings relating to national security issues?

Yes. The (c)(1) exemption for national security is identical to that in the FOIA.[1a] (See chapter 4).

Are meetings relating to internal agency rules and practices open under the Sunshine Act and the FACA?

Sunshine and FACA exemption (c)(2) is identical to the second exemption of the FOIA.[1b] (See chapter 4.) The D.C. Circuit has found that this exemption cannot be used to close Sunshine meetings held by the Nuclear Regulatory Commission (NRC) to discuss its budget, because such budgeting does not relate "solely" to internal personnel matters.[2]

Can agencies invoke other statutes governing public access in order to close a meeting?

Yes. Sunshine and FACA exemption (c)(3)[2a] closely parallels the (b)(3) exemption of the FOIA. (See chapter 4.)

Can agencies close a meeting where trade secrets, or commercial or financial information, will be discussed?

Yes. Exemption (c)(4) of the Sunshine Act and the FACA is identical to the (b)(4) exemption of the FOIA[3]. (See chapter 4.)

Can meetings be closed when sanctions will be considered against an individual or a corporation?

Yes. The Sunshine Act and FACA allow agencies to close meetings at which discussion would be likely to "involve accusing any person of a crime or formally censuring any person."[3a] The Sunshine Act (c)(5) exemption does not have a parallel in the FOIA. Since the mere fact that an agency was considering making an accusation may damage a reputation, the purpose of the (c)(5) Sunshine Act exemption is to protect persons (including businesses) if the agency decides there was insufficient basis for accusing them.[4]

According to the legislative history of the Sunshine Act, agencies should not use this exemption every time a meeting might put a company in a bad light—some formal agency action must actually be under discussion before a meeting can be properly closed by citing (c)(5). It is meant to include meetings to discuss whether a particular case should be referred to the Department of Justice for prosecution, or whether the agency should issue a "formal reprimand."

Can meetings be closed in order to protect personal privacy?

Yes. The Sunshine Act and FACA exemption (c)(6) allows agencies to close meetings that would "disclose information of a personal nature where disclosure would constitute a clearly unwarranted invasion of personal privacy."[4a]

This is very similar to the (b)(6) exemption for personal privacy found in the FOIA.[5] (See chapter 4.)

If a meeting is closed by citing Sunshine and FACA exemption (c)(6) for personal privacy, can the individual whose privacy is being protected insist that the meeting be an open one?

Yes. If the individual involved wants the issues dealt with at an open meeting, the agency cannot invoke the (c)(6) privacy exemption to close the meeting.[6] (The meeting, of course, could still be closed if the agency could claim some other Sunshine Act exemption.)

This does not, however, give individuals the power to insist that matters concerning them be handled at meetings. The agencies could still use the procedure of passing memos around for notation.

Can meetings be closed if matters contained in law enforcement records are to be discussed?

Yes. The Sunshine Act and the FACA (c)(7) exemption for law enforcement records is based on the FOIA exemption for such records. Under the Sunshine Act and the FACA, the meetings may be closed if the discussion to be held would be likely to disclose certain kinds of law enforcement investigatory records.[6a] The only significant distinction between this exemption and the FOIA's (b)(7) exemption (discussed in chapter 4) is that the Sunshine Act exemption protects oral as well as written law enforcement material.

The FOIA's Exemption 7, by contrast, specifies protection for only *records,* but since the FOIA only provides access to records (and not to oral statements as they are being made and before they have been transcribed, summarized, or otherwise recorded) the issue was not important when the FOIA provision was drafted.

Do high government officials have the same privacy protections under Sunshine Act and FACA exemptions as lower-level employees and private citizens?

Like the FOIA, the Sunshine Act and FACA privacy exemptions (c)(6) and (c)(7)(C) provide for a balancing test. The agency or committee may decide that the public's interest in knowing about some personal matters may outweigh the privacy interests of the individual. But in addition to the general balancing test, the legislative history suggests that high government officials may have fewer privacy rights than lower officials and private citizens.[7]

Can Sunshine and FACA meetings be closed if they deal with reports about financial institutions?

Yes. The (c)(8) Sunshine and FACA exemption[7a] is identical to the (b)(8) exemption of the FOIA and should be interpreted the same way.[8] (See chapter 4.)

Can Sunshine and FACA meetings be closed if the discussion could lead to financial speculation or financial instability?

Yes. Part A of exemption (c)(9) allows the closing of a Sunshine Act or FACA meeting that would be likely to

disclose information the premature disclosure of which would—

   (A) in the case of an agency which regulates currencies, securities, commodities, or financial institutions, be likely to (i) lead to significant financial speculation in currencies, securities, or commodities, or (ii) significantly endanger the stability of any financial institution.[8a]

Exemption (c)(9)(A) is designed to prevent potential invest-ors from learning of future government policies in time to make investments that would permit windfall profits. It is also intended to prevent panic reactions with investors pull-ing money out of financial institutions. Financial institutions include

banks
savings and loan associations
credit unions
brokers and dealers in securities or commodities
exchanges dealing in securities or commodities (such as the
    New York Stock Exchange)
investment companies
investment advisors[9]

Some of the agencies that can claim Sunshine Act exemp-tion (c)(9)(A) are the Federal Reserve Board, the Securi-ties and Exchange Commission (SEC), the Federal Deposit Insurance Corporation (FDIC), and the Commodity Credit Corporation.

Since this exemption applies only where there is "significant" danger, the agency must estimate whether the impact is significant enough to outweigh the public's interest in attend-ing an open meeting. You might argue, then, that no "significant" danger exists.

Can a Sunshine Act or FACA meeting be closed if it is claimed that an open meeting would frustrate a proposed agency action?
Yes, but within limitations. Part B of (c)(9) provides that agencies can close meetings if the discussion would

disclose information the premature disclosure of which would . . .
    (B) in the case of any agency, be likely to significantly
    frustrate implementation of a proposed agency action,
except that subparagraph (B) shall not apply in any in-stance where the agency had already disclosed to the public the content or nature of its proposed action, or where the agency is required by law to make such disclo-sure on its own initiative prior to taking final agency action on such proposal.[9a]

This is a difficult exemption for both sides to interpret, because agencies could probably argue that, if the public knew the full range of the internal agency controversies, agency goals could be "frustrated." The fact that this exemption can be claimed by any government agency or advisory committee, and not just one that deals with, say, financial regulation, also makes this a potentially very sweeping exemption. The Sunshine Act's (c)(9)(B) exemption, then, must be applied narrowly or the entire statute would be effectively gutted. Its scope is limited since it applies only to "significant" frustrations of agency action; any possible hindrances that are less than significant cannot be the basis for a (9)(B) exemption.

The legislative history provides some concrete examples of the kinds of effects that the (9)(B) exemption is meant to prevent. For example, if an agency is considering placing an embargo on certain goods, and if this became public knowledge before the proposal went into effect, then the embargo could be frustrated by shipping the goods quickly.[10] Or public disclosure of agency bargaining positions might make it impossible to reach an agreement.[11] Or if it were revealed in advance that the agency was committing itself to making a particular purchase, a quick investor might be able to make a windfall profit.[12]

Some applications have been more controversial. The Office of Management and Budget (OMB), for instance, has argued that an agency can close a meeting that will discuss the agency's budget before it is submitted to Congress.[13] This position, however, was struck down when Common Cause challenged the Nuclear Regulatory Commission's decision to close its budget deliberations.[14]

In situations where the proposed action is already public knowledge or is supposed to be public knowledge, can a Sunshine Act or a FACA meeting be closed by claiming that openness would frustrate agency action?

No. While a Sunshine Act or a FACA meeting can be closed if the substance of the proposed action has only "leaked" out unofficially,[15] Sunshine Act and FACA exemption (c)(9)(B) cannot be used to close a meeting dealing with actions that have already been made public. By the same token, an agency may be required by some other statute to announce its proposals before taking action, and in such situations it could not close a meeting.[16]

Can Sunshine Act and FACA meetings be closed when they deal with an agency's role in some adversary proceeding, such as a lawsuit or an administrative hearing?

Yes. Sunshine Act and FACA exemption (c)(10) allows agencies to close meetings that would be likely to reveal information that would

> specifically concern the agency's issuance of a subpoena, or the agency's participation in a civil action or proceeding, an action in a foreign court or international tribunal, or an arbitration, or the initiation, conduct, or disposition by the agency of a particular case or formal agency adjudication pursuant to the procedures in section 554 of this title or otherwise involving a determination on the record after opportunity for a hearing.[16a]

In other words, an agency does not have to open meetings that would reveal its own legal strategy; nor should it be engaging in public discussions of the guilt or innocence of some other party.

However, an agency cannot cite exemption (c)(10) for closing a general discussion of its legal strategies and policies. To justify closing a particular meeting, an agency must cite *specific* cases, ones that are either actually pending or under consideration.[17] For example, the Postal Service Board of Governors was able to close a Sunshine Act meeting by citing exemption (c)(10) when it scheduled discussions of a postal rate hike. A court was persuaded that the possibility that litigation might arise over a rate increase was enough to justify closing the meeting.[18]

The Sunshine Act and FACA exemption (c)(10) overlaps in some ways with the FOIA exemption (b)(5) insofar as it deals with attorney-client and attorney-work product material.

In summary, what are the major differences between the exemptions of the FOIA and those of the Sunshine Act and FACA?

First, in practice the Sunshine Act and FACA exemptions are broader than the FOIA exemptions because they deal with what might be discussed, rather than with what is already on record. When dealing with a written record, a particular bit of information either does or does not appear; there is no speculation about its existence or probability. The Sunshine Act and FACA exemptions, by contrast, permit agencies to close a meeting "likely to disclose" exempt material (meaning that disclosure "is more likely than not" to occur).[19] And while this standard for closing meetings is not so broad as agency proposals during the drafting of the Sunshine Act, it will be hard indeed for you to prove where honest caution ends and abuse takes place. Similarly, while the FOIA permits the deletion of an exempt sentence or paragraph while the rest of the record is released, it is not possible to delete words or phrases from an ongoing meeting.

The FOIA also differs from the Sunshine Act and the FACA exemptions in that the latter's fifth exemption does not cover advice and predecisional material. This is a major shift. Instead, the Sunshine Act and FACA (c)(5) exemption provides protection for any person being considered for possible accusations or censure.

The FOIA's ninth exemption protects oil wells. The Sunshine Act and the FACA make no mention of such a category of protected information. Instead, Sunshine Act and FACA exemption (c)(9) relates to financial matters (particularly to financial matters on which an agency might have an impact) and to frustration of agency actions. This exemption has no FOIA parallel.

The Sunshine Act and the FACA's tenth exemption, protecting agency plans in adversarial proceedings, also has no clear FOIA parallel, although it does overlap in many ways with the FOIA's exemption (b)(5), protecting some material involving the attorney-client privilege and the attorney-work product.

NOTES

1. 5 U.S.C. Section 552b(c).
1a. 5 U.S.C. Section 552b(c)(1).
1b. 5 U.S.C. Section 552b(c)(2). *See also,* U.S., Congress, House, *Conference Report on the Government in the Sunshine Act*, 94th Cong., 2d sess., Aug. 26, 1976, H. Rept. 94–1441, p. 15, reprinted in *Conference Report on the Government in the Sunshine Act*, 94th Cong., 2d, sess., Aug. 26, 1976, H. Rept. 94–1441, p. 15, reprinted in Christine M. Marwick, ed., *The 1981 Edition of Litigation under the Federal Freedom of Information and Privacy Acts* (Washington,

D.C.: Center for National Security Studies, 1980. *Also see, Dept of the Air Force v. Rose*, 425 U.S. 352 (1976).

2. *Common Cause v. NRC*, 67 F.2d 921 (D.C. Cir. 1982).

2a. 5 U.S.C Section 552b(c)(3).

3. 5 U.S.C. Section 552b(c)(4); *See also Conference Report*, note 1b at 15.

3a. 5 U.S.C. Section 552b(c)(5).

4. Rep. 94–354, 94th Cong., 1st sess., 1975, p. 22.

4a. 5 U.S.C. Section 552b(c)(6).

5. S. Rept. 94–354, *supra* note 4, at 21.

6. *Id.* at 22; U.S., Congress, House, Government Operations Committee, 94th Cong., 2d sess., 1976, H. Rept. 94–880, p.7. *See also* Richard K. Berg and Stephen N. Klitzman, *An Interpretive Guide to the Government in the Sunshine Act*, (Washington, D.C.: Administrative Conference of the U.S., June 1978), p.2.

6a. 5 U.S.C. Section 552b(c)(7).

7. S. Rept. 94–354, *supra* note 4, at 21–22; H. Rept. 94–880, *supra* note 6, at 11.

7a. 5 U.S.C. Section 552b(c)(8).

8. S. Rept. 94–354, *supra* note 4, at 25.

8a. 5 U.S.C. Section 552b(c)(9)(A).

9. S. Rept. 94–354, *supra* note 4, at 24.

9a. 5 U.S.C. Section 552b(c)(9)(B).

10. S. Rept. 94–354, *supra* note 4, at 24.

11. *Id.*

12. *Conference Report, supra* note 1b, at 15.

13. OMB Circular No. A-10, Section 7 (revised, Nov. 12, 1976); *See* Berg and Klitzman, *supra* note 6, at 25.

14. *Common Cause, supra* note 2.

15. *Conference Report, supra* note 1b, at 15.

16. S. Rept. 94–354, *supra* note 4, at 25.

16a. 5 U.S.C. Section 552b(c)(10).

17. S. Rept. 94–354, *supra* note 4, at 26.

18. *Time, Inc. v. U.S. Postal Service*, 667 F.2d 329 (2d Cir. 1981).

19. *Conference Report, supra* note 1b, at 15.

IX

The Federal Advisory Committee Act

What was Congress's intention in enacting the Federal Advisory Committee Act (FACA)?

Congress had found that while there were a great many federal advisory committees, there was very little regulation to ensure that they accomplished something useful. In the early 1970s, when the FACA was under consideration, there were estimated to have been as many as 3,200 advisory committees, costing about $75,000,000 a year. It was found that obsolete committees were sometimes never phased out, and that many committees produced recommendations that were completely ignored and reports that were lost to the public. There was also a threat that some committees, composed as they are of people from outside the government, might end up representing their own private interests rather than working for the well-being of the general public. Congress became concerned that they were quite possibly exercising excessive influence on government decision-making.[1]

To counterbalance this risk of undue influence, the 1972 FACA includes a provision that opens meetings of federal advisory committees to the public. But as mentioned earlier, opening up proceedings to the scrutiny of outside critics was only one of the benefits the act set out to accomplish. The FACA's main focus was the general regulation of such committees. And as a result, the procedures for enforcing the open meeting provisions are weaker than those of the Sunshine Act, which goes into considerably more detail about how open meetings are to come about. By contrast, the FACA's open meeting provisions are extremely brief, and they lack self-enforcing mechanisms. The law's omissions point up how strong the other access statutes are.

What is a "federal advisory committee" covered by the terms of the FACA?

The FACA broadly defines a *federal advisory committee* as "any committee, board, commission, council, conference, panel, task force, or similar group" that has been set up so that federal officials, including the President, can obtain advice and recommendations. The definition also includes any subgroups of such bodies. To qualify as a FACA committee, the group cannot be a federal agency, which is to say that its function must be limited to giving advice, rather than also exercising some authority.[2] In addition, there must be some formality to the creation of or utilization of a FACA committee: it must be either set up by a federal statute or by a reorganization plan, or it must be set up or utilized by the President or an agency. And the committee membership cannot consist entirely of full-time federal employees; it must be at least partially outside the federal government.[2a]

Are any advisory committees, or categories of advisory committees, explicitly exempted from the provisions of the FACA?

Yes. The FACA specifically exempts a number of committees that might otherwise have been covered.

In addition to exempting committees that are composed entirely of federal employees, it exempts both the Advisory Committee on Intergovernmental Relations and the now defunct Commission on Government Procurement.[2b]

Committees that have been established or utilized by the Central Intelligence Agency (CIA) or the Federal Reserve System are also exempt.[2c]

The FACA specifically states that none of its provisions apply to

> any local civic group whose primary function is that of rendering a public service with respect to a Federal program, or any State or local committee, council, board, commission, or similar group established to advise or make recommendations to State or local officials or agencies.[2d]

The act also states that, when Congress establishes federal advisory committees, it may also set up provisions different from those of the FACA in order to regulate those particular committees.[2e] This means that it may sometimes be necessary to find out about a committee's origin in order to determine if it is in compliance with the law. If a committee is established by executive branch action it must follow FACA provisions (unless it falls under one of the classes of exemptions just mentioned). If the committee was established by statute after 1972, there *may* be some variation in the requirements.

In addition, the FACA's legislative history makes it clear that the act does not apply to federal contractors, even where they might function very much like an advisory committee.[3]

It should be fairly clear that these definitions and exceptions create some rather large gray areas. There are after all a great many private groups and clusters of citizens, both formal and informal, that put considerable effort into giving the government advice. Some groups may exist for the purpose of giving the government a torrent of advice and yet not fall under the FACA's definition of an *advisory committee*. Such a group may have been established for the purpose of improving communications generally, and the FACA does not address communications generally. The two key factors in deciding whether a group should be considered an FACA committee seem to be whether it has an established structure and whether it has a defined purpose for which an agency intends to use it. Casual, informal groups, brought together without a request for specific recommendations do not fall under the act.[4]

This gray area is important because the FACA gives the public the right to insist that all advisory committees that fit its definition be formally chartered and follow the procedures that the act lays out. If some group seems to be an undeclared advisory committee, it may be possible to challenge the propriety of its status in court and get an injunction against future meetings with the agency unless it abides by the FACA provisions.[5] This may be particularly useful if you are disputing the advice the group is giving the agency or if you feel that some "informal" gray area group is exerting excessive influence. Some groups have been disbanded rather than meet FACA rules.[6] As with the other access statutes, agencies have sometimes shown resistance that goes beyond a simple exploitation of gray areas.[7]

How do I find out about the functions of a particular advisory committee?

Whether a committee is set up by statute, by presidential action, or by an agency head, the FACA places certain requirements on their creators: they are supposed to formally charter the committee. The act specifies that committees are not supposed to meet or take action unless a charter has been filed with either the Director of the Office of Management and Budget (OMB) or (in the case of presidential committees) with the head of the agency to which the committee reports. Among other things, this charter is supposed to specify the objectives of the committee, the time period in which it is supposed to operate, its duties and cost, the agency or people to whom it reports, the estimated number of meetings it will hold, and its estimated termination date.[7a]

These charters may prove helpful if you want to learn about committee functions in order to find out whether you want to attend its meetings, and they also provide a starting point for challenging a committee that has not been properly established or that goes beyond its original mandate.

What kinds of information does the FACA require be published?

The FACA requires that certain categories of information be published in the *Federal Register*. When an advisory committee is established, notice of the fact is supposed to be published in the *Federal Register*.[7b] "Timely notice" of each advisory committee meeting is also supposed to be published in the *Federal Register*.[7c]

To someone using the FACA, the timely notice requirement is ordinarily the more important of the two publication provisions.

This advance notice of meetings is supposed to include a description of the meeting's schedule and location, and whether or not the meeting is to be closed. If the meeting is closed, the notice is supposed to state the exemption or exemptions that authorize closing. (This will be discussed in more detail later on in this chapter.)

This "timely notice" requirement does not apply, however, "when the President determines otherwise for reasons of national security." This presidential exception is not defined in the statute, so it can be applied quite broadly. Since it is undefined, it does not depend on the possible discussion of "properly classified" material, as does the Sunshine Act and FACA exemption for closing meetings.[8]

The FACA also leaves unsaid how much advance warning actually constitutes "timely notice" of a scheduled event. The OMB Guidelines for the implementation of the FACA suggest fifteen days' advance notice,[9] and various court decisions suggest thirty days' notice,[10] but agencies have been faulted for not complying with either standard.[11]

Are advisory committees supposed to make use of informal means of announcing an upcoming meeting, in addition to publication in the *Federal Register*?

Yes. Regulations are supposed to ensure that other forms of notice are used, so that "all interested persons are notified."[11a]

What kinds of advisory committee meetings are supposed to be open to the public?

The FACA establishes that "each advisory committee meeting shall be open to the public,"[11b] except for portions that are likely to involve the discussion of matters protected by the exemptions enumerated in the Government in the Sunshine Act.

As mentioned in the preceding chapter, the provisions for closing meetings in the Sunshine Act and in the FACA have been identical since 1976. (The FACA exemptions were at first pegged to those of the FOIA, but that was changed when the Sunshine Act was passed.) (See chapter 8.)

Does the FACA provide the public the right to participate in open advisory committee meetings?

No. The public is permitted to attend strictly as an observer, even though the FACA states, "[I]nterested persons shall be permitted to attend, appear before, or file statements with any advisory committee, subject to such reasonable rules or regulations as the Director [of OMB] may prescribe."[11c] This language is tantalizing, for it seems to suggest that members of the public may choose, at their discretion, to participate in such meetings. But this is not the case. This subsection of the FACA is merely an affirmation that advisory committees can of course ask for advice or accept advice offered by interested parties or by outside experts. It does not add up to the right to participate in the committee meetings, except insofar as the committee or agency chooses.[12]

This provision does present a challenge in that it reminds the public that it can and should make greater efforts to influence agency and committee deliberations. Those who feel that they have something to contribute to an advisory committee's review of some issue can always request to appear before the committee and can file position papers. But the committee does not have to read what is submitted or grant an appearance.

Can an advisory committee meeting that started out as an open meeting be suddenly adjourned?

Yes. The FACA establishes that all advisory committee meetings held under the provisions of the act *must* be chaired or attended by a designated federal employee or officer. This official is authorized by the act to adjourn a meeting "whenever he determines it to be in the public interest" to do so.[12a]

What kinds of records does the FACA require agencies and advisory committees to compile concerning FACA committee operations and meetings?

The FACA requires several kinds of records and reports to be compiled.

1. The President is required to submit a yearly report to Congress each March 31. This report is supposed to include information on all advisory committees that existed the preceding calendar year. For each committee, this report is supposed to set out whether the committee is a continuing or an *ad hoc* body; the committee's functions; information concerning committee reports; the dates of its meetings; names and occupations of each committee's members; and so on. If any information is withheld for national security reasons, the presidential report must say so.[12b]

2. As previously discussed, each committee is supposed to have a charter.

3. If meetings are closed, each advisory committee is supposed to issue an annual report concerning such closures.

4. Agencies are supposed to keep detailed financial records of their advisory committees' operations and the support services provided to them.[12c]

5. "Detailed minutes" of meetings must be kept. These

are supposed to include a record of who attended, copies of reports "received, issued, or approved," and a "complete and accurate description" of what was discussed.[12d]

6. Finally, and certainly not least, advisory committees are supposed to produce reports, which are to contain the committee's recommendations for the agency or the President. These reports, together with "appropriate background papers," are supposed to be filed with the Library of Congress, and made available to the public under the provisions of the FOIA.[12e]

Does the public have the right of access to the written records (including meetings) of FACA committees?

Yes. The public may request FACA records under the provisions of the FOIA. The FACA specifies that "records, reports, transcripts, minutes, appendixes, working papers, drafts, studies, agenda, or other documents" that are used by an advisory committee must be made available under the provisions of the FOIA.[12f]

This creates something of a paradox, since the FOIA's exemptions apply to agency *records* and are not identical to the Sunshine Act and FACA exemptions (see chapter 8), which specify the grounds for closing agency *meetings*. This means that two different standards apply to the same material, depending on whether it is on paper or under discussion at a meeting.

For example, the FOIA's exemption (b)(5) permits agencies to withhold information that would reveal advice contained in memoranda within the executive branch. But this exemption does not carry over to Sunshine Act and FACA meetings: advisory committee meetings may not be closed because advice is likely to come up for discussion. However, even though the advice privilege does not provide grounds for closing a meeting, when that same advice appears in the written transcript of a meeting and is reviewed under the standards of the FOIA, it may be deleted by citing exemption (b)(5). Of course, since the FOIA exemptions do not protect information that has been previously released, nothing concerning advice that was said at an *open* meeting would be exempt. But many FACA meetings are closed on other grounds, and the advice contained in the transcripts of closed meetings may be withheld when reviewed under the FOIA.

Is there an official at each agency who has the primary responsibility for seeing that that agency's advisory committees comply with the FACA?

Yes. The FACA sets up a number of management controls for advisory committees. Among others, the act requires that each agency have an Advisory Committee Management Officer. This officer controls and supervises that agency's advisory committees; is in charge of all advisory committee reports, records, and so on; and is responsible for handling FOIA requests for the advisory committees' materials.[12g]

The Advisory Committee Management Officer is the person to contact when questions arise, but may not be as helpful as members of the public might wish. Indeed, these officers may see their primary job as making sure that the committees' interests run smoothly and quietly, rather than openly. This varies from agency to agency, of course.

What recourse is available if an advisory committee is violating the provisions of the FACA, such as closing meetings without a basis for doing so, or not being properly chartered as a committee?

The FACA fails to provide a simple and easy basis for citizen's suits, in the way that the other access statutes do. In fact, it is quite silent on the subject.

However, suits have been brought successfully under the Administrative Procedure Act (APA).[13] But, as explained in the discussion of reverse FOIA lawsuits in chapter 6, it is more difficult to bring a suit under the APA than under the FOIA or the Privacy Act. Under the APA, you must be able to prove that you have standing to sue—a clear investment in the outcome of the case. A plaintiff must be able to "allege and prove a 'distinct and palpable injury to himself' as the threshold requirements for standing to sue."[14] Public interest organizations may sometimes be able to establish such standing.[15]

By comparison, the FOIA, the Privacy Act, and, for that matter, the Sunshine Act, all permit "any person" to sue in federal court; you do not have to establish anything beyond the fact that you want access to certain information or a certain meeting and have been denied that access.

NOTES

1. U.S., Congress, Senate, 92d Cong., 2d sess., 1972, S. Rept. 92–1098, p. 6: "The lack of public scrutiny of the activities of advisory committees was found to pose the danger that subjective influences not in the public interest could be exerted on Federal decisionmakers." *See also*, U.S., Congress, House, Committee on Government Operations, Subcommittee on Special Studies, *Presidential Advisory Committee Hearings*, 91st Cong., 2d sess., 1970; U.S., Congress, House, 91st Cong., 2d sess., 1970, H. Rept. 91–1731. Christine M. Marwick, ed., *The 1981 Edition of Litigation under the Federal Freedom of Information Act and Privacy Act* (Washington, D.C.: Center for National Security Studies, 1980) contains a bibliography of FACA cases and material on Appendix pp. 132–133; James T. O'Reilly, *Federal Information Disclosure* (Colorado Springs: McGraw-Hill, Shepards, 1977) contains a chapter on the FACA; *Government Disclosure Service* (Englewood Cliffs, N.J.: Prentice-Hall, 1979) contains a brief summary. The enactment of the FACA is largely the result of the efforts of Rep. John S. Monagan (D.-Conn.) and Sen. Lee Metcalf (D.-Mont.).

2. The FACA's definition of an *agency* appears at 5 U.S.C. Section 551(1). It is a narrower definition than that in the FOIA, 5 U.S.C. Section 552(e), which also includes government-controlled corporations.

2a. 5 U.S.C. Appendix I, Section 3(2).

2b. Id.

2c. 5 U.S.C. Appendix I, Section 4(c).

2d. Id.

2e. 5 U.S.C. Appendix I, Section 4(a).

3. *Lombardo v. Handler*, 397 F. Supp. 792 (D.D.C. 1975) (neither the American Academy of Sciences nor its subgroups are subject to either the FACA or the FOIA).

4. *Nader v. Baroody*, 396 F. Supp. 1231 (D.D.C. 1975), *vacated as moot*, No. 75–1969 (D.C. Cir. Jan. 10, 1077).

5. *Gates v. Schlesinger*, 360 F. Supp. 797 (D.D.C. 1973).

6. U.S., Congress, Senate, Committee on Government Affairs, *Study of Federal Regulation: Volume III, Public Participation in Regulatory Agency Proceedings*, 95th Cong., 1st sess., 1977, p. 157.

7. There is, for example, a fairly dramatic account of two Senate staffers who tried to attend a FACA meeting and ran into the following obstacles: they were lied to (told no space was available when there was, and told that the meeting had already adjourned when it had not); they were told it was an open meeting, which happened to be held in the controlled-access Executive Office Building to which (Catch-22) they could not be given access; and they were implicitly threatened when a security guard conspicuously loaded his revolver as they were trying to negotiate access to the meeting. *Id.* at 149–150, citing 119 *Congressional Record*, S. 19,371 (daily ed., Oct. 18, 1973) (remarks of Senator Metcalf).

7a. 5 U.S.C. Appendix I, Section 9(c).

7b. 5 U.S.C. Appendix I, Section 9(a)(2)

7c. 5 U.S.C. Appendix I, Section 10(a)(2).

8. 5 U.S.C. Section 552b(c)(1).

9. 39 *Fed. Reg.* 12,390 (1974).

10. *Gates supra* note 5.

11. For a comprehensive critique of the way in which the FACA has been poorly implemented, *see* Barbara Tuerkheimer, "Veto by Neglect: The Federal Advisory Committee Act," 25 *Amer. U. L. Rev.* 53 (1975); for a discussion of implementation of FACA notice provision in particular, *see* p. 73 of the Tuerkheimer article.

11a. 5 U.S.C. Appendix I, Section 10(a)(2).

11b. 5 U.S.C. Appendix I, Section 10(a)(1).

11c. 5 U.S.C. Appendix I, Section 10(a)(3).

12. *Gates supra,* note 5. "Plaintiffs have not pointed out, however, any statutory language creating a right of public participation in advisory committees, and the Court can find none. The Court will order that the meeting be open to the public as observers."

12a. 5 U.S.C. Appendix I, Section 10(e).

12b. 5 U.S.C. Appendix I, Section 6(c).

12c. 5 U.S.C. Appendix I, Section 12.

12d. 5 U.S.C. Appendix I, Section 10(c).

12e. 5 U.S.C. Appendix I, Section 13

12f. 5 U.S.C. Appendix I, Section 10(b).

12g. 5 U.S.C. Appendix I, Section 8(b).

13. 5 U.S.C. Section 706. See *Gates,* supra, note 5

14. *Metcalf v. National Petroleum Council,* 407 F. Supp. 257 (D.D.C. 1976), aff'd, 553 F.2d 176, 187 (D.C. Cir. 1977); *Mulqueeny v. National Commission on the Observation of International Women's Year,* 549 F.2d 1115 (7th Cir. 1977).

15. *Nader v. Baroody, supra* note 4.

Appendix A:

Sample Letters

This section provides samples of some of the kinds of letters that people requesting access to information regularly write. A few caveats on writing your own letters should be helpful here.

1. There is no magic formula for writing request letters, appeal letters, and all the other items in the paper war that getting access can sometimes become. These sample letters are meant as suggestions; in fact, they fall a long way short of covering every possible situation.

2. These samples can and should be shortened, lengthened, altered and otherwise tinkered with in order to fit each particular situation. A reasonably careful reading of the earlier sections of this book will suggest other points you might prefer to make, or might have to make.

3. The only ironclad rule is to try to be clear. There is no reason to assume, just because the letters and material you receive from the government may be couched in bureaucratic obfuscation, that government employees can themselves decipher vague or evasive letters that they may receive.

4. In writing your letters while referring to these samples, don't be confused by the parentheses and brackets—include what's in the curved parentheses; follow the italic instructions in square brackets.

Request for General Information under the FOIA

> [*Your Name*
> *Address*
> *Daytime Phone Number*
> *Date* _____

Address your FOIA request to the FOIA
Office of the appropriate agency
or agencies; see Appendix D.

Dear Sir or Madam:

This is a request under the Freedom of Information Act (5 U.S.C. Section 552.)

I write to request a copy of [*give a clear description of the material that you want; include whatever information you think might make the agency's search easier*].

[*Optional paragraph, to be adapted if you believe it would help identify the material requested*]: To help avoid any misunderstanding of what records are being requested, I am enclosing a copy of a news account [*or government report, or book, whatever*] which refers to this material.

If the requested records are not in the possession of your agency, I ask that you forward this request to any agency that you believe may have records that are responsive to this request. In the alternative, I ask that you inform me of other agencies that might have such records.

As you know, the FOIA provides that even if some requested material is properly exempt from mandatory disclosure, all segregable portions must be released [5 U.S.C. Section 552(b)]. If all material covered by this request is withheld, please inform me of the specific exemptions that are being claimed.

If the requested material is released with deletions, I ask that each deletion be marked to indicate the exemption(s) being claimed to authorize each particular withholding.

In addition, I ask that your agency exercise its discretion to release information that may be technically exempt but where withholding would serve no important public interest.

[*If you are not requesting the material for a commercial purpose, you can ask for a waiver or reduction of fees*]: As you know, the FOIA provides that agencies may reduce or waive fees if it would be "in the public interest because furnishing the information can be considered as primarily benefitting the public." [5 U.S.C. Section 552(a)(4)(A)]. I believe release of this material would be of benefit to the public because _____[*Add a brief explanation of the public benefit; you can always follow through with a more detailed fee waiver letter—see the following sample.*] I therefore ask that you waive any fees relating to this request. If you rule otherwise, and if the fees will total more than $_____, I ask that you inform me of the charges before you fill my request.

[*Include this paragraph if your request is for a great many documents and you expect that you will not want copies of all of them. You must be prepared to travel to the location where the records are kept*]: If you do not grant my request for a fee waiver, and if the copying fees are more than $_____, I ask that provision be made so that I may review the records I am requesting and without incurring duplication costs, select those documents that I want copied.

If you have any questions regarding this request, please telephone me at the above number. I would be happy to discuss ways in which this request could be clarified or somewhat redesigned to reflect the agency's filing system and speed the search for records.

As provided under the FOIA, I will expect a reply within 10 working days.

Sincerely,

[*Your Signature
Name
Title, if writing on behalf of an
    organization*]

[*No need to have signature notarized
or to provide identification if you
are not requesting your own files.*]
[*Mark envelope*]: Attn:
Freedom of Information Unit

Request for Personal Records under the FOIA/PA

> [*Your Name*
> *Address*
> *Daytime Phone Number*
> *Date*]

Address your request to the FOIA/PA
Office of the appropriate agency
or agencies; see Appendix D.

Dear *Sir or Madam:*

This is a request under the Freedom of Information Act (5 U.S.C. Section 552) and the Privacy Act (5 U.S.C. Section 552a).

I write to request a copy of all agency records relating to me.

[*Add this paragraph if you are writing to the FBI*]: Please inform me if your index or indexes show that there are "See References" indicating that my name appears in files under captions other than my name, so that I can decide whether to have such files searched. [*If you know of particular filing systems within the agency that are likely to contain information about you, add an identification of these systems; when writing the FBI, for example, you might want to say*]: My request includes, but is not limited to, any material regarding me that may be found in your main files, electronic surveillance indexes, and "Do Not File" files, which are described by the Church Committee Report on Intelligence Activities, S. Rept. 94–755.

In order to help your search for these materials, I am including the following information. [*Include whatever additional information you believe would help locate and identify your particular records; for example*]:

Other names I have used:_____. [*Include nicknames; variations of your name, with or without the middle initial; names reflecting previous marital statuses; even women who have never used their husband's name should ask for a check of such variations as Mrs. John Doe, Mrs. Jack Doe, and Mrs. Mary Doe.*]

Other places I have lived, worked or visited:_____. [*Include dates.*]

I have applied for government employment or worked for

the government in the following capacities:_____. [*Mention government offices, programs, contracts, grants, and so forth*.]

I specifically ask that you check the political surveillance records from the following programs:_____, particularly in regard to the following events_____and organizations_____. [*You might want to add dates and locations*.]

My date of birth is_____; my place of birth is_____; my Social Security number is_____; my government employment number [*if applicable*] is_____.

The following information may also be of use in locating and identifying my records:_____. [*Be creative in helping the searchers*.]

[*If you are not writing field offices separately, include this sentence*]: This request includes a search for additional records in your agency's field or regional offices in the following locations: _____. [*Remember, with some agencies such as the FBI, each such office must be written separately. FBI field office addresses are included in Appendix D*.]

As you know, the FOIA requires that even if some material is properly exempt from mandatory disclosure, all segregable portions must be released. If all material covered by this request is withheld, please inform me of the specific exemptions that are being claimed; if material is being released with deletions, I ask that each deletion be marked to indicate which exemption(s) is (are) being claimed to authorize each particular withholding. In addition, I ask that your agency exercise its discretion to release information that may be technically exempt but where withholding would serve no important public interest.

I am prepared to pay reasonable fees for the material that I am requesting. However, I ask that if the fees will total more than $_____ that I be informed before the fees are incurred.

In addition, the FOIA states that fees should be reduced or waived when release of information would be of benefit to the public. Since the release of files to the subjects of those files is important for the protection of personal privacy in our society, I believe that the fees that would be incurred by this request should be waived, or, in the alternative, reduced.

[*If you know that you will not want your complete file, if you want to save copying fees, and if you are prepared to go to the location where the records are kept, you can include this sentence*]: If you do not grant my request for a fee waiver, and if the copying fees will be more than $_____, I ask that provisions be made so that I can review the records I am requesting and to select those documents that I want copied.

If you have any questions regarding this request, please contact me at the above number. I would be happy to discuss ways in which this request could be clarified or redesigned to speed the search for records.

As provided under the FOIA, I will expect a reply within ten working days.

> Sincerely,
>
> *[Your Notarized signature*
> *Name*
> *Social Security Number*
> *Date and Place of Birth]*

[If you are not sure what personal
identification the particular agency
requires, have your signature notarized.
The bottom of the letter should include this
formula for the convenience of the notary.];

Sworn to me on the _____day of _____, 19____, before me

_____.

Notary Public

Privacy Waiver

Note: A privacy waiver is sometimes useful when records are being requested on behalf of an organization. Individuals involved in that organization may want to inform the agency that their names should not be deleted from such materials when the request is processed. Privacy waivers from individuals would then be attached either to the initial request for the records, or to an appeal letter that is arguing against various deletions. The text of such a letter might read:

> *[Your Name*
> *Address*
> *Daytime Phone Number*
> *Date]*

[*Address your privacy waiver letter
to the same official that the initial
request letter or the appeal letter is
addressed to.*]

Re: Request Number_____[*Add the Request Identification
Number if you know the number the request has been
assigned.*]

Dear *Sir or Madam:*

I am writing in regard to the request under the Freedom of
Information Act (5 U.S.C. Section 552) by [*name of person
making request,*] dated[_____], for records of [*brief description of requested material*]. Copies of the relevant correspondence are included with this letter.

In regard to this specific Freedom of Information Act request,
I hereby waive my privacy interests under FOIA exemptions
(b)(6) and (b)(7)(c) and under the Privacy Act (5 U.S.C. Section
552a), and authorize your agency to release to [*name of
requester*] agency records containing my name or other material relating to me that might otherwise be protected from
release in the interests of personal privacy.

Please contact me at the above number if you have any
questions.

Sincerely,

[*Your Notarized signature
Name
Social Security Number
Date and Place of Birth*]

[*If you are not sure what personal
identification the particular agency
requires, have your signature notarized.
The bottom of the letter should include this
formula for the convenience of the notary.*]:

Sworn to me on the_____day
of_____, 19_____, before me
_____.
Notary Public

Request for Transcript under the FOIA and the Sunshine Act

> [*Your name*
> *Address*
> *Daytime Phone Number*
> *Date*]

[*Address your FOIA and Sunshine Act request to the office of the correct agency; see Appendix D*.]

Dear *Sir or Madam:*

This is a request under the Freedom of Information Act (5 U.S.C. Section 552) and the Government in the Sunshine Act (5 U.S.C. Section 552b).

I write to request a copy of the transcript of the meeting of [*date*] held by your agency members. [*If you want only a particular part of the transcript, you might want to reduce your copying fees by narrowing your request*.]: My request is limited to the portion or portions of that meeting that was discussed [*describe the subject that you are interested in as clearly as possible*].

If any portions are deleted under the provisions of 5 U.S.C. Section 552b(c), I ask that all portions that are not exempt be released. If any material is withheld, I ask that you specify under what Sunshine Act exemptions your agency has authority to do so. As you know, the FOIA provides that all segregable portions of a record that are not specifically exempted from mandatory disclosure must be released [5 U.S.C. Section 552(b)].

If the requested material is released with deletions, I ask that each deletion be marked to indicate the exemption(s) being claimed to authorize each particular withholding.

In addition, I ask that your agency exercise its discretion to release information that may be technically exempt but where withholding would serve no important public interest.

[*If you are not requesting the material for a commercial purpose, you can ask for a waiver or reduction of fees*.]: As you know, the FOIA provides that agencies may reduce or waive fees if it would be "in the public interest because furnishing the information can be considered as primarily benefitting the public." [5 U.S.C. Section 552(a)(4)(A)]. I believe release of this material would be of benefit to the public because_____. [*Add a brief explanation of the public benefit;*

you can always follow through with a more detailed fee waiver letter—see the following sample.] I therefore ask that you waive any fees relating to this request. If you rule otherwise, and if the fees will total more than $_____, I ask that you inform me of the charges before you fill my request.

[*Include this paragraph if your request is for a great many documents and you expect that you will not want copies of all of them. You must be prepared to travel to the location where the records are kept.*] If you do not grant my request for a fee waiver, and if the copying fees are more than $_____, I ask that provisions be made so that I can review the records I am requesting and select those documents I want copied.

If you have any questions regarding this request, please contact me at the above number. I would be happy to discuss ways in which this request could be clarified or somewhat redesigned to reflect the agency's filing system and speed the search for records.

As provided in the Freedom of Information Act, I will expect a reply within 10 working days.

> [*Your Signature*
> *Name*
> *Title, if writing on behalf of an*
>   *organization*]

[*No need to have signature notarized
or to provide identification if you
are not requesting records that relate
to you personally.*]
[*Mark envelope*]: Attn:
Freedom of Information Unit

Request for Transcript under the FOIA and the FACA

> [*Your name*
> *Address*
> *Daytime Phone Number*
> *Date*]

[*Address your FOIA and FACA request to the office of the correct agency; see Appendix D.*]

Dear Sir or Madam:

This is a request under the Freedom of Information Act (5 U.S.C. Section 552), and the Federal Advisory Committee Act (FACA) (5 U.S.C. Appendix I).

I write to request a copy of the transcript of the meeting of [*date*] held by the [*name of committee*]. [*If you want only a particular part of the transcript, you might want to reduce your copying fees by narrowing your request.*]: My request is limited to the portion(s) of that meeting that discussed [*describe the subject that you are interested in as clearly as possible*].

If any portions are deleted under the provisions of 5 U.S.C. Section 552(b), I ask that all portions that are not exempt be released. If any material is withheld, I ask that you specify under what exemptions your agency has authority to do so. As you know, the FOIA provides that a 11 segregable portions of a record that are not specifically exempted from mandatory disclosure must be released [5 U.S.C. Section 552(b)].

If the requested material is released with deletions, I ask that each deletion be marked to indicate the exemption(s) being claimed to authorize each particular withholding.

In addition, I ask that your agency exercise its discretion to release information that may be technically exempt but where withholding would serve no "important public interest."

[*If you are not requesting the material for a commercial purpose, you can ask for a waiver or reduction of fees.*]: As you know, the FOIA provides that agencies may reduce or waive fees if it would be "in the public interest because furnishing the information can be considered as primarily benefiting the public" [5 U.S.C. Section 552(a)(4)(A)]. I believe release of this material would be of benefit to the public because_____. [*Add a brief explanation of the public benefit; you can always follow through with a more detailed fee waiver letter—see the following sample.*] I therefore ask that you waive any fees relating to this request. If you rule otherwise, and if the fees will total more than $_____, I ask that you inform me of the charges before you fill my request.

[*Include this paragraph if your request is for a great many documents and you expect that you will not want copies of all of them. You must be prepared to travel to the location where the records are kept.*]: If you do not grant my request for a fee waiver, and if the copying fees are more than $_____, I ask that provisions be made so that I can review the records I am requesting and select those documents I want copied.

If you have any questions regarding this request, please contact me at the above number. I would be happy to discuss ways in which this request could be clarified or somewhat redesigned to reflect the agency's filing system and speed the search for records.

As provided in the Freedom of Information Act, I will expect a reply within ten working days.

> [*Your Signature*
> *Name*
> *Title, if writing on behalf of an*
>   *organization*]

[*No need to have signature notarized*
or to provide identification if you
are not requesting records that relate to you personally.]
[*Mark envelope*]: Attn:
Freedom of Information Unit

Request for a Waiver of Reduction of Fees

Note: People who are not requesting material for commercial purposes may qualify for a waiver or reduction of fees (see chapter 1). A fee waiver request is sent first to the official handling your initial request, and then, if not granted, to the agency's appeal office. If you are appealing both withheld material and a refusal to grant a fee waiver, you can combine both your arguments against withholding and for a waiver in the same letter, or you can write two separate letters.

> [*Your name*
> *Address*
> *Daytime Phone Number*
> *Date*]

[*Send fee waiver request to the*
appropriate agency or agencies.

Dear Sir or Madam [*or name if you know it, of official handling the request*]:

I am writing to request a waiver of fees in connection with my Freedom of Information Act request of [*date*] for [*brief description of requested material*].

> [Note: *Use either one or the other of the next two paragraphs, depending on whether the documents have been provided or are being held up for search fees*.]:

[*First alternative paragraph*]: As you know, you have provided me with the requested material [*or with some of the requested material*] and have assessed a cost of $_____ to cover search and copying fees.

[*Second alternative paragraph*]: As you know, you have advised me that your agency will not process my request until it receives $_____ to cover the search fees. However, as I am sure you are aware, the FOIA provides that search fees are to be waived—even before the requested documents are located and reviewed for possible exemptions—if the prospective release of any such material could be expected to benefit the public. [See *Eudey v. CIA*, 478 F. Supp. 1175 (D.D.C. 1979).]

I have requested and here repeat my request that you waive these fees because "furnishing the information can be considered as primarily benefiting the general public" [5 U.S.C. Section 552(a)(4)(A)].

The language of the FOIA makes clear that Congress intended that fees not be a bar to private individuals or public interest organizations seeking access to government records. At the same time, it permitted that fees be charged to corporations and individuals using the act for private gain.

The legislative history of the FOIA fee waiver/reduction provision calls for a liberal interpretation of the phrase "primarily benefitting the public." This suggests that all fees should be waived whenever the release of the information contributes to public debate on an important policy issue and when the person requesting the information is doing so with the intention of contributing to the uninhibited, robust, and wide-open debate that Congress intended to encourage.

This means that all fees should be waived if two criteria are met. First, the information will contribute to public debate on important policy issues. And second, the information is requested so that it can be used for this purpose.

This release of this information would benefit the public because_____. [*Here add an explanation of the benefits to the public that would follow from the release. Take as much spuce as needed. If you are writing on behalf of an organization, add something about your group's service to the public. If it is a tax-exempt nonprofit organization, you should say so and include your tax-exemption number. If you are a member of the press or writing a scholarly work, say so.]*

I intend to make the information available to the public. [*Add an explanation of how you would make the material public. Do you plan to give it to a library or to the press? If possible, attach letters from the representatives of such institutions confirming that they have an interest in the material requested.*]

[*Members of the press may be entitled to a fee waiver even if they expect a financial gain. They should however omit this sentence.*]: The release of this information would not result in a financial benefit to me.

[*If possible, cite specific instances where similar requests have been granted a waiver or reduction of fees, demonstrating that such material is of recognized interest to the public.*]

Since this request is for material that clearly is of interest to the public, other persons will undoubtedly be requesting these records. It would be unfair if the first requester were to bear the full financial burden of the initial search, and therefore the search fees should be waived or reduced.

[*Use this paragraph in a fee waiver appeal letter if you have already been refused a reduction of fees and if the fees seem excessively high.*]: If my appeal for a waiver of fees is not substantially granted, I request an itemization of the charges I am being assessed. As you know, the FOIA permits fees to be charged only for the search and copying costs and not for the review of the material.

[*Use this paragraph only if you intend to travel to the location where the documents are kept, and know that you do not, in fact, want copies of all documents covered by the request.*]: As an alternative to being assessed copying fees, I ask to be granted access to the records that are responsive to my request so that I may review them without incurring duplication costs and may select those that I want copied. As you are aware, subsection (a)(3) of the FOIA requires agencies to make documents "promptly available" and subsection (a)(4) permits "recovery of only the direct costs of such search and duplication." Therefore, agencies are required by law to make documents available for inspection, but may not require the purchase of copies of documents.

Since the information that is the subject of this letter fits the criteria spelled out by Congress for waiving fees in the public interest, I believe that your agency should waive such fees, or, at the very least, reduce them substantially.

If you have any questions regarding this request, please contact me at the above number.

> [*Your Signature*
> *Name*
> *Title, if writing on behalf of an*
>   *organization*]

[*No need to have signature notarized.*]

Response When an Agency Asks You to Wait

> [*Your Name*
> *Address*
> *Daytime Phone Number*
> *Date*]

[*Address your request to the*
official who wrote the letter
advising you of the delay.]

Re: Request number_____ [*Add the Request Identification Number if one has been assigned.*]

Dear Sir or Madam [*or name, if you know it, of official handling the FOIA request*]:

I am writing in response to your letter of [*date*] informing me that there would be a delay in processing my request of [*date*] under the FOIA (5 U.S.C. Section 552) for records pertaining to [*brief description of requested material.*]

Thank you for informing me of this delay. As you know, the FOIA requires that an agency must make an initial determination regarding an FOIA request within ten working days, and may take an additional ten working days in unusual circumstances. I am reserving my right to appeal the failure to meet the statutory deadlines.

I am willing to accept a reasonable delay in the processing

of this FOIA request; however, I ask that I be informed of the date by which my request will be processed.

In addition, I am asking for the name and telephone number of the official in your office who will actually be handling this request and to whom I can address further inquiries on its progress.

If there is any way that my request can be clarified or somewhat redesigned to reflect the agency's filing system and speed the search for the records, I will be happy to discuss matters.

If you have any questions regarding this request, please contact me at the above phone number.

> [*Your Signature*
> *Name*
> *Title, if writing on behalf of an*
>   *organization*]

[*No need to have signature notarized.*]

Appeal When an Agency Fails to Meet Time Limits

[Note: See chapter 2 for information about the time limits under the FOIA.]

> [*Your Name*
> *Address*
> *Daytime Phone Number*
> *Date*]

[*Address your appeal letter to*
the address given in the agency's
letter informing you of the delay,
or to the appropriate appeals
office; see appendix D.]

Re: Request number _____ [*Add the Request Identification Number if one has been assigned.*]

Dear *Sir or Madam* [*or name, if you know it, of official who handles FOIA appeals*]:

This is an appeal under the Freedom of Information Act [5 U.S.C. Section 552(a)(6)].

[Use this paragraph if the agency has made no response to your request, and if the statutory time limits, plus time in the mails, have elapsed.]: On *[date]* I sent your agency a letter requesting access under the FOIA to records concerning *[brief description of requested material.]* To date, I have received no response to my request.

[Use this paragraph instead if you have received a letter advising you of delays in processing your request but the agency has not yet made a determination even though the promised date has elapsed.]: On *[date]* I received an acknowledgement from *[name of official signing that letter]* explaining that my FOIA request of *[date]* for *[brief description of requested material]* had been received but that I would have to await the results of "processing." I have now waited *[period of time]* but my request has not yet been processed. *[If a "promise date" has gone by, say so.]*

As you know, the FOIA provides that an agency must make an initial determination of whether to comply with an FOIA request within ten working days of receiving the request. An additional ten working days is permitted in "unusual circumstances" [5 U.S.C. Section 552(a)(6)(A)]. Since I have allowed a more than reasonable time for compliance with the statutory requirements, I am treating your agency's failure to meet the FOIA's deadlines as a denial of my request. This letter is a formal appeal of that denial.

I am enclosing a copy of my request letter *[if applicable, you can also include any other correspondence or your notes of phone conversations in which agency officials may have made promises or refused to abide by the statutory provisions]* for your convenience so that you can see what materials are under request.

As provided under the FOIA, I will expect a reply to this appeal within twenty working days.

Sincerely,
[Your Signature
Name
Title (if any)]

[No need to have signature notarized.]
[Mark envelope]: Attn: Freedom of
Information Appeals

Appeal for Material that Is Withheld

Note: This appeal letter provides examples of somewhat sophisticated arguments in favor of further disclosure, but the essential part of the appeal letter is contained in the first paragraph. The rest of the letter is optional and should be adapted to suit the particular request for access. See chapter 5 for a discussion of administrative appeal letters.

[Your Name
Address
Daytime Phone Number
Date]

[Address your administrative appeal letter
to the person or office mentioned in the
agency's denial letter.]

Re: Request number _____ *[Include this if the agency has*
assigned your request a reference number].

Dear *[Name of official handling appeals]*:

I am writing under the appeal provisions of the FOIA, 5 U.S.C. Section 552(a)(6). On *[date]* I received a letter from *[name]* of your agency denying me my request under the FOIA for *[briefly describe the requested records.]* This letter informed me that a letter of appeal should be directed to you. I am attaching copies of my correspondence regarding this request so that you can see precisely what I have requested and the grounds on which it is claimed that this information is exempted from mandatory disclosure under the FOIA. I hereby ask that you overrule the initial decision to deny this information and now release to me all the requested material that has been withheld.

As provided under the FOIA, I expect to receive a reply within twenty working days.

[Below are sample paragraphs that might be adapted to
your own FOIA request. Consult chapters 4 and 5 to
help determine if they apply to your particular request,
and, if these do not apply, what alternative arguments
for release you might make.]

[*Use this paragraph if the agency has withheld all or nearly all of the requested material*]: Because your agency has withheld all [*or nearly all*] of the information that I requested, I believe that it is not adhering to the FOIA provision that requires that "any reasonably segregable portion of a record shall be provided to any person requesting such a record after deletion of the portions that are exempt" [5 U.S.C. Section 552(b)]. I hereby request that your agency release all such segregable portions.

[*You should also explain why you believe that various of the exemptions have been improperly claimed. Here we include some samples of common arguments. Others can be drawn from the discussions in chapter 4.*]

I also believe that upon reconsideration, you will determine that the material that has been withheld under the following exemptions [*list the exemptions cited in the denial*] do not actually meet the standards for lawful withholding under the FOIA.

[*Sample argument, to be used if the agency has claimed the (b)(6)—in the case of the Sunshine/FACA exemption, the (c)(6)—(or exemption for personal privacy, but where the release of the information would make an important contribution to public debate.*]: I believe that your agency has used the (b)(6) exemption to delete information concerning high government officials who are suspected of improper conduct and substandard performance. As you know, the case law holds that such individuals are not protected by the privacy exemption to the same degree that private citizens are. *Arieff v. Dept. of the Navy*, 712 F.2d 1462 (D.C. Cir. 1983). In the case of [*briefly describe the information requested*], the contribution that the material would make to public debate clearly outweigh the possible damage to personal privacy. [*If possible, add an explanation of why this particular information is important to public debate, and why damage would be unlikely or not significant. You might want to attach news clips or cite articles, books or reports to demonstrate public interest in the subject and/or the fact that little or no damage would follow release. Then explain how releasing the records to you would contribute to public debate.*] If this material is released to me, I intend to make it available for public debate by [*writing an article or book, depositing the documents in a library, giving it to the press or interested scholars, or whatever applies in your particular case. You should attach letters from such interested librarians, journalists, scholars, and so forth*].

[*Sometimes an agency will delete only portions of documents that they release. If the agency has not marked the specific exemption(s) used to justify each deletion, you should appeal the failure to do so. If you know the specific exemptions claimed, you can then argue from the contexts in which they occur that the exemptions do not actually apply in those instances. There is no reason why you cannot go line by line through all the material received and then, item by item, explain why you think exemptions have been incorrectly applied. Here are some examples of such arguments. Other arguments can be drawn from the discussion of the exemptions in chapter 4.*]

[*Sample paragraph, showing an argument about a particular deletion*]: On the memo dated [_____] [*or provide some other precise description of the particular deletion*], the second paragraph appears to describe a foreign policy discussion at an open meeting of the [_____] organization. Since this was an informal gathering of students, none of whom had security clearances, it is impossible that this information can be properly classified under the (b)(1) exemption. And since more than fifty people attended this meeting, the (b)(7)(D) exemption protecting confidential sources cannot be used because there is no way that an account of such a large meeting could be traced to any particular source.

[*Since FOIA withholdings are mandatory in only a few situations, it is often possible to argue for a discretionary release.*]

As you know, the FOIA does not require that information falling within some particular exemption *must* be withheld; the FOIA permits agencies to exercise their discretion and to release information that may in fact be technically exempt. If, after reviewing the requested material, you determine that there is in fact some arguable legal basis for withholding, I ask that the records nevertheless be released because there is no important public interest in continuing to withhold the material. [*For instance, if the material is old or the subject deceased, you should argue that its release would no longer cause any of the harms enumerated in the exemptions to the access statutes. And if the information would be of benefit to public debate, you should explain that fact.*]

If, after careful review of my appeal letter, you decide to continue to withhold some or all of the information that I have been denied by your agency in my initial request, I ask that you give me an index of the withheld material, together with specific justifications for denying release of each item still withheld.

[*Finally, you have the option of threatening to go to court, if that is your intention.*]: If this appeal letter is denied in full or in part, and if a satisfactory explanation of why the withheld information is in fact properly exempt is not offered, I intend to file suit to compel disclosure. [*In a somewhat softer alternative, you could say that you will consider filing suit to compel disclosure. See chapter 6 for background on such lawsuits.*]

If you have any questions regarding this request, please contact me at the above number.

Sincerely,

[*Your Signature
Name
Title, if writing on behalf of an
  organization*]

[*No need to have signatures on
appeal letters notarized.*]

[*Mark envelope*]:
Attn: Freedom of Information Appeals

Appendix B:

The Federal Freedom of Information Act—Text 5 U.S.C. Section 552

§552. Public information; agency rules, opinions, orders, records, and proceedings.

(a) Each agency shall make available to the public information as follows:

(1) Each agency shall separately state and currently publish in the Federal Register for the guidance of the public—

(A) descriptions of its central and field organization and the established places at which, the employees (and in the case of a uniformed service, the members) from whom, and the methods whereby, the public may obtain information, make submittals or requests, or obtain decisions;

(B) statements of the general course and method by which its functions are channeled and determined, including the nature and requirements of all formal and informal procedures available;

(C) rules of procedure, descriptions of forms available or the places at which forms may be obtained, and instructions as to the scope and contents of all papers, reports, or examinations;

(D) substantive rules of general applicability adopted as authorized by law, and statements of general policy or interpretations of general applicability formulated and adopted by the agency; and

(E) each amendment, revision, or repeal of the foregoing.

Except to the extent that a person has actual and timely notice of the terms thereof, a person may not in any manner be required to resort to, or be adversely affected by, a matter required to be published in the Federal Register and not so published. For the purpose of this paragraph, matter reasonably available to the class of persons affected thereby is deemed published in the Federal Register when incorporated by reference therein with the approval of the Director of the Federal Register.

(2) Each agency, in accordance with published rules, shall make available for public inspection and copying—

(A) final opinions, including concurring and dissenting opinions, as well as orders, made in the adjudication of cases;

(B) those statements of policy and interpretations which have been adopted by the agency and are not published in the Federal Register; and

(C) administrative staff manuals and instructions to staff that affect a member of the public;

unless the materials are promptly published and copies offered for sale. To the extent required to prevent a clearly unwarranted invasion of personal privacy, an agency may delete identifying details when it makes available or publishes an opinion, statement of policy, interpretation, or staff manual or instruction. However, in each case the justification for the deletion shall be explained fully in writing. Each agency shall also maintain and make available for public inspection and copying current indexes providing identifying information for the public as to any matter issued, adopted, or promulgated after July 4, 1967, and required by this paragraph to be made available or published. Each agency shall promptly publish, quarterly or more frequently, and distribute (by sale or otherwise) copies of each index or supplements thereto unless it determines by order published in the Federal Register that the publication would be unnecessary and impracticable, in which case the agency shall nonetheless provide copies of such index on request at a cost not to exceed the direct cost of duplication. A final order, opinion, statement of policy, interpretation, or staff manual or instruction that affects a member of the public may be relied on, used, or cited as precedent by an agency against a party other than an agency only if—

(i) it has been indexed and either made available or published as provided by this paragraph; or

(ii) the party has actual and timely notice of the terms thereof.

(3) Except with respect to the records made available under paragraphs (1) and (2) of this subsection, each agency, upon any request for records which (A) reasonably describes such records and (B) is made in accordance with published rules stating the time, place, fees (if any), and procedures to be followed, shall make the records promptly available to any person.

(4) (A) In order to carry out the provisions of this section, each agency shall promulgate regulations, pursuant to notice and receipt of public comment, specifying a uniform schedule of fees applicable to all constituent units of such agency. Such fees shall be limited to reasonable standard charges for documents search and duplication and provide for recovery of only the direct costs of such search and duplication. Documents shall be furnished without charge or at a reduced charge where the agency determines that waiver or reduction of the fee is in the public interest because furnishing the information can be considered as primarily benefiting the general public.

(B) On complaint, the district court of the United States in the district in which the complainant resides, or has his principal place of business, or in which the agency records are situated, or in the District of Columbia, has jurisdiction to enjoin the agency from withholding agency records and to order the production of any agency records improperly withheld from the complainant. In such a case the court shall determine the matter de novo, and may examine the contents of such agency records in camera to determine whether such records or any part thereof shall be withheld under any of the exemptions set forth in subsection (b) of this section, and the burden is on the agency to sustain its actions.

(C) Notwithstanding any other provision of law, the defendant shall serve an answer or otherwise plead to any complaint made under this subsection within thirty days after service upon the defendant of the pleading in which such complaint is made, unless the court otherwise directs for good cause shown.

(D) Except as to cases the court considers of greater importance, proceedings before the district court, as authorized by this subsection, and appeals therefrom, take precedence on the docket over all cases and shall be assigned for hearing and trial or for argument at the earliest practicable date and expedited in every way.

(E) The court may assess against the United States reasonable attorney fees and other litigation costs reasonably incurred in any case under this section in which the complainant has substantially prevailed.

(F) Whenever the court orders the production of any agency records improperly withheld from the complainant and assesses against the United States reasonable attorney fees and other litigation costs, and the court additionally issues a written finding that the circumstances surrounding the withholding raise questions whether agency personnel acted arbitrarily or capriciously with respect to the withholding, the Civil Service Commission shall promptly initiate a proceeding to determine whether disciplinary action is warranted against the officer or employee who was primarily responsible for the withholding. The Commission, after investigation and consideration of the evidence submitted, shall submit its findings and recommendations to the administrative authority of the agency concerned and shall send copies of the findings and recommendations to the officer or employee or his representative. The administrative authority shall take the corrective action that the Commission recommends.

(G) In the event of noncompliance with the order of the court, the district court may punish for contempt the responsible employee, and in the case of a uniformed service, the responsible member.

(5) Each agency having more than one member shall maintain and make available for public inspection a record of the final votes of each member in every agency proceeding.

(6) (A) Each agency, upon any request for records made under paragraph (1), (2), or (3) of this subsection, shall—

(i) determine within ten days (excepting Saturdays, Sundays, and legal public holidays) after the receipt of any such request whether to comply with such request and shall immediately notify the person making such request of such determination and the reasons therefor, and of the right of such person to appeal to the head of the agency any adverse determination; and

(ii) make a determination with respect to any appeal within twenty days (excepting Saturdays, Sundays, and legal public holidays) after the receipt of such appeal. If on appeal the denial of the request for records is in the whole or in part upheld, the agency shall notify the person making such request of the provisions for judicial review of that determination under paragraph (4) of this subsection.

(B) In unusual circumstances as specified in this subparagraph, the time limits prescribed in either clause (i) or clause (ii) of subparagraph (A) may be extended by written notice to the person making such request setting forth the reasons for such extension and the date on which a determination is expected to be dispatched. No such notice shall specify a date that would result in an extension for more than ten working days. As used in this subparagraph, 'unusual circumstances' means, but only to the extent reasonably necessary to the proper processing of the particular request—

(i) the need to search for and collect the requested records from field facilities or other establishments that are separate from the office processing the request;

(ii) the need to search for, collect, and appropriately examine a voluminous amount of separate and distinct records which are demanded in a single request; or

(iii) the need for consultation, which shall be conducted with all practicable speed, with another agency having a substantial interest in the determination of the request or among two or more components of the agency having substantial subject-matter interest therein.

(C) Any person making a request to any agency for records under paragraph (1), (2), or (3) of this subsection shall be deemed to have exhausted his administrative remedies with respect to such request if the agency fails to comply with the applicable time limit provisions of this paragraph. If the Government can show exceptional circumstances exist and that the agency is exercising due diligence in responding to the request, the court may retain jurisdiction and allow the agency additional time to complete its review of the records. Upon any determination by an agency to comply with a request for records, the records shall be made promptly available to such person making such request. Any notification of denial of any request for records under this subsection shall set forth the names and titles or positions of each person responsible for the denial of such request.

(b) This section does not apply to matters that are—

(1) (A) specifically authorized under criteria established by an Executive order to be kept secret in the interest of national defense or foreign policy and (B) are in fact properly classified pursuant to such Executive order;

(2) related solely to the internal personnel rules and practices of an agency;

(3) specifically exempted from disclosure by statute (other than section 552b of this title), provided that such statute (A) requires that the matters be withheld from the public in such a manner as to leave no discretion on the issue, or (B) establishes particular criteria for withholding or refers to particular types of matters to be withheld;

(4) trade secrets and commercial or financial information obtained from a person and privileged or confidential;

(5) inter-agency or intra-agency memorandums or letters which would not be available by law to a party other than an agency in litigation with the agency;

(6) personnel and medical files and similar files the disclosure of which would constitute a clearly unwarranted invasion of personal privacy;

(7) investigatory records compiled for law enforcement purposes, but only to the extent that the production of such records would (A) interfere with enforcement proceedings, (B) deprive a person of a right to a fair trial or an impartial adjudication, (C) constitute an unwarranted invasion of personal privacy, (D) disclose the identity of a confidential source and, in the case of a record compiled by a criminal law enforcement authority in the course of a criminal investigation, or by an agency conducting a lawful national security intelligence investigation, confidential information furnished only by the confidential source, (E) disclose investigative techniques and procedures, or (F) endanger the life or physical safety of law enforcement personnel;

(8) contained in or related to examination, operating, or condition reports prepared by, on behalf of, or for the use of an agency responsible for the regulation or supervision of financial institutions; or

(9) geological and geophysical information and data, including maps, concerning wells.

Any reasonably segregable portion of a record shall be provided to any person requesting such record after deletion of the portions which are exempt under this subsection.

(c) This section does not authorize withholding of information or limit the availability of records to the public, except as specifically stated in this section. This section is not authority to withhold information from Congress.

(d) On or before March 1 of each calendar year, each agency shall submit a report covering the preceding calendar year to the Speaker of the House of Representatives and President of the Senate for referral to the appropriate committees of the Congress. The report shall include—

(1) the number of determinations made by such agency not to comply with requests for records made to such agency under subsection (a) and the reasons for each such determination;

(2) the number of appeals made by persons under subsection (a)(6), the result of such appeals, and the reason for the action upon each appeal that results in a denial of information;

(3) the names and titles or positions of each person responsible for the denial of records requested under this section, and the number of instances of participation for each;

(4) the results of each proceeding conducted pursuant to subsection (a)(4)(F), including a report of the disciplinary action taken against the officer or employee who was responsible for improperly withholding records or an explanation of why disciplinary action was not taken;

(5) a copy of every rule made by such agency regarding this section;

(6) a copy of the fee schedule and the total amount of fees collected by the agency for making records available under this section; and

(7) such other information as indicates efforts to administer fully this section.

The Attorney General shall submit an annual report on or before March 1 of each calendar year which shall include for the prior calendar year a listing of the number of cases arising under this section, the exemption involved in each case, the disposition of such case, and the cost, fees, and penalties assessed under subsection (a)(4)(E), (F), and (G). Such report shall also include a description of the efforts undertaken by the Department of Justice to encourage agency compliance with this section.

(e) For purposes of this section, the term 'agency' as defined in section 551(1) of this title includes any executive department, military department, Government corporation, Government controlled corporation, or other establishment in the executive branch of the Government (including the Executive Office of the President), or any independent regulatory agency.

Appendix C:

Where to Go for Legal Help

The organizations described in this section are *sometimes* able to provide legal assistance to people with FOIA/PA or Sunshine/FACA problems. (See chapter 6.) If they cannot handle your case, they can often refer you to someone in private practice.

American Civil Liberties Union Affiliates.
The ACLU has state and local affiliates across the country. One near you may be able to help. These chapters can also provide information about state FOI, "Open Records," and privacy laws, if you are interested in getting nonfederal government records. The national office of the ACLU can give you the address of your nearest affiliate.

ACLU
32 W. 43 St.
New York, N.Y. 10036
(212) 244-9800

The Campaign for Political Rights.
The Campaign is a coalition of more than 80 religious, environmental, civic, and labor organizations working to end intelligence abuses directed against political targets. The Campaign coordinates a Task Force on the FOIA, which brings together a variety of groups to discuss FOIA-related legislation. It has helped groups in using the FOIA as a means of gathering documentation on improper surveillance and similar programs. They have a special interest in helping campus groups obtain records on intelligence activities at colleges and

universities. In addition, they can give advice on how to publicize material showing improper intelligence operations. They have an eight page pamphlet, *FOIA as an Organizing Tool*, and a monthly newsletter, *Organizing Notes* which covers FOIA-intelligence matters.

The Campaign for Political Rights
201 Massachusetts Ave., N.E.
Washington, D.C. 20002
(202) 547–4705

The Center for National Security Studies

Jointly sponsored by the American Civil Liberties Union Foundation and the Fund for Peace, the CNSS has had extensive experience dealing with the FOIA. It is the publisher of a technical manual for attorneys, *Litigation under the Federal Freedom of Information and Privacy Acts* (which covers the full range of FOIA issues). The CNSS also publishes a pamphlet, *Using the Freedom of Information Act: A Step-by-Step Guide*. The Center's litigation arm, the ACLU National Security Project, can take only a very few cases, and then only those that relate to national security. Legal representation will be considered only after you have exhausted the administrative process of requests and appeals. You can then communicate in writing by sending the CNSS copies of your correspondence with the agency, together with a cover letter explaining the importance of the documents requested.

CNSS
122 Maryland Ave., N.E.
Washington, DC 20002
(202) 544–5380

Freedom of Information Clearinghouse

The Clearinghouse is a project of Ralph Nader's Center for the Study of Responsive Law. It can provide legal and technical assistance to public interest groups, journalists, and individuals. The Clearinghouse has been one of the most active FOIA watchdog groups and has brought in numerous cases relating to health, environment, and tax records. The Clearinghouse can offer advice and refer people to private lawyers; it can actually take cases, however, only where a significant point of law is involved.

Freedom of Information Clearinghouse
P.O. Box 19367
Washington, DC 20036
(202) 785–3704

Fund for Open Information and Accountability, Inc.

FOIA, Inc. maintains an expanding library of releases under the FOIA that have social and political importance. It publishes pamphlets, research reports, and a newsletter; maintains a speakers bureau; works with teachers in developing educational materials; supports selected FOIA lawsuits (including the Rosenberg case); and helps individuals, scholars, and organizations in securing and interpreting files, particularly those of the FBI.

FOIA, Inc.
36 W. 44 St., Rm. 312
New York, N.Y. 10036
(212) 730–8095

Law Schools.

Law schools around the country have clinics that provide legal services as part of their training program for their students. Consult those schools near you. Here we mention two in Washington, D.C. Since all FOIA suits may be filed in the District of Columbia, these schools are sometimes willing to take suits from around the country.

The civil-litigation section of Antioch Law School's public interest Intake Office will provide assistance to groups and individuals writing request and appeal letters. Clients can be referred to private attorneys.

Antioch School of Law
Intake Office
1624 Crescent Place, N.W.
Washington, DC 20009
(202) 265–9500

The Institute is an example of a public-interest law firm; it operates out of Georgetown University Law School, and is staffed by three full-time lawyers and several law students. It does not handle request or appeal letters, but can provide representation (usually charging for court costs only) to individuals or groups involved in significant FOIA disputes.

Institute for Public Interest Representation
Georgetown University Law Center
600 New Jersey Ave., N.W.
Washington, DC 20001
(202) 624–8390

National Lawyers Guild.
The Guild will help individuals and groups with general questions about FOIA or Privacy Act procedures. Those with specific problems or needing legal representation will be referred to a law firm or private lawyer. The Guild has a number of offices:

509 C Street, N.E.
Washington, DC 20002
(202) 547–0880

853 Broadway, 17th Fl.
New York, N.Y. 10003
(212) 260–1360

712 Grandview
Los Angeles, CA. 90057
(213) 380–3180

The National Prison Project of the American Civil Liberties Union Foundation.
The Prison Project cannot provide individual representation, but it does have a comprehensive outline for prisoners seeking presentence investigation reports, prison files, medical records, and personal files held by the Federal Bureau of Prisons and by the U.S. Parole Commission. The Prison Project can refer prisoners to local legal-aid groups when requests for information from state authorities are involved.

National Prison Project
1346 Connecticut Ave., N.W. Suite 1031
Washington, DC
(202) 331-0500

The Reporters Committee for Freedom of the Press, FOI Service Center.

The FOI Service Center is available for reporters and other professional journalists. It deals with federal and state FOIA and provides a telephone hotline, legal advice, research memos, representation assistance, a State-Federal FOI Research Library, draft complaints and briefs, legal citations and analyses, and a variety of publications.

FOI Service Center
% Reporters Committee
1125 15th St., N.W.
Washington, DC 20005
(202) 466–6312

Appendix D:

Addresses of Federal FOIA/PA Offices

When searching for a particular agency, bear in mind that it may be listed under its larger organizational grouping. The Social Security Administration, for example, is listed as a branch of the Department of Health and Human Services.

For each agency (whether an independent agency or part of a larger department), the address for the requests is given on the left; the address for appeals, if different, is given on the right.

Write in the lower left corner of your envelope "FOIA Request" or "FOIA Appeal," as applicable. Some agencies require this, but even if it is not required it often helps the agency mail room deliver it.

Finally, please remember that names, titles, addresses, and telephone numbers change frequently. If you are in a hurry, and want to avoid mail room delays, you should call to confirm that these are still the correct addresses.

Addresses for FOIA Request Letters and Appeals

(Note: All addresses, telephones and agencies are subject to change)

Label envelopes "FOIA Request" or "FOIA Appeal"

Agency	Requests	Appeals
Action	Director of Administrative Services ACTION 806 Connecticut Ave., N.W. Room P314 Washington, DC 20525 (202) 254-8105	Director of Administrative Services ACTION 806 Connecticut Ave., N.W. Room P314 Washington, DC 20525 (202) 254-8105

Agency	Requests	Appeals
Administrative Conference of U.S.	Executive Secretary Administrative Conference of U.S. 2120 L. St. NW Washington, DC 20037 (202) 254-7020	Executive Secretary Administrative Conference of the U.S. 2120 L. St., NW Washington, DC 20037 (202) 254-1021
Department of Agriculture/		
Agricultural Marketing Service	FOIA Officer Agricultural Marketing Service, Room 3054 14th Independence Ave. SW Washington, DC 20250 (202) 447-4366	Administrator Agricultural Marketing Service Dept. of Agriculture Washington, DC 20250 (202) 447-5115
Agricultural Stabilization and Conservation Service	Director-Management Services Division Dept. of Agriculture P.O. Box 2415 Washington, DC 20013 (202) 447-2717	Director-Management Services Division Dept. Of Agriculture P.O. Box 2415 Washington, DC 20013 (202) 447-2717
Animal and Plant Health Inspection Service	FOIA Coordinator Animal and Plant Health Inspect. Service Fed. Bldg., Room 711 6505 Bellcrest Rd. Hyattsville, MD 29782 (301) 436-7239	FOIA Coordinator Animal and Plant Health Inspec. Service Fed. Bldg., Room 711 6505 Bellcrest Rd. Hyattsville, MD 29782 (301) 436-7239
Economic Statistics and Cooperatives Service	Chief of Records Systems Analysis Branch Economic Statistics and Cooperative Service South Agriculture Bldg. Room 1419 14th & Independence Ave., S.W. Washington, DC 20250 (202) 447-4611	Chief of Records Systems Analysis Branch Economic Statistics and Cooperative Service South Agriculture Bldg. Room 1419 14th & Independence Ave., S.W. Washington, DC 20250 (202) 447-4611
Extension Service	FOIA Coordinator Science and Education Administration South Agriculture Bldg. Room 436 Washington, DC 20250 (202) 447-2076	Director Science and Education Administration USDA Washington, DC 20250 (202) 447-5923
Farmers Home Administration	Director Management Information Systems Division Farmers Home Admin. 103 Auditors Bldg. Washington, DC 20250 (202) 436-7800	Administrator Farmers Home Administration South Agricultural Bldg. Room 5014 Dept. of Agriculture Washington, DC 20250 (202) 447-7967

Agency	Requests	Appeals
Foreign Agricultural Service	Asst. Administrator for Management Foreign Agricultural Service South Agriculture Bldg. Room 5095 14th & Independence Ave., S.W. Washington, DC 20250 (202) 447-3138	Administrator Foreign Agricultural Service South Agriculture Bldg. Room 5071 14th & Independence Ave., S.W. Washington, DC 20250 (202) 447-3935
Forest Service	Address to any level— District Ranger, Research Station Director, etc. (202) 447-6661	Chief U.S. Forest Service P.O. Box 2417 Washington, DC 20013 (202) 447-6661
Office of the Inspector General	Assistant Inspector General for Administration Dept. of Agriculture Washington, DC 20250 (202) 447-6915	Inspector General Dept. of Agriculture Washington, DC 20250 (202) 447-8001
Rural Electrification Administration	Director REA Information Rural Electrification Administration Dept. of Agriculture 14th & Independence Ave., S.W., Room 4042 Washington, DC 20250 (202) 447-5606	Administrator Rural Electrification Administration Dept. of Agriculture Washington, DC 20250 (202) 447-2791
American Battle Monuments Commission	Director of Operations & Finance American Battle Monuments Commissions 5127 Pulaski Bldg. 20 Massachusetts Ave., N.W. Washington, DC 20314 (202) 272-0533	Secretary American Battle Monuments Commission 5127 Pulask Bldg. 20 Massachusetts Ave., N.W. Washington, DC 20314 (202) 693-6067
Arms Control and Disarmament Agency	FOIA Officer Arms Control and Disarmament Agency Dept. of State Bldg. Washington, DC 20451 (202) 632-0760	Executive Officer Arms Control and Disarmament Agency Dept. of State Bldg. Washington, DC 20451 (202) 632-0760
Board for International Broadcasting	Administrative Officer Board for International Broadcasting Suite 430 1030 Fifteenth St., N.W. Washington, DC 20008 (202) 254-8040	Executive Director Board for International Broadcasting Suite 430 1030 Fifteenth St., N.W. Washington, DC 20008 (202) 254-8040

Agency	Requests	Appeals
Central Intelligence Agency	Information and Privacy Coordinator Central Intelligence Agency Washington, DC 20505 (703) 351-1100	Information and Privacy Coordinator Central Intelligence Agency Washington, DC 20505 (703) 351-1100
Civil Aeronautics Board	Office of the Secretary Civil Aeronautics Board 1825 Connecticut Ave., N.W. Washington, DC 20428 (202) 673-5068	Managing Director Civil Aeronautics Board 1825 Connecticut Ave., N.W. Washington, DC 20428 (202) 673-5980

Commerce, Department of

Agency	Requests	Appeals
Bureau of the Census	Associate Director of Admin. & Field Operations Bureau of the Census Washington, DC 20233 (202) 763-5238	Director Bureau of the Census Washington, DC 20233 (202) 763-5190
Information Management Division	Information Management Division Office of Organization and Management System Department of Commerce Washington, DC 20230 (202) 377-4217	Assistant Secretary for Administration Department of Commerce Washington, DC 20230 (202) 377-2112
Commission on Civil Rights	Solicitor Commission on Civil Rights Room 700 1121 Vermont Ave., N.W. Washington DC 20425 (202) 254-7381	Staff Director Commission on Civil Rights 1121 Vermont Ave., N.W. Washington, DC 20425 (202) 254-7381
Commission on Fine Arts	Secretary Commission on Fine Arts 708 Jackson Pl., N.W. Washington, DC 20006 (202) 566-1066	Chairman Commission on Fine Arts 708 Jackson Pl., N.W. Washington, DC 20006 (202) 566-1066
Commodity Futures Trading Commission	Deputy Director Office of Public Info. 2033 K St., N.W. Washington, DC 20581 (or appropriate regional office) (202) 254-8630	Commodity Futures Trading Commission 2033 K St., N.W. Washington, DC 20581 (202) 254-8630
Community Services Administration	FOIA Records Officer Office of Administration Community Services Administration Room 426 1200 19th St., N.W. Washington, DC 20506 (202) 254-5794	Assistant Director for Management Community Services Administration 1200 19th St., N.W. Washington, DC 20506 (202) 254-5794

Agency	Requests	Appeals
Consumer Product Safety Commission	Office of the Secretary Consumer Product Safety Commission 1111 18th St., N.W. Suite 300 Washington, DC 20207 (202) 634-7700	Office of the Secretary Consumer Product Safety Commission 1111 18th St., N.W. Suite 300 Washington, DC 20207 (202) 634-7700

Defense, Department of

Department of the Air Force/Force & Staff	Freedom of Information Manager HQ, USAF/DADF Washington, DC 20330 (202) 697-3467	Freedom of Information Manager HQ, USAF/DADF Washington, DC 20330 (202) 697-3467 (or as directed in denial notice.)
Department of the Air Force/Policy and Procedures	HQ, USAF/DADMD Washington, DC 20330 (202) 767-4502	HQ, USAF/DADMD Washington, DC 20330 (202) 767-4502 (or as directed in denial notice.)
Department of the Army	Office of the FOI HQDA (SAPA-POI) The Pentagon Washington, DC 20310 (202) 697-4122	Secretary of the Army Attn: General Counsel The Pentagon Washington, DC 20310 (202) 697-8029
Defense Communications Agency	FOIA Officer Defense Communications Agency Code 104 Washington, DC 20305 (202) 692-2007	Director Defense Communications Agency Code 100 Washington, DC 20305 (202) 692-0018
Defense Contract Audit Agency	Records Administrator Defense Contract Audit Agency Cameron Station, Room 4A380 Alexandria, Virginia 22314 (703) 274-7310	Asst. Director, Resources Defense Contract Audit Agency Cameron Station Alexandria, Virginia 22314 (703) 274-7285
Defense Intelligence Agency	Director Defense Intelligence Agency Attn: RTS-2A Washington, DC 20301 (202) 692-5766	Director Defense Intelligence Agency Attn: SC (PA 1974) Washington, DC 20301 (202) 692-5766
Defense Investigative Service	Director Defense Investigative Service (D0020) 1900 Half St., S.W. Washington, DC 20324 (202) 693-1740	Director Defense Investigative Service (D0020) 1900 Half St., S.W. Washington, DC 20324 (202) 693-1740

Agency	Requests	Appeals
Defense Logistics Agency	Director Defense Logistics Agency DLA-XA Cameron Station Alexandria, Virginia 22314 (703) 274-6250	Director Defense Logistics Agency ATTN: DLA:G Cameron Station Alexandria, Virginia 22314 (703) 274-6250
Defense Mapping Agency	Director Defense Mapping Agency Bldg. 56 Naval Observatory Washington, DC 20305 (202) 254-4431	Director Defense Mapping Agency Bldg. 56 Naval Observatory Washington, DC 20305 (202) 254-4431
Defense Nuclear Agency	Director Public Affairs Office Defense Nuclear Agency Washington, DC 20305 (202) 325-7095	Director Public Affairs Office Defense Nuclear Agency Washington, DC 20305 (202) 325-7095
Marine Corps	CNC Code MPI-60 HQMC Washington, DC 20380 (202) 694-4309	Navy JAG Code 14 200 Stovall St. Alexandria, VA 22332 (703) 325-9870
Department of the Navy	Chief of Naval Operations OP-09-BIF Room 4D471, Pentagon Washington, DC 20350 (202) 697-1459	JAG (Code 14) Navy Department Washington, DC 20370 (202) 694-4028
National Security Agency	Director, NSA National Security Agency Central Security Service Fort Meade, MD 20755 (301) 688-6524	Appeals Authority National Security Agency Central Security Service Fort Meade, MD 20755 (301) 688-6311
Office of the Secretary of Defense/ Office of the Joint Chiefs of Staff	Office of the Asst. Secretary of Defense (Public Affairs) Director, FOI and Security Review Pentagon, Room 2C757 Washington, DC 20301 (202) 697-1160	Secretary of Defense Department of Defense Pentagon Washington, DC 20301 (202) 697-1160
Delaware River Basin Commission	FOIA Officer Delaware River Basin Commission P.O. Box 7360 West Trenton, NJ 08628 (609) 883-9500	Executive Director Delaware River Basin Commission P.O. Box 7360 West Trenton, NJ 08628 (609) 883-9500

Agency	Requests	Appeals
Education, Dept. of (formerly HEW)	FOI Officer Public Affairs Office Dept. of Education Room 4169 Federal Office Bldg. 6 400 Maryland Av., S.W. Washington, DC 20202 (202) 426-6573	Executive Secretary of Education 400 Maryland Ave., S.W. Washington, DC 20202 (202) 426-6420
Energy, Department of	Director of FOI & PA Activities AD-43 1000 Independence Ave., S.W. Washington, DC 20585 (202) 252-5955	Director Office of Hearings and Appeals Department of Energy 2000 M St., N.W. Washington, DC 20461 (202) 653-4077
Environmental Protection Agency	FOI Officer Environmental Protection Agency A-101, Room 1132 401 M St., S.W. Washington, DC 20460 (202) 755-2764	FOI Officer Environmental Protection Agency A-101, Room 1132 401 M St., S.W. Washington, DC 20460 (202) 755-2764
Equal Employment Opportunity Commission	Office of Public Affairs Equal Employment Opportunity Commission 2401 E St., N.W., Room 4202 Washington, DC 20506 (202) 634-6460	Office of Public Affairs Equal Employment Opportunity Commission 2401 E St., N.W., Room 4202 Washington, DC 20506 (202) 634-6460
Export-Import Bank of the U.S.	Senior VP-Research & Communications Export-Import Bank of the U.S. 811 Vermont Ave., N.W. Washington, DC 20571 (202) 566-8907	Export-Import Bank of the U.S. ATTN: General Counsel 811 Vermont Ave., N.W. Washington, DC 20571 (202) 566-8111
Farm Credit Administration	Director of Public Affairs Office of Administration Public Affairs Division Farm Credit Administration 490 L'Enfant Plaza East, S.W. Suite 4000 Washington, DC 20578 (202) 755-2170	Director of Public Affairs Office of Administration Public Affairs Division Farm Credit Administration Suite 400 Washington, DC 20578 (202) 755-2170
Federal Communications Commission	Executive Director Federal Communications Commission 1919 M St., N.W. Washington, DC 20554 (202) 632-6390	Executive Director Federal Communications Commission 1919 M St., N.W. Washington, DC 20554 (202) 632-6390

Agency	Requests	Appeals
Federal Deposit Insurance Corporation	Executive Secretary Records Unit, FDIC 550 17th St., N.W. Washington, DC 20429 (202) 389-4446	Executive Secretary Records Unit, FDIC 550 17th St., N.W. Washington, DC 20429 (202) 389-4446
Federal Election Commission	Office of Public Records Federal Election Commission 1325 K St., N.W. Washington, DC 20463 (202) 523-4181	Office of Public Records Federal Election Commission 1325 K St., N.W. Washington, DC 20463 (202) 523-4181
Federal Emergency Management Agency	FOIA Officer Fed. Emergency Management Agency 1725 I St. N.W., Room 807 Office of Public Affairs Washington, DC 20472 (202) 634-6772	FOIA Officer Fed. Emergency Management Agency 1725 I St., N.W., Room 807 Office of Public Affairs Washington, DC 20472 (202) 634-6772
Federal Energy Regulatory Commission	FOI Officer Office of Public Information Federal Energy Regulatory Commission 825 N. Capital St., N.E. Room 1000 Washington, DC 20426 (202) 357-8055	FOI Officer Office of Public Information Federal Energy Regulatory Commission 825 N. Capital St., N.E. Room 1000 Washington, DC 20426 (202) 357-8055
Federal Home Loan Bank Board	Federal Home Loan Bank Board Information Systems Division Information Disclosure Section 1700 G St., N.W. Washington, DC 20552 (202) 377-6138	Secretary Federal Home Loan Bank Board 1700 G St., N.W. Washington, DC 20552 (202) 337-6250
Federal Labor Relations Authority	General Counsel Federal Labor Relations Authority 1900 E. St., N.W. Washington, DC 20573 (202) 632-6264	General Counsel Federal Labor Relations Authority 1900 E. St., N.W. Washington, DC 20573 (202) 632-6264
Federal Maritime Commission	Secretary Federal Maritime Commission 1100 L St., N.W. Washington, DC 20573 (202) 523-5725	Chairman Federal Maritime Commission 1100 L St., N.W. Washington, DC 20573 (202) 523-5911
Federal Mediation and Conciliation Service	General Counsel Federal Mediation and Conciliation Service 2100 K St., N.W. Room 908 Washington, DC 20427 (202) 653-5290	General Counsel Federal Mediation and Conciliation Service 2100 K St., N.W. Room 908 Washington, DC 20427 (202) 653-5290

Agency	Requests	Appeals

Federal Reserve System	Office of Public Affairs
	Federal Reserve System
	Federal Reserve Bldg.
	20th St. and Constitution Ave.,
	   N.W., Room B-2117B
	Washington, DC 20551
	(202) 452-3204
		Office of Public Affairs
		Federal Reserve System
		Federal Reserve Bldg.
		20th St., and Constitution Ave.,
		   N.W., Room B-2117B
		Washington, DC 20551
		(202) 452-3204

Federal Trade Commission	Office of the Secretary FOIA Office Federal Trade Commission 6th and Pennsylvania Ave., N.W. Washington, DC 20580 (202) 523-3582	Office of the Secretary FOIA Office Federal Trade Commission 6th and Pennsylvania Ave., N.W. Washington, DC 20580 (202) 523-3582

Foreign Claims Settlement Commission of the U.S.	General Counsel
	Foreign Claims Settlement
	   Commission of the U.S.
	1111 20th St., N.W.
	Washington, DC 20579
	(202) 653-5883
		General Counsel
		Foreign Claims Settlement
		   Commission of the U.S.
		1111 20th St., N.W.
		Washington, DC 20579
		(202) 653-5883

General Services Administration	FOI Officer Office of External Affairs General Services Administration 18th and F. St., N.W. Room 6111 Washington, DC 20405 (202) 566-1231	FOI Officer Office of External Affairs General Services Administration 18th and F. St., N.W. Room 6111 Washington, DC 20405 (202) 566-1231
Health and Human Services, Department of (formerly Department of Health, Education, and Welfare)		
Food and Drug Administration	Asst. Commissioner for Public Affairs Food and Drug Admin. Parklawn Bldg., Room 12A16 5600 Fishers Lane Rockville, Maryland 20852 (301) 443-4813	Asst. Secretary for Health Humphrey Bldg., Room 716G 200 Independence Ave., S.W. Washington, DC 20201 (202) 245-7694
General Administration and Office of the Secretary	FOIA Officer HHS Humphrey Bldg., Room 645F Washington, DC 20201 (202) 245-6221	Asst. Secretary for Management and Budget Humphrey Bldg., Room 510A Washington, DC 20201 (202) 245-6396

Health Care Financing Administration	Director, Office of Public
	   Affairs
	Health Care Financing
	   Administration
	East Highrise Bldg., Room 656
	6401 Security Blvd.
	Baltimore, MD 21235
	(301) 594-7030
		Administrator
		Health Care Financing
		   Administration
		Humphrey Bldg.,
		200 Independence, S.W.
		Washington, DC 20201
		(202) 245-6726

Agency	Requests	Appeals
Social Security Administration	FOIA Officer Social Security Administration Altmeyer Bldg. 6401 Security Blvd. Room 124 Baltimore, MD 21235 (301) 594-1995	Commissioner Humphrey Bldg. 200 Independence, S.W. Room 613 Washington, DC 20201 (202) 245-6764
Housing and Urban Development, Department of	Central Information Center Dept. of Housing and Urban Development 451 7th St., S.W., Room 1104 Washington, DC 20410 (202) 755-6420	Central Information Center Dept. of Housing and Urban Development 451 7th St., S.W., Room 1104 Washington, DC 20410 (202) 755-6420
Interior, Department of		
Bureau of Indian Affairs	Director of the Office of Administration Bureau of Indian Affairs 1951 Constitution Ave., N.W. Washington, DC 20240 (202) 343-7445	Office of Information Resources Management Dept of the Interior 18th & E St., N.W. Washington, DC 20240 (202) 343-6669
Bureau of Land Management	Office of Public Affairs Bureau of land Management Interior Bldg., Room 5619 Washington, DC 20240 (202) 343-5717	Office of Information Resources Management Dept. of the Interior 18th & E. St., N.W. Washington, DC 20240 (202) 343-6669
Bureau of Mines	Chief, Office of Mineral Information Bureau of Mines Columbia Plaza, Room 1035 Washington, DC 20241 (202) 634-1001	Office of Information Resources Management Dept. of the Interior 18th & E. St., N.W. Washington, DC 20240 (202) 343-6669
Fish and Wildlife Service	Fish and Wildlife Service 1717 H St., N.W. Washington, DC 20240 (202) 343-8914	Office of Information Resources Management Dept. of the Interior 18th & E. St., N.W. Washington, DC 20240 (202) 343-6669
Geological Survey	Director Geological Survey Dept. of the Interior USGS National Center 12201 Sunrise Valley Dr. Reston, VA 22092 (703) 860-7411	Office of Information Resources Management Dept. of the Interior 18th & E. St., N.W. Washington, DC 20240 (202) 343-6669

Agency	Requests	Appeals
Heritage Conservation and Recreation Service	Office of Communications Heritage Conservation and Recreation Service Pension Bldg. 4th and G St. Washington, DC 20001 (202) 343-5726	Office of Information Resources Management Dept. of the Interior 18th & E. St., N.W. Washington, DC 20240 (202) 343-6669
National Park Service	Office of Communications National Park Service Interior Bldg., Room 3043 Washington, DC 20240 (202) 343-7394	Office of Information Resources Management Dept. of the Interior 18th & E. St., N.W. Washington, DC 20240 (202) 343-6669
Office of the Secretary (and other offices not listed here)	Office of Public Affairs Dept. of the Interior 18th and E St., N.W. Washington, DC 20240 (202) 343-8687	Office of Information Resources Management Dept. of the Interior 18th & E. St., N.W. Washington, DC 20240 (202) 343-6669
Office of Territorial Affairs	Office Manager Office of Territorial Affairs Dept. of Interior Washington, DC 20240 (202) 343-6971	Office of Information Resources Management Dept. of the Interior 18th & E. St., N.W. Washington, DC 20240 (202) 343-6669
Office of Water Research and Technology	Director Office of Water Research and Technology Dept. of Interior 18th and E St., N.W. Washington, DC 20240 (202) 343-8687	Office of Information Resources Management Dept. of the Interior 18th & E. St., N.W. Washington, DC 20240 (202) 343-6669
Inter-American Foundation	FOIA Officer 1515 Wilson Blvd. Rosslyn, VA 22209 (703) 841-3869	FOIA Officer 1515 Wilson Blvd. Rosslyn, VA 22209 (703) 841-3869
International Communications Agency	FOIA Request International Communications Agency Room 1019 1750 Pennsylvania Ave., N.W. Washington, DC 20547 (202) 724-9103	FOIA Appeal for Access to Records Congressional and Public Liaison Office Room 1019 1750 Pennsylvania Av., N.W. Washington, DC 20547 (202) 724-9103

Agency	Requests	Appeals
International Cooperation Agency, U.S.	Office of Public Affairs IDCA 320-21st St., N.W. Washington, DC 20523 (202) 632-8150	Office of Public Affairs IDCA 320-21st St., N.W. Washington, DC 20523 (202) 632-8150
International Trade Commission	Secretary U.S. International Trade Commission 701 E St., N.W. Washington, DC 20436 (202) 523-0161	Secretary U.S. International Trade Commission 701 E St., N.W. Washington, DC 20436 (202) 523-0161
Interstate Commerce Commission	FOIA Officer Interstate Commerce Commission 12th St., and Constitution Ave., N.W. Room 3887 Washington, DC 20423 (202) 275-7076	FOIA Officer Interstate Commerce Commission 12th St., and Constitution Ave., N.W. Room 3887 Washington, DC 20423 (202) 275-7076

Justice, Department of

Bureau of Prisons	General Counsel Bureau of Prisons 320 First St., N.W. Washington, DC 20534 (202) 724-3062	Office of FOI Appeals Dept. of Justice 10th and Pennsylvania Ave., N.W. Washington, DC 20530 (202) 739-4672
Federal Bureau of Investigation (Headquarters)	Director Federal Bureau of Investigation ATTN: FOIA and Privacy Acts Branch Washington, DC 20535 (202) 324-5520	Office of Privacy and FOI Appeals Dept. of Justice 10th and Pennsylvania Ave., N.W. Washington, DC 20530 (202) 739-4672

FBI Field Offices
Address initial requests to
Special Agent in Charge,
FBI, at address below

Field Divisions of the Federal Bureau of Investigation

Division	Office Phone	Address, with zip code
1 Albany, New York	518-405-7551	502 U. S. Post Office and Court House 12207
2 Albuquerque, New Mexico	505 247-1555	301 Grand Avenue NE 87102
3 Alexandria, Virginia	703 683-2680	Room 500, 300 North Lee Street 22314
4 Anchorage, Alaska	907 276-4441	Federal Building, Room E-222, 701 C Street 99513
5 Atlanta, Georgia	404 521-3900	275 Peachtree St., N.E. 30303

Field Divisions of the Federal Bureau of Investigation

6 Baltimore, Maryland	301 265-8080	7142 Ambassador Rd. 21207
7 Birmingham, Alabama	205 252-7705	Room 1400-2121 Building 35203
8 Boston, Massachusetts	617 742-5533	John F. Kennedy Federal Office Building, 02203
9 Buffalo, New York	716 856-7800	Room 1400-111 W. Huron St., 14202
10 Butte, Montana	406 792-2304	115 U. S. Court House and Federal Building 59701
11 Charlotte, North Carolina	704 372-5484	1120 Jefferson Standard Life Building, 307 Tyron St., 28202
12 Chicago, Illinois	312 431-1333	Room 905, Everett McKinley Dirksen Building 60604
13 Cincinnati, Ohio	513 421-4310	400 U. S. Post Office and Court House Building, 45202
14 Cleveland, Ohio	216 522-1400	3005 Federal Office Building 44199
15 Columbia, South Carolina	803 254-3011	1529 Hampton St. 29201
16 Dallas, Texas	214 741-1851	1801 North Lamar, Suite 300 75202
17 Denver, Colorado	303 629-7171	Room 18218, Fed. Office Building 80202
18 Detroit, Michigan	313 965-2323	Patrick V. McNamara Building, 477 Michigan Avenue 48220
19 El Paso, Texas	915 533-7451	202 U. S. Court House Building, 79001
•20 Honolulu, Hawaii	808 521-1411	Kalanianaole Fed. Building, Room 4307, 300 Ala Moana Blvd. 96850
21 Houston, Texas	713 224-1511	6015 Fed. Building and U. S. Court House 77002
•22 Indianapolis, Indiana	317-639-3301	Room 679, 575 North Pennsylvania St. 46204
23 Jackson, Mississippi	601 948-5000	Federal Building, Rm. 1553, 100 W. Capital Street 39201
24 Jacksonville, Florida	904 721-1211	Oaks V. 4th Floor, 7820 Arlington Expressway 32211
25 Kansas City, Missouri	816 221-6100	Room 300, U.S. Courthouse 64106
26 Knoxville, Tennessee	615 588-8571	Room 800, 1111 Northshore Drive 37919

Field Divisions of the Federal Bureau of Investigation

27 Las Vegas, Nevada	702 385-1281	Room 219, Fed. Office Building 89101
28 Little Rock, Arkansas	501 372-7211	215 U.S. Post Office Building 72201
29 Los Angeles, California	213 272-6161	11000 Wilshire Boulevard 90024
30 Louisville, Kentucky	502 583-3941	Room 502, Fed. Building 40202
31 Memphis, Tennessee	901 525-7373	841 Clifford Davis Fed. Building 38103
32 Miami, Florida	305 573-3333	3801 Biscayne Boulevard 33137
33 Milwaukee, Wisconsin	414 276-4684	Room 700, Fed. Building and U. S. Court House 53202
34 Minneapolis, Minnesota	612 339-7861	392 Fed. Building 55401
35 Mobile, Alabama	205 438-3674	520 Fed. Building 36602
36 Newark, New Jersey	201 622-5613	Gateway 1, Market Street 07101
37 New Haven, Connecticut	203 777-6311	Fed. Building 150 Court Street 06510
38 New Orleans, Louisiana	504 522-4670	701 Loyola Ave., 70113
39 New York, New York (New Rochelle) (Brooklyn-Queens)	212 553-2700 914 576-3300 212 450-3140	26 Fed. Plaza 10007 (MRA) 1 Sheraton Plaza, 9th Floor 10801 (MRA) 95-25 Queens Boulevard, Rego Park, N.Y. 11374
40 Norfolk, Virginia	804 023-3111	Room 830, 200 Cranby Mall 23510
41 Oklahoma City, Oklahoma	405 842-7471	50 Penn Place, Suite 1600 73118
42 Omaha, Nebraska	402 348-1210	Rm. 7401, Federal Bldg., U. S. Post Office and Courthouse, 215 N. 17th Street 68102
43 Philadelphia, Pennsylvania	215 629-0800	8th Floor Fed. Office Building, 600 Arch Street 19100
•44 Phoenix, Arizona	602 279-5511	2721 North Central Avenue 85004
45 Pittsburgh, Pennsylvania	412 471-2000	1300 Fed. Office Building 15222
46 Portland, Oregon	503 224-4181	Crown Plaza Building 97201
47 Richmond, Virginia	804 644-2631	200 W. Grace Street 23220
48 Sacramento, California	916 481-9110	Fed. Building, 2800 Cottage Way 95825
49 St. Louis, Missouri	314 241-5357	2704 Fed. Building 63103

Field Divisions of the Federal Bureau of Investigation

50 Salt Lake City, Utah	801 355-7521	3203 Fed. Building 84138
51 San Antonio, Texas	512 225-0741	433 Post Office Building 78296
52 San Diego, California	714 231-1122	Fed. Office Bldg., Room 6S-31, 800 Front Street 92168
53 San Francisco, California	415 552-2155	450 Golden Gate Ave., 94102
•54 San Juan, Puerto Rico	809 754-6000	U. S. Courthouse & Fed. Building, Room 526 Hato Rey, P.R. 00918
55 Savannah, Georgia	912 354-9911	5401 Paulsen St., 31405
56 Seattle, Washington	206 622-0460	915 Second Ave., 98174
57 Springfield, Illinois	217 522-9675	535 W. Jefferson Street 62702
58 Tampa, Florida	813 228-7661	Room 610, Fed. Office Building 33602
59 Washington, D.C.	202 324-3000	FBI, Washington Field Office, Washington, D.C. 20535
60 Quantico, Virginia	703 640-6131	Fed. Bureau of Investigation Academy 22135

Appeal letters should be sent to:
Office of Privacy & FOI Appeals
Dept. of Justice
10th & Pennsylvania, N.W.
Washington, D.C. 20530
(202) 739-4672

Agency	Requests	Appeals
Law Enforcement Assistance Admin.	Asst. Administrator Office of Operations Support 633 Indiana Ave., N.W., Rm. 1042 Washington, DC 20531 (202) 724-7733	Office of Privacy & FOI Appeals Dept. of Justice 10th & Pennsylvania, N.W. Washington, DC 20530 (202) 739-4672
All other Divisions and Offices	Administrative Counsel Justice Management Division Dept. of Justice 10th & Pennsylvania, Ave., N.W. Washington, DC 20530 (202) 633-3452	Office of Privacy & FOI Appeals Dept. of Justice 10th & Pennsylvania, N.W. Washington, DC 20530 (202) 739-4672
Labor, Dept. of	Assistant Secretary for Administration & Management Dept. of Labor 200 Constitution Ave., N.W. Washington, DC 20210 (202) 523-8065	Solicitor of Labor Dept. of Labor 200 Constitution Ave., N.W. Washington, DC 20210 (202) 523-7675

Agency	Requests	Appeals
Marine Mammal Commission	General Counsel Marine Mammal Commission 1625 I St., N.W., Rm. 307 Washington, DC 20006 (202) 653-6237	General Counsel Marine Mammal Commission 1625 I St., N.W., Room 307 Washington, DC 20006 (202) 653-6237
Merit Systems Protection Board	FOIA Office Merit Systems Protection Board 1717 H St., N.W. Washington, DC 20419 (202) 632-4525	Executive Assistant Merit Systems Protection Board 1717 H St., N.W. Washington, DC 20419 (202) 632-4525
National Aeronautics and Space Administration	Information Center National Aeronautics and Space Admin. 400 Maryland Ave., S.W Washington, DC 20546 (202) 755-8341	Administrator and National Aeronautics and Space Administration 400 Maryland Ave., S.W. Washington, DC 20546 (202) 755-3918
National Archives and Records Service	Archivist of the United States National Archives and Records Service 8th & Pennsylvania Ave., N.W. Washington, DC 20408 (202) 523-3134	Deputy Archivist of the United States National Archives & Records Service 8th & Pennsylvania Ave., N.W. Washington, DC 20408 (202) 523-3132
National Capital Planning Commission	Secretary National Capital Planning Commission 1325 G St., N.W. Washington, DC 20576 (202) 724-0206	Chairman National Capital Planning Commission 1325 G St., N.W. Washington, DC 20576 (202) 724-0206
National Credit Union Administration	Deputy Asst. Administrator For Administration National Credit Union Administration 1776 G St., N.W. Washington, DC 20456 (202) 357-1235	Deputy Asst. Adminstrator For Administration National Credit Union Administration 1776 G St., N.W. Washington, DC 20456 (202) 357-1235
National Foundation on the Arts and Humanities	General Counsel National Endowment for the Arts OR National Endowment for the Humanities 2401 E St., N.W. Washington, DC 20506 (202) 634-6588	Chairman National Endowment for the Arts OR National Endowment for the Humanities 2401 E St., N.W. Washington, DC 20506 (202) 634-6588

Agency	Requests	Appeals
National Labor Relations Board	FOIA Officer National Labor Relations Board Legal Research and Policy Planning 1717 Pennsylvania Ave., N.W. Rm. 1100 Washington, DC 20570 (202) 254-9350	General Counsel National Labor Relations Board 1717 Pennsylvania Ave., N.W. Washington, DC 20570 (202) 254-9128
National Mediation Board	Executive Secretary National Mediation Board 1425 K St., N.W. Washington, DC 20572 (202) 523-5343	Executive Secretary National Mediation Board 1425 K St., N.W. Washington, DC 20572 (202) 523-5343
National Science Foundation	Freedom of Info. Officer National Science Foundation 1800 G St., N.W. Washington, DC 20550 (202) 357-9498	Deputy Director National Science Foundation 1800 G St., N.W. Washington DC 20550 (202) 357-9498
National Security Council	Staff Secretary National Security Council Old Executive Office Bldg. Washington, DC 20506 (202) 395-3116	Staff Secretary National Security Council Old Executive Office Bldg. Washington, DC 20506 (202) 395-3116
National Transportation Safety Board	Director Bureau of Admin. (AD1) National Transportation Safety Board 800 Independence Ave., S.W. Washington, DC 20594 (202) 472-6111	Managing Director National Transportation Safety Board 800 Independence Ave., S.W. Washington, DC 20594 (202) 472-6011
Nuclear Regulatory Commission	Director Office of Administration U.S. Nuclear Regulatory Commission Washington, DC 20555 (202) 492-8133	Executive Secretary Office of Administration U.S. Nuclear Regulatory Commission Washington, DC 20555 (202) 492-8133
Occupational Safety and Health Review Commission	Office of Information & Publications Occupational Safety and Health Review Commission 1825 K St., N.W. Washington, DC 20006 (202) 634-7943	Chairman Occupational Safety and Health Review Commission 1825 K St., N.W. Washington, DC 20006 (202) 634-7946

Agency	Requests	Appeals
Office of Management and Budget	Assistant to the Director for Administration OMB Old Executive Office Bldg., Rm. 243 Washington, DC 20503 (202) 395-4790	Assistant to the Director of Administration OMB Old Executive Office Bldg., Rm. 243 Washington, DC 20503 (202) 395-4790
Office of Personnel Management (formerly U.S. Civil Service Commission)	Director Office of Management Office of Personnel Mgmt. 1900 E St., N.W. Washington, DC 20233 (202) 632-6161	Same
Office of the U.S. Trade Representative	FOIA Officer Office of the U.S. Trade Representative 1800 G St., N.W., Rm. 720-A Washington, DC 20506 (202) 395-3432	FOIA Appeals Committee Office of the U.S. Trade Representative 1800 G St., N.W. Washington, DC 20506 (202) 395-3432
Overseas Private Investment Corp.	Vice President for Public & Congressional Affairs Overseas Private Investment Corp. 1129-20th St., N.W. Washington , DC 20527 (202) 653-2800	General Counsel Overseas Private Investment Corp. 1129-20th St., N.W. Washington, DC 20527 (202) 653-2925
Panama Canal Commission	Panama Canal Commission Office of the Secretary 425 13th St., N.W., Room 312 Washington, DC 20004 (202) 724-0104	Same
Pennsylvania Ave. Development Corp.	Public Info. Officer Pennsylvania Ave. Development Corp. Pennsylvania Bldg. 425 13th St. N.W., Suite 1148 Washington, DC 20004 (202) 566-1218	Same
Pension Benefit Guaranty Corp.	Director, Office of Communications Pension Benefit Guaranty Corp. 2020 K St., N.W. Washington, DC 20006 (202) 254-4827	Same

Agency	Requests	Appeals
Postal Rate Commission	Secretary Postal Rate Commission 2000 L St., N.W. Washington, DC 20268 (202) 254-3830	Same
Postal Service, U.S.	Records Officer U.S. Postal Service 475 L'Enfant Plaza Washington, DC 20260 (202) 245-4142	Same
Railroad Retirement Board	Chief Executive Officer Railroad Retirement Board 844 Rush St., Rm. 536 Chicago, Ill. 60611 (312) 751-4930	Same
Securities & Exchange Commission	FOIA Officer Securities & Exchange Commission 1100 L St., N.W. Washington, DC 20549 (202) 535-5798	Same
Selective Service System	National Headquarters Selective Service System 600 E St., N.W. Washington, DC 20435 (202) 724-0846	Director Selective Service 600 E St., N.W. Washington, DC 20435 (202) 724-0424
Small Business Administration	Director Office of Public Info. Small Business Administration 1441 L St., N.W. Washington, DC 20416 (202) 653-6460	Asst. Administrator for Advocacy and Public Communications Small Business Admin. 1441 L St., N.W Washington, DC 20416 (202) 653-6460
State, Dept. of	Information and Privacy Coordinator Dept. of State 2201 C St. N.W., Rm. 1239 Washington, DC 20520 (202) 632-1267	Chairman, Appeal Review Panel Dept. of State 2201 C St., N.W. Washington, DC 20520 (202) 632-9437
Agency for International Development	Chief, Public Inquiry Staff OPA/PI Agency for International Development Rm. 2849 21st & Virginia Ave., N.W. Washington DC 20523 (202) 632-1850	Administrator Agency for International Development 21st & Virginia Ave., N.W. Washington, DC 20523 (202) 632-9620

Agency	Requests	Appeals
Tennessee Valley Authority	Director of Information Tennessee Valley Authority Knoxville, Tenn. 37902 (615) 632-3257	General Manager Tennessee Valley Authority 400 Commerce St. Knoxville, Tenn. 37902 (615) 632-3257
Transportation, Dept. of		
Coast Guard	Public Affairs, U.S. Coast Guard Department of Transportation Washington, DC 20593 (202) 426-2419	Commandant (G-APA) U.S. Coast Guard Washington, DC 20591 (202) 426-2419
Federal Aviation Administration	Asst. Administrator for Public Affairs Federal Aviation Admin. 800 Independence Ave., S.W. Washington, DC 20591 (202) 426-3485	Same
Federal Highway Administration	Office of Organization and Management Federal Highway Administration 400 7th St., S.W. Washington, DC 20590 (202) 426-0534	Same
Federal Railroad Administration	Chief Counsel Federal Railroad Administration Dept. of Transportation 400 7th St., S.W., Rm. 5418 Washington, DC 20590 (202) 426-0881	Same
Highway Traffic Safety Administration	Executive Secretary Highway Traffic Safety Administration 400 7th St., S.W. Washington, DC 20590 (202) 426-1834	Associate Administrator for Administration Highway Traffic Safety Administration 400 7th St., S.W. Washington, DC 20590 (202) 426-1789
Research and Special Programs	Administrator Research & Special Programs Dept. of Transportation 400 7th St., S.W. Washington, DC 20590 (202) 755-4972	Same
St. Lawrence Seaway Corp.	Chief, Management Info. Division St. Lawrence Seaway Corp. P.O. Box 520 Messina, NY 13662 (315) 764-0271	Same

Agency	Requests	Appeals
Office of the Secretary	Director, Public and Consumer Affairs Office of the Secretary Dept. of Transportation 400 7th St., S.W. Washington, DC 20590 (202) 426-4488	General Counsel Dept. of Transportation 400 7th St., S.W. Washington, DC 20590 (202) 426-4702
Urban Transportation Administration	Director of Public Affairs Urban Transportation Admin. 400 7th St., S.W. Washington, DC 20590 (202) 426-4043	Chief Counsel Urban Transportation Administration 400 7th St., S.W. Washington, DC 20590 (202) 426-4043
Treasury, Dept. of.		
Alcohol, Tobacco, and Firearms	Assistant to the Director (Disclosure) Bureau of Alcohol, Tobacco and Firearms 12th & Pennsylvania, N.W., Rm. 4407 Washington, DC 20226 (202) 566-7118	Same
Comptroller of the Currency	Director, Communications (FOI) Comptroller of the Currency 490 L'Enfant Plaza East, S.W. Washington, DC 20219 (202) 447-1800	Same
Customs Service, U.S.	U.S. Customs Service Office of Chief Counsel 1301 Constitution Ave., N.W. Washington, DC 20229 (202) 566-5476	Same
Internal Revenue Service	To the office controlling the record or to the appropriate district office, OR Director, Disclosure Operations Division 1111 Constitution Ave., N.W. Rm. 1603 Washington, DC 20224 (202) 566-4263	Commissioner of Internal Revenue Disclosure, Litigation Division CC: D, Rm. 3701 1111 Constitution Ave., N.W. Washington, DC 20224 (202) 566-4109
Office of the Secretary	Office of the Secretary Dept. of Treasury 1500 Pennsylvania Ave., N.W. Washington, DC 20220 (202) 566-5573	Same

Agency	Requests	Appeals
Secret Service	U.S. Secret Service 1800 G St., N.W. Washington, DC 20223 (202) 535-5798	Same
Veterans' Administration	To the office having jurisdiction of the record OR Central Office Veteran's Administration 810 Vermont Ave., N.W. Washington, DC 20420 (202) 389-3632	Administrator of Veteran's Affairs Veterans' Administration Central Office 810 Vermont Ave., N.W. Washington, DC 20420 (202) 389-3632
Water Resources Council	FOI Officer Water Resources Council 2121 L St., N.W. Washington, DC 20037 (202) 254-8290	General Counsel Water Resources Council 2121 L St., N.W. Washington, DC 20037 (202) 254-6303

AMERICAN CIVIL LIBERTIES UNION HANDBOOKS

SPECIAL MONEY SAVING OFFER

Now you can have an up-to-date listing of Bantam's hundreds of titles plus take advantage of our unique and exciting bonus book offer. A special offer which gives you the opportunity to purchase a Bantam book for only 50¢. Here's how!

By ordering any five books at the regular price per order, you can also choose any other single book listed (up to a $4.95 value) for just 50¢. Some restrictions do apply, but for further details why not send for Bantam's listing of titles today!

Just send us your name and address plus 50¢ to defray the postage and handling costs.

We Deliver!
And So Do These Bestsellers.